The John Colet Archive · 2

The John Colet Archive
of American Literature
1620-1920

Number 2, Summer 1974

Alexander Hill Everett

Prose Pieces
and
Correspondence

Edited by Elizabeth Evans

THE JOHN COLET PRESS

The John Colet Archive of American Literature,
a quarterly series, presents the tangible yields of
current scholarly inquiry into the distant reaches
of American literary history. By the selective
recovery of near-forgotten works in compact,
inexpensive modern editions, the Archive is
intended to enrich, modestly but measurably, the
working literary heritage of the American people.
Correspondence may be addressed to The Director,
The John Colet Press, Box 80101, Como Station,
St. Paul, Minnesota 55108.

Preface

A representative selection of Alexander Hill Everett's
journalism and correspondence is gathered in this volume,
intended to help secure Everett's recognition as a highly
competent figure, albeit a minor one, in the growth of American literature during the first half of the nineteenth century.
The five articles and twenty letters printed here are only a
fraction of Everett's literary output, but together they give
a clear impression of their author's broad education, his
sense of humor and of irony, and his lively attentiveness to
an exceptionally wide range of human affairs.

The body of this edition is a literal transcription of the
sources in nineteenth-century prints and manuscripts; my
choice and treatment of copy-texts are discussed in the introduction, below. The text of each article and of the correspondence as a whole is followed by practical annotation—
translations of unfamiliar words and phrases, chronological
information, and brief comments on various persons and
events of more than passing interest to Everett but no longer
universally recognizable. The bibliography is a comprehensive checklist, rather than an exhaustive inventory, of Everett's known literary remains. The index of personal names
which concludes the volume is limited for the most part to
historical personages identifiable in modern works of general reference.

In preparing this edition I have incurred numerous debts
of gratitude. For their kind assistance and for permission
to publish letters from their holdings, I am grateful to
Stephen T. Riley and Malcolm Freiberg of the Massachusetts

Historical Society; to Kenneth C. Cramer of the Dartmouth
College Library; to W. H. Bond of the Harvard University
Library; to Thompson R. Harlow of the Connecticut Histori-
cal Society; and to Arthur Monke of the Bowdoin College
Library.

I wish also to thank David B. Comer III, James P. Smith,
George Walker, and Louis Zahn, colleagues of mine at the
Georgia Institute of Technology, for their help. Ruth Hale
and Jean Kirkland of the Georgia Institute of Technology Li-
brary were of invaluable assistance in bibliographic matters.
Lucia Ramey and Marie Lampkin were faithful proofreaders.

I am most grateful to the Georgia Tech Foundation for a
grant which aided substantially in the preparation of this
edition.

Elizabeth Evans

Georgia Institute of Technology
Atlanta, Georgia
1974

Contents

Introduction

Alexander Hill Everett (1790-1847), son of Oliver Everett and Lucy Hill Everett, was raised in Boston and educated at Harvard. He began his diplomatic career at St. Petersburg in 1809, in the company of John Quincy Adams, then United States minister to Russia. Nine years later, Everett's principal vocation was in full stride; from 1818 to 1823 he served as secretary to the American legation and later as chargé d'affaires in the temporarily united Netherlands, and from 1825 to 1829 he was United States minister to Spain. A literary interlude of a decade ensued, during which Everett edited the North American Review (1830-1835). In 1840 he resumed his political career as a special envoy sent to Havana to investigate misaction in slave-ship dealings. In 1847 he sailed for China as the first United States commissioner under the treaty of 1844. Forced to return because of ill health when he first set out, Everett finally reached China and died there on May 29, 1847.

    Having rejected the role of clergyman (his father's profession and the one in which his younger brother Edward first distinguished himself) and of lawyer (though he had prepared himself for it in the law offices of John Quincy Adams), Everett pursued the dual roles of diplomat and writer almost all his life, a choice by no means unique to him but fairly common among his contemporaries. A great deal of his writing is thus in the form of official correspondence and reports to Washington officials, a matter of public record-keeping and only of incidental significance in his literary career. His long years of foreign service are remembered

chiefly because of his personal and public association with
John Quincy Adams and various other officials. Episodes of
concern to the historian are discussed by Samuel Flagg
Bemis,[1] and Everett's excursions into state politics during
his years as editor of the North American Review are examined in the general political context of his era by A. B.
Darling.[2] Everett's life as a politician and diplomat has not
been entirely neglected, then, but neglect is practically the
case for his career as a man of letters. In this capacity he
is remembered almost exclusively as the friend of Washington Irving, George Ticknor, and William H. Prescott—con-
vincing Irving to come to Spain to work on the material for
his Columbus, and procuring valuable Spanish books which
Ticknor and Prescott needed in their studies.

Everett is one of many shadowy figures mentioned in Harry Hayden Clark's Transitions in American Literary History,[3]
sharing relative obscurity with William Dunlap, Robert
Walsh, Julian Verplanck, E. P. Whipple, P. S. duPonceau,
J. G. Percival, Edward S. Gould, James A. Hillhouse,
Samuel Batchelder, John Palfrey, and even Jared Sparks—
names that hardly leap into recognition. It is only through
the patient sifting of personal correspondence and published
articles in such journals as the North American Review, the
Democratic Review, and the American Quarterly Review,
that one can rescue such men from oblivion and restore
them to a minor but significant position in American letters.
Considerable talent and good fortune assure the reputations
of the Coopers, the Irvings, the Longfellows; but the great
majority of journeymen whose productions served useful
purposes in their day have been ignored with the passing of
time and the redirection of tastes and styles. What was comparatively innovative in their writings (Everett's fledgling
moves from strict neoclassic criteria to a more marked
romantic reaction in evaluating Byron, for example) is now
so commonplace that the effort goes unnoticed and, of course,
unread.

Certainly it is neither feasible nor necessary to make extravagant claims for Everett's work, but an examination of

his writing does show that his achievements deserve more
than the scant notice thus far accorded them. In addition to
sizeable collections of personal correspondence, Everett's
legacy consists of three books of political interest—Europe
(1822), New Ideas on Population (1823), and America
(1827); two brief biographies (the lives of Joseph Warren
and Patrick Henry in Jared Sparks's series, The Library of
American Biography); more than seventy articles in the
North American Review; numerous articles in other journals; at least a dozen published addresses; two volumes of
collected essays, culled from the journal writings; and a
small book of verse.

The three political books embody Everett's observations
and analysis of conditions and trends in Europe and in North
and South America, and his disagreement with Malthus and
Godwin regarding theories of population growth. Although
the three volumes attracted modest praise and were translated into several foreign languages, Everett remarked in a
letter of September 14, 1839, to Lydia Sigourney, that he
could not furnish her with copies of Europe and America because they had long been out of print. These works need not
be despised, even though the judgments they express may
today seem pallid and obvious; much of the writing is good
and the information worthwhile. The two biographies are the
weakest of Everett's performance; by comparison with modern research and documentation, his approach to biography
seems haphazard and even naïve. Nevertheless, his efforts
suited the "American Plutarch," Jared Sparks, editor of
the biographical series and a former editor of the North
American Review.

Although Everett's books have their importance, it is in
his articles, his years of work as editor of the North American Review, and his fascinating correspondence with a host
of notable figures that one may see him as a competent representative of his age. In the course of his diplomatic appointments at Brussels and Madrid, Everett had acquired a
Continental outlook, and was much sought after by Jared
Sparks in the 1820's to contribute articles on a regular basis
to the North American Review. Many of Everett's articles

are book reviews, perhaps better described as essay-
reviews since Everett often took the occasion to indulge in
lengthy digressions on matters suggested by the book. The
single essay-review included in this volume, "Irving's Columbus," is a typical reflection of Everett's critical skill
and taste, but others of his essay-reviews are of comparable
importance, particularly in showing Everett's knowledge of
Continental figures and subjects. Limitations of space pre-
clude my illustrating in this edition a very common practice
of Everett's, the inclusion of voluminous extracts in a review as an introduction to the book at hand. In his twenty-
five-page review of J. P. Kennedy's Swallow Barn, for
example, Everett confined his pertinent comments to four
pages; the twenty-nine-page review of Carlyle's Sartor
Resartus had twenty-one pages of extracts. Such an approach
to reviewing is of course no longer acceptable, but at a time
when books, especially foreign books, were not readily
available everywhere, the practice was clearly justifiable.

The titles of Everett's essay-reviews reflect his far-
ranging literary interests: "Rémusat's Chinese Grammar,"
"Memoirs of the Queen of France," "Lord Byron," "Life
and Works of Canova," "Geoffroy on Dramatic Literature."
Others of his surviving articles register his thoughts on
nearly every aspect of early nineteenth-century culture; few
subjects seem to have been utterly foreign to him. It is perhaps understandable that material of this sort in nineteenth-
century journals should remain untouched unless specific
research leads to it: the articles are generally long, the
pages tightly printed, the topics often unfamiliar or uninvit-
ing. But we label this writing dull at our peril, for a careful
reading of it provides an indispensable index to the critical
temper of its day, and the articles of a single writer often
supply the clearest possible impression of his literary per-
sonality.

Five substantial pieces chosen from among these occasional writings of Everett's are here made available to
modern readers—a mere sampling of their author's output,
but a fair representation of his wide-ranging interests, his
critical acumen, and his wit. The first item is one of Ever-

ett's energetic "paper war" pieces, "The Tone of British
Criticism," which appeared in the North American Review
in 1830, the first year of Everett's editorship. The "war"
raged between journalists in England and America during the
early nineteenth century; the caustic tone of Everett's article, and of the quoted insults to which he responds, exemplifies the overstated chauvinism that prevailed for a time in
cultural relations between the adolescent States and their
mother country.

"Irving's Columbus" is characteristic of Everett's essay-
reviews, although it has none of the ponderous excerpts of
the material under discussion that accompany much of his
critical writing. Everett surveys Irving's work in leisurely
fashion; his criticism may today appear mild and commonplace, but he does point out specific weaknesses, personal
friendship notwithstanding, in what Irving had published by
1829.

"Lord Vapourcourt," a droll narrative, gently satirizes
the domestic-sentimental problems of great wealth and great
poverty. The piece is of indeterminate genre, one of Everett's few attempts to produce fiction of a sort. Its wholly
unlikely plot is based on coincidences and a happy ending.

"An Exhibition of Pictures" reviews the Fourth Exhibition
in the gallery of the Boston Athenaeum. Apart from his co-
herent and well-informed observations on the paintings displayed, Everett demonstrates his specialized knowledge of
Spanish artists, a by-product of his years as a diplomat in
Madrid.

"The Present State of Polite Learning in England and
America," one of Everett's published addresses, was deliv-
ered on September 3, 1834, to the Phi Beta Kappa Society of
Bowdoin College and printed in the same year by Charles
Bowen of Boston. The observations recorded here are cer-
tainly more objective than the strident complaints issued in
"The Tone of British Criticism," and quietly summarize
Everett's sound if rather conventional literary views.

The selected correspondence which concludes this edition
covers the years 1809 to 1842; the travel descriptions,
anecdotes, and ideas are an intimate illustration of Everett's

tastes and interests. The recipients are Everett's family and acquaintances, including those whose fame eventually outstripped his own—his brother Edward and his particular friends Ticknor, Prescott, and Longfellow.

Each of the five long prose pieces below is a word-for-word transcription of the latest print published under Everett's authority. "The Tone of British Criticism" and "An Exhibition of Pictures" are preserved only in quarterly issues of the North American Review. "Irving's Columbus" and "Lord Vapourcourt" were republished among Everett's Critical and Miscellaneous Essays some fifteen years after their initial appearance in the North American Review and the Token, respectively; the collected volume thus supplies the copy-text for this edition. "The Present State of Polite Learning in England and America" is extant only as a separate pamphlet. In all cases, Everett's typographers maintained a high standard of accuracy; both substantive and accidental errors are very few, corrected here by bracketed editorial marks. Idiosyncratic spellings and punctuations acceptable in the nineteenth century, if not in the twentieth, are reproduced without comment. Detailed information on the original print of each article accompanies the annotation following the text.

Everett's surviving correspondence is deposited in at least fifteen research libraries from New Hampshire to Georgia. The institution owning the original of each letter in this volume is noted at the foot of the letter. Of the twenty items of correspondence printed here, thirteen are autographs. The letters to Longfellow, Lydia Sigourney, Andrews Norton, and Everett's wife Lucretia, and all but one to George Ticknor, bear signatures and outside addresses. The letters to Jared Sparks lack outside addresses but are identifiable by Everett's signature.

The remaining seven letters are preserved as copies of Everett's original: December 31, 1809 to Lucy Everett; January 1, 1810 and July 17, 1822 to his brother Edward; December 17, 1821 to John Pickering; September 5, 1827 to William H. Prescott; July 12, 1828 to George Ticknor;

and August 19, 1828 to Secretary Salmon. None of these letters is signed, but internal evidence clearly denotes each as
Everett's. On January 5, 1848, Sally Everett (Mrs. Nathan
Hale) wrote to Edward Everett urging him to follow the
Hales in relinquishing any claim to their brother Alexander's
estate so it might go to his wife Lucretia, who, Sally added,
"has always been his clerk and copyist. . . ." Thus it may
be that most of the letters after 1816 (the year of Alexander's marriage) are in Lucretia's hand. The penmanship
differs among the letters, however, and it is not possible to
identify each copyist with certainty.

All of Everett's scribal errors—notably his erratic spelling of foreign words and his haphazard punctuation—are
transcribed intact, with an absolute minimum of editorial
sic's and other interpolations. Several words are nearly il-
legible in the source; each doubtful reading is followed by a
question mark in brackets. Occasionally Everett struck
through a word, apparently at the time of writing and not as
a result of careful revision; such words are suppressed
without comment in the edition.

When Everett remarked in a letter to George Ticknor that
he was somewhat disappointed by the contents of N. A. Haven's Remains, which Ticknor had edited, he noted that
"what is not prepared for publication can seldom be completely fitted for it." So it is with Everett's letters. Apparently he never envisioned their publication, but they are
presented here in careful transcription—the casual thoughts
of a widely educated man in the morning of his country's
intellectual life.

Notes

1. Samuel Flagg Bemis, John Quincy Adams and the Foundations of American Foreign Policy (New York, 1956).
2. A. B. Darling, Political Changes in Massachusetts, 1824-1848 (New Haven, 1925).
3. Harry Hayden Clark, Transitions in American Literary History (1954; rpt. Durham, N.C., 1967).

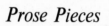

Prose Pieces

The Tone
of British Criticism

It is always more or less provoking to be made the subject
of abuse and sarcasm with or without just cause; and it is
painful enough to see the character of the relations between
two great countries vitiated by the paltry prejudices of a few
obscure scribblers; but it is nevertheless curious, as a
matter of philosophical study, and at times sufficiently
amusing to mark the influence of national pride and jealousy
on the tone of the British periodical writers in regard to the
United States. We have already on several preceding occa-
sions, adverted to this subject, and we rarely open a review, magazine, or newspaper from the mother country,
without observing some new effect of the same cause. As
regularly as their successive numbers issue from the press,
each and all of them continue to carry on this—as they probably conceive—very pious warfare, according to their various measures of ability and habitual modes of handling the
topics that come before them. The Quarterly reviles us,
the Edinburgh sneers at us, Blackwood bullies us,[1] the
magazines show us up under no very brilliant colors in
imaginary travels and journals from Kentucky;—even the
poor bookseller's drudge, who gets up that humblest of all
periodicals, the Literary Gazette, can afford to be merry at
the expense of Jonathan.[2] In short we are daily, weekly,
monthly, and quarterly, from one year's end to the other,
accused before these self-created courts of sundry high
crimes and misdemeanors, and to all these indictments we

are regularly expected to plead guilty, at least by a silent
acquiescence in the charges made upon us. If in reply to
this continual attack, an American writer happen to venture
upon a few words in the way of recrimination, or even simple self-defence, we are forthwith proclaimed by the same
general chorus of voices to be the most susceptible and
thin-skinned of all the dwellers upon earth. It is perhaps but
justice to add, that the Radicals, who, like us, though for
different reasons, are constantly run upon by almost every
other sect and party in the kingdom, appear to have a sort
of fellow-feeling with us, and that we are occasionally pa-
tronized in the Westminster Review, the Black Dwarf, and
Cobbett's Register.

Such is, and has been for many years past, the habitual
tone of the British critics in regard to this country. In the
mean time the real head and front of our offending—as is
perfectly well understood on both sides—is nothing more
than this, that we happen by the act of God, and the valor
and virtue of our fathers, without any merit or fault of our
own, to be placed in such a situation, political, geographi-
cal, and statistical, that we are more likely than any other
power to rival or surpass Great Britain, first, in those
commercial and maritime pursuits, which have hitherto
constituted the chief elements of her greatness, and at a
more remote period in population, wealth and national importance. Now we put it to the conscience of any reflecting
statesman in the mother country, or even any honest and
fair-minded man among the more irritable race of authors,
to decide—and we are willing to abide by the sentence—
whether this be a just ground for so much abuse. It is, no
doubt, natural enough, that a comparative view of the respective positions of the two countries should excite a good
deal of jealousy in British minds; but we appeal to the sober
sense and considerate judgment of our transatlantic brethren to say, whether it be right and proper to indulge this
sentiment, and exhibit it so plainly as they do in their language and actions. Is the petulant and peevish spirit, which
they regularly show in regard to this subject, such a one as
we should naturally expect from a great and gallant nation,

that still maintains, though in the wane of her fortunes, a lofty standing among the leading powers of the world? Is it not more like the petty spite of a faded beauty, who would gladly, if she dared, tear out the eyes of a younger rival, because she feels that their lustre eclipses that of her own? Or, omitting any question of justice and propriety, is it not the dictate of policy and correct taste to suppress these base emotions, and to render a manly and honorable tribute to merit of every description wherever we meet with it? Is not this, after all, the best and surest method of fully securing our own deserts, whatever they may be? Is it possible to give a more significant proof of conscious weakness, than by constantly carping at, and exaggerating petty blemishes in the characters of others; putting the worst construction upon doubtful passages; and passing over in silence, or 'damning with faint praise' the good qualities and actions that cannot be disputed? When we see an individual in private life pursuing this course, do we not pronounce him at once and without hesitation to be a sour, sorry, poor-spirited creature, and generally conclude that he is a disappointed and broken-down man? The same principles apply to the intercourse of nations; and if individuals, so insignificant as ourselves, might venture to suggest any thing in the nature of advice to our brethren on the other side of the water, we would, in all humility, respectfully give it as our opinion, that they would better consult their own interest and comfort, as well as ours, by putting a good face upon this matter, and accustoming themselves to look with complacency and satisfaction, instead of a mean and paltry jealousy, upon the rising greatness and exuberant prosperity of our young and flourishing republic.

The abuse, which they lavish upon us, although it may give us at times some passing annoyance, really does us very little injury, while the indulgence of the feelings, in which it has its origin, must be to them, unless the best ethical philosophers are at fault, a perpetual source of internal uneasiness and disquiet. On the other hand, if they could persuade themselves to take a different view of the subject, they might derive a satisfaction of the highest and

most liberal kind from the very circumstances, which now
change the milk of human kindness, that should naturally
flow in their bosoms for a kindred people, into wormwood
and gall. Is there nothing, in fact, to approve, to admire,
to rejoice at, to sympathise with in the mighty developement
of wealth and population—the creation, as it were, of a new
human race—which is now going on upon our vast territory?
And is it no just ground of pride and pleasure to an Englishman that all these wonders are the work of English hands,
and were performed under the influence of English habits,
feelings, and principles? Can the friend of learning in England find no joy in reflecting that the language he loves and
cultivates—the language, which conveyed to his infant ear
the soft accents of maternal affection—to his young heart the
tender avowals of passionate love—to his manly mind the
sublime strains of parliamentary and pulpit eloquence, will
be spoken in a future age by hundreds of millions, inhabiting
a distant foreign land, and will enliven with its rich and
noble music the now solitary regions of another quarter of
the globe? Is it nothing, for example, to the enthusiastic admirer of Shakspeare—and every Englishman is or ought to
be one—that the madness of Lear will hereafter rend the
concave of a thousand theatres from Maine to California;
the sorrows of Juliet draw forth floods of sympathy from
bright eyes in the valleys of the Rocky Mountains, or on the
banks of the river Columbia; and the mournful melody of the
harp of Ariel move upon the bosom of the smooth Pacific
'in notes by distance made more sweet' than they ever could
have been, even in the fancy of the poet, upon the shores of
the 'still vexed Bermoothes?' Here, too, Liberty has found
a home and a throne, and Liberty is or was the god of the
idolatry of every true-born Englishman. Is it nothing to the
countryman of Hampden, Sidney, and Russell, that the
principles of 'the glorious constitution,' for which they
gave up their 'golden years' to exile and prison, or their
lives upon the block, are to flourish hereafter in all their
beauty, purified and perfected, according to the illustrious
Fox, by the experience of a thousand years, in four and
twenty—in the sequel we know not how many more—inde-

pendent states? Is it nothing to the friend of good government, social order, law, and humanity, that the problem of
perpetual peace has at length been solved, and that these
four and twenty states have bound themselves together by a
mysterious but indissoluble tie of union, which preserves to
them at once the beneficial activity of independent sover-
eignties and the untroubled harmony of a single community?
Is it nothing to a Scotchman—a friend of Erskine—that the
Trial by Jury is to spread its banner of protection over the
head of the unfortunate, and perhaps innocent prisoner—that
the potent sound of Habeas Corpus, like the sesame of the
Arabian fable, is to burst the doors, which arbitrary power
shall have closed—if such a case should ever happen here—
in regions which might, and probably would, if they had not
been settled by Englishmen, have been subjected to a ruthless Spanish despotism? Finally, is it a matter of indifference to the Christian—this is not, we are aware, an argu-
mentum ad hominem, when addressed to the writers in the
Edinburgh Review—but is it, after all, a matter of indifference to the friend of pure and undefiled religion under any
of its forms, that the beautiful feet of those that bring good
tidings, that publish peace, that say unto Zion, Thy God
reigneth, are already traversing in every direction the
sandy shores of the Atlantic, the blue summits of the Alle-
ghanies, and the green savannahs of the West, that they are
climbing the precipices of the Rocky Ridge, and will soon
reach the distant borders of the South Sea? Is all this world
of wonders, this magnificent display of the full bloom and
glory of civilization, bursting forth, as it were instantaneously, from the depth of barbarism, like a Lapland spring
out of the icy bosom of winter, to be held as nothing, and
worse than nothing, not because it is not the work of Englishmen—for that in the main it is—but because it is not performed by the Englishmen, who inhabit a little island on the
eastern side of the Atlantic? Is it not a burning shame, a
crying sin, that under the influence of this paltry motive,
the greatest achievements and characters are to be habitually depreciated, the purest and most amiable sentiments
mocked and jeered at, and this too by men of high pretensions

for talent, education, and philosophy? We know not what
others may say in answer to these questions, or what doctrines and sentiments may be fashionable in the mother
country, where a selfish system seems in fact to be the order of the day: but for ourselves, we must avow without
hesitation, that we consider the tone of criticism, to which
we have here alluded, as very strongly marked by bad principle, bad feeling, bad taste, and bad policy. We believe
that our transatlantic brethren, who adopt it, are great los-
ers by it, on the score, not only of honor and conscience,
but of national advantage, as well as mere personal comfort
and pleasure. We really think that an Englishman of right
feeling and good understanding, instead of exhibiting a miserable jealousy of the progress of this great offset from the
parent stock, ought to take as much pride in it as in any of
the more direct developements of the resources of his country. We conceive that the victory over our western wilderness, which has been won by English hands and English
hearts, ought to fill his mind with as high a satisfaction as
the blockade of the whole coast of the European continent by
the British navy: and that he ought to view the marvellous
increase of population that is going on among us, the hitherto unexampled multiplication of human life and human happiness, which is taking place, for instance, in the State of
Ohio, with even more delight than the glorious waste of
blood and treasure at Trafalgar or Waterloo.

Of the various attacks that have been from time to time
directed against this country in the British journals, few, if
any, have been more offensive to the public feeling than the
article upon American Literature, which appeared in the
ninety-ninth number of the Edinburgh Review. The works of
the Rev. Dr. Channing,[3] form the immediate subject of it,
and its principal aim appears to be to depreciate the talent
and destroy the reputation of this justly eminent divine.
Several other writers of great merit are also shewn up under a ludicrous point of view, and an attempt is made to cast
a general slur upon the intellectual character of the country.
The spirit in which the article is executed corresponds very
well with the nature of its purpose, and is distinguished by

a more than usual portion of the malignant and cold hearted flippancy, which has always been one of the leading traits in the style of this, in many respects, valuable journal. We are not of [the] opinion, that it is necessary to the honor of the country, or the reputation of the individuals particularly interested, to repel every attack of this description. The best and only sufficient reply to foreign calumny, is annually and hourly given in the constantly progressive greatness and glory of the United States. There are, however, some cases that seem to form an exception to this remark, and we have been given to understand that a notice of the article alluded to, would be acceptable to many of our readers. We could have wished, that the task had fallen into more competent hands, but shall cheerfully execute it to the best of our ability, and shall endeavor, if our limits should permit, to point out the errors in one or two other articles of a similar kind, that have lately appeared in other British journals.

The reviewer commences by remarking, that the only American writers who have hitherto been heard of in England, are Irving, Brown, and Cooper, to whose names must now be added, that of Dr. Channing. On farther tasking his memory, it occurs to him that there lived half a century ago such a man as Dr. Franklin, who, as the Quarterly had previously informed us, possessed some skill in grinding his electrical machine; that Jonathan Edwards wrote some rather remarkable treatises on metaphysics, and finally, that there appeared in the United States, just before the revolutionary war, an anonymous work, entitled 'A Farmer's Letters,'[4] which gives a tolerably correct description of certain local scenes and incidents. The works of these writers compose, according to the reviewer, the whole body of American literature.

Now we have no hesitation in pronouncing this to be a very poor and silly piece of affectation. It is much as if an American, in giving a summary account of British literature, should say, that we had heard in this country of no modern writers of much distinction excepting Scott, Moore, and Southey, and more recently, Dr. Chalmers; but that we had reason to suppose, that Newton had made some important

discoveries in astronomy at the beginning of the last century; that 'one Locke,' as Lord Sunderland called him, had
published about the same time, a pretty valuable essay on
the human understanding; and finally, that there appeared in
London, soon after the close of the seven years' war, a
very agreeable little collection of letters on miscellaneous
subjects, published under the feigned name of 'Fitzosborne.'
This caricature, though somewhat more extravagant, is in
point of taste and correctness, precisely parallel to that of
the Review. To attempt to remove an ignorance, which is
obviously affected, would of course be superfluous, and we
shall therefore spare ourselves the trouble of completing
this very elaborate catalogue of American authors. We may
remark, however, that at the moment when the reviewer
was telling us, that he could only recollect the few names
above quoted, that of JEFFERSON was ringing through the
newspapers of his country, and filling the mouths of men of
science, taste, and liberal curiosity throughout the civilized
world. The memoirs and correspondence of this illustrious
statesman, philosopher, scholar, and author, were probably on his table at the time when he wrote the passage in
question. Does the reviewer mean to tell us that the name of
Jefferson will not be ranked hereafter among the principal
ornaments of the literature and philosophy of the present
day? Does he really suppose that the author of the declaration of independence of the United States, the Notes on Virginia, and the vast body of political, literary, and scientific
works, which emanated from the same prolific pen, will be
eclipsed in the judgment of posterity by Hector St. John, or
by either of the four writers, justly distinguished as they
all are, whom the critic has thought proper to mention? He
ought to be aware, whether he is or not, that Mr. Jefferson
will occupy an elevated place in the very highest order of
writers—the one of which Cicero and Burke are the great
exemplars in ancient and modern times—writers, who by
combining literary and active pursuits, and exhibiting in
both a first-rate talent, furnish in their works the most
complete reflection that can possibly be given, of the finished man. A person, who could forget the name of Jefferson

in the present noon-day of his glory, and go back half a century to rake out Hector St. John from the dust of his barn-
yard, would not feel the difference between Tacitus and Tom
Thumb, and would have talked to you of Goody Two Shoes
the morning after the first publication of the Reflections on
the French Revolution.

By the side of the Memoirs and Correspondence of Jefferson lay, or should have lain, upon the table of our critic, at
the time when he was writing, among the other new publications, the first volume of the American translation with an
accompanying commentary of the Mécanique Celeste. Is the
name of BOWDITCH[5] unknown to the countrymen of Napier,
Playfair, and Leslie? If so, is it our fault or theirs that they
are ignorant of the existence and labors of one of the first
mathematicians of the age? It will not answer for the critic
to tell us, that he intended to limit his view of our literature
to the departments of poetry and romance, since the very
publication which was immediately before him belongs to
that of moral philosophy. Charity itself requires that we
should compliment his memory and understanding at the expense of his honesty, and believe that his pretended ignorance is, as we have already intimated, a mere piece of
silly affectation.

We shall not, as we have said before, undertake to complete the catalogue which this writer has left in so defective
a state, but will mention a few other names which would
naturally have occurred to any person disposed to do us justice, and moderately versed in our political and literary
history; and continuing to look at the same great department
of science, to which the works of Dr. Channing and those of
Mr. Jefferson belong, we would venture to ask our critic
whether, with his universal knowledge of men and things,
past, present, and to come, he ever heard of two such persons as JOHN ADAMS and JOHN QUINCY ADAMS? If not,
we have the honor to apprise him, that the former, who under a coincidence of singularly beautiful and affecting circumstances a few years since terminated his earthly pilgrimage—and the latter, who is still living in the full vigor
of his powers and brightness of his glory, have occupied

successively, during their long and brilliant careers of half
a century each, the highest places in philosophy, taste, and
learning, as well as in the administration of the government
of their country, and the esteem of their fellow citizens;
that though they were constantly engaged in the most urgent
and momentous political affairs, creating constitutions,
representing the people in legislative halls and foreign
courts, encountering, in short, responsibility and toil of
every description, until they finally stood before the world
as the elected Rulers of our great and rising empire, they
still found leisure—like the admired statesmen and sages of
antiquity—to cultivate letters in the intervals of business—
published voluminous works, the results of thorough researches into the most intricate branches of political philosophy—taught in our colleges the noble arts they practised in
the Senate, and maintained an extensive correspondence
with most of the distinguished individuals of the age. Of
them and their works the reviewer, according to his own
account, is profoundly ignorant. Whether his ignorance,
real or affected, be more discreditable to himself or to
them, is a question which we may safely leave to the reader
to decide. Again; did our critic never hear of FISHER
AMES?[6] If not, we recommend to his perusal the Speech on
the British Treaty, and the Eulogy on Hamilton. He will soon
perceive that the views they set forth are similar to those
that are generally taken in England on the same subjects;
and having thus ascertained that he can praise them with a
good conscience, we have little doubt that he will admit
them to be fully equal to the most successful efforts of Can-
ning or Mackintosh; HAMILTON himself, with his illustrious
fellow laborers, MADISON and JAY, the joint Numas of our
modern Rome; did the reviewer never hear of them, or
does he suppose that their works will be winked out of the
view of the world by the voluntary blindness of an anonymous Scotch journalist? To take a more 'modern instance,'
has our critic, in the singular shortness of his memory,
forgotten the name of ROBERT WALSH,[7] who has been several times noticed with extraordinary favor in the Edinburgh
Review itself, has contributed to its pages, and was pro-

nounced by its conductors to be one of the best writers in the
language, until he undertook the task of defending his country against British slander, after which it was pretty soon
discovered, that he did not write so well as he did before;
who now publishes a review that would be disparaged by being placed on an equality with most of the leading English
journals of the same description? We will mention but one
more name, and only further ask, whether it would not have
been natural for one who was taking a general view of American literature, in connexion with a particular notice of the
works of Dr. Channing, to revive the recollection of his
friend and colleague in the ministry of divine truth, the be-
loved, the admired, the lamented BUCKMINSTER[8] —a miracle of genius, cut off indeed in the early morning of his
brilliant promise, but not till he had produced works which
may well be compared with the mature efforts of the highest
talents in the same departments of learning? His discourses,
of which a volume was published soon after his death in
1813, and a second has just passed through the press, are
among the most elegant, finished, and really valuable productions of their class to be found in the language. They
combine the powerful thinking of the English divines, more
directly applied to practical life, with the fervid eloquence
of the French school, chastened by the purest and most delicate taste. With all their merit they give us, no doubt, as
we read them, a very inadequate idea of the delightful effects which they produced, when the impression was aided
by the charming intonations, the graceful movements, and
the radiant visage of the accomplished speaker; but considered simply as written sermons, they are undoubtedly superior to any that have appeared in England since the beginning of the present century. To say this, is giving them,
indeed, but scanty praise, and it would be easy to show, if
we had room and opportunity to make the comparison, that
the standard of pulpit eloquence, and we may add, of biblical
criticism and most other branches of theology, is higher in
this country than it is in Great Britain. In these respects,
we are at least sufficiently advanced to know what has been
done and is doing on the continent of Europe, which does not

appear to be the case with our worthy brethren of the 'fast anchored isle.'

If the object of the reviewer, in reducing the number of American authors of any reputation to three or four, were to do the greater honor to those, whom he is willing to acknowledge as such, his proceeding, if not justifiable, would be rather more natural. We all have our favorites among the various pretenders to different kinds of distinction, and are apt enough, in our partiality for those we prefer, to overlook the just claims of others. Such, however, is not the motive of this writer. After limiting in this way the number of our authors, he next proceeds to a malignant and studied depreciation of the merit of those whom he is pleased to enumerate. Messrs. Irving, Brown, and Cooper, and Dr. Channing, are successively noticed in a tone of insolent and contemptuous levity, which would suit well enough with an inquiry into the merit of a doubtful rope-dancer or the rival pretensions of the two Fire-Kings, but which really seems to us to be out of place in a discussion that involves the honor and interest of some of the most highly gifted and respectable individuals of the day. Messrs. Irving and Cooper—although not precisely of equal pretensions—stand, as our readers do not require to be informed, quite at the head of polite literature. Their reputation and popularity are not confined to England and the United States, but extend through the civilized world. With the exception of a few veterans in the wane of their powers, though still in the fulness of their fame, such as Goethe and Châteaubriand on the continent, and Scott, Moore, Southey, and some others in England, that properly belong to another generation, we really know no writers, who, in the line in which they labor and excel, can come in competition with our distinguished countrymen. Their eminence is not the passing effect of an accidental burst of popular favor, obtained by low and unworthy arts, but rests securely on the labors and successes of a series of years. Dr. Channing, on the other hand, though at present somewhat less extensively known, possesses claims to respect of a still higher order, resulting from a still more marked superiority of talent, and enhanced by the

sacred nature of his calling and the exemplary purity of his
life. The delicacy, which we deem it proper to observe in
speaking of a living character, a neighbor, and a personal
friend, prevents us from dwelling so much as we should otherwise gladly do upon the merits of this divine. Suffice it to
say, that if first-rate powers, directed with a steady, unwearied, and enthusiastic effort to the promotion of the
noblest ends by the noblest means, can entitle a man to the
gratitude of others, Dr. Channing has a fair right to claim
that distinction. We are happy, for the honor of our country,
to add, that the public favor has, in this case at least, been
awarded with discernment, and that few, if any, of our citizens, are more admired and respected by all classes of the
community.

Such are the persons, whose literary merits are the subject of discussion in the article before us. Let us now see
the manner in which they are treated.

Mr. Irving, who had hitherto been petted, and, as it were,
clapped on the back by these sturdy censors, is now 'deficient in nerve and originality,' he 'brought nothing with him
from home,' and his sketches, taken in England, are only
'copies of our favorite authors'—'patterns, taken on silk
paper from our classic writers.' The applause bestowed
upon his works, was not so much a tribute to his merit, as
an acknowledgment of the assiduous homage, with which he
courted the favor of the British public. 'He gasped for British popularity.' 'The national politeness (?) owed him some
return, for he imitated, admired, deferred to us, and was
ready to sacrifice every thing to obtain a smile or a look of
approbation.' Such is the liberal construction put by the
critic upon the amiable and romantic, but perfectly honest
and even natural delusion in regard to the refinement and
generosity of the British aristocracy, under which Mr.
Irving appears to have labored on his arrival in England,
and which certainly gave a false coloring to many passages
in the second series of his writings.

Mr. Cooper is treated with still less ceremony. He is
'the drudge of his materials,' he 'labors under an epilepsy
of the fancy,' he is 'not aware of the infinite divisibility

of <u>mind</u> and matter.' Is the reviewer, by the bye, quite certain himself of the truth of this principle as respects the
former substance? He 'anatomizes his subjects'—'he runs
riot in an account of the dishes at a boarding-house, as if it
were a banquet of the gods, and recounts the overturning of
a stage-waggon with as much impetuosity, turbulence, and
exaggerated enthusiasm, as if it were the fall of Phaëton.'
One of his works is, however, a masterpiece, but the merit
even of this appears to result in a great measure from the
circumstance of its containing a single fine description.
And what, gentle reader, do you suppose to be the subject of
this description, which has the effect of elevating one of
these abortions of an epileptic fancy into a literary <u>chef-
d'oeuvre</u>? Neither more nor less than the 'white topsail of
an English man-of-war.' 'The description of the guiding of
the vessel by the Pilot through the narrow strait left for her
escape, the sea-fight, and the incident of the <u>white topsail
of the English man-of-war</u> appearing above the fog, where
it is first mistaken for a cloud, are of the first order of
graphic composition. <u>The rest is commonplace.</u>' Our critic
traverses in the wake of his adventurous author a thousand
leagues of land and pathless ocean—numberless incidents
and changes of many-colored life invite his attention without
success. 'Tis all barren because 'tis all foreign. But no
sooner does the 'white topsail of an English man-of-war'
rise upon his fancy, like the welcome vision of the Heavenly
Twins upon the weary eyes of the tempest-tost mariners in
Horace, than all is well, and he is ready to exclaim with
honest Larry in the Absentee, 'There spoke the true thing—
now my own heart's satisfied.' '<u>The rest is commonplace.</u>'
    This we think excellent. We know nothing better in the
same way, unless it be a subsequent passage in the article
in which the reviewer represents himself as having heard
or <u>said</u> beforehand all the good things in Dr. Channing's
Essay on Milton. 'Our author's criticisms seem to be in a
great measure borrowed from our own lucubrations.' 'All
this we have heard or said before. We are not edified at all,
nor are we greatly flattered by it. It is as if we should convey a letter to a friend in America, and should find it tran-

scribed and sent back to us with a heavy postage.' Our reviewer, whatever may be his other errors, can hardly be charged with hiding his light under a bushel. Montesquieu tells us in one of his Persian letters, that on a visit to a friend's house in the country, he met with two persons who talked more than the rest of the company. The conversation of one resolved itself into this phrase, <u>Cela est vrai parceque je l'ai dit</u>—'that is true, for I have said as much myself'; that of the other into the following, <u>Cela n'est pas vrai parceque je ne l'ai pas dit</u>—'that cannot be true, for I never said any such thing.' The former was considered a pleasant fellow, while the other passed for an insufferable coxcomb. Our critic employs the converse of the first of these forms. <u>Cela est vrai, donc je l'ai dit</u>—'that is true, therefore I said it myself.' He has not the most remote conception that any body else in the world can originate a good thing. If there be a bright thought in Dr. Channing's Essay on Milton, it was of course borrowed from the article on the same subject which appeared about the same time in the Edinburgh Review, although the latter unluckily did not reach this country until after Dr. Channing's was published. Talleyrand, upon reading one day in a newspaper some new repartee, which was attributed, as usual, to himself, is said to have exclaimed, <u>Voila encore un bon mot, que je suis bien aise d'avoir dit</u>.[9] The reviewer, we think, might say as much with great propriety in the present instance, for Dr. Channing's article, wherever it may have come from, is the better of the two. With equal simplicity he firmly believes, that all the books that are published throughout the world are intended solely and exclusively for the perusal of his fraternity, and if they contain any allusion to, or extract from 'the Review,' they are thus far in the nature of a letter, which returns to its writer with the burden of double postage. With all this, our critic can talk very pointedly and properly in the same article on the folly of <u>selfishness</u>. 'This paltry <u>self</u>, looking upon <u>itself</u> as of more importance than all the rest of the world, fancies <u>itself</u> the centre of the universe, and would have every one else look upon it in the same light.' We entirely agree in the doctrine

here stated by this writer, which is so distinctly expressed
as to relieve us from the trouble of seeking epithets, to
characterize his practice.

So much for the manner in which Messrs. Irving and
Cooper, and in part Dr. Channing, are treated in the article
before us. As respects the last of these writers, he not only
borrows all his good sayings from the Edinburgh Review,
but 'endeavors to trim to all opinions and unite all suf-
frages,'—'calculates the vulgar clamor and venal sophistry
of the British press for the meridian of Boston,'—'keeps an
eye to both worlds, kisses hands to the reading public all
round, and does his best to stand well with all the different
sects and parties.' 'He is a Unitarian, but disclaims all
connexion with Dr. Priestley as a materialist; he denounces
Calvinism and the Church of England, but to show that this
proceeds from no want of liberality, makes the amende honorable to Popery and Popish divines—is an American Republican and a French Bourbonist—abuses Bonaparte, and observes a profound silence with respect to Ferdinand.' 'He
likes wit, provided it is serious.' Because he speaks of
Milton, Bacon, and Shakspeare, as superior in the order of
intellect to the Duke of Wellington and Admiral Nelson, he
is compared to Abraham Adams, in Fielding's novel, who
'thought a schoolmaster the greatest character in the world,
and himself the greatest of all schoolmasters'; and is represented as 'gravely dividing greatness into different sorts,
and placing himself at the top.' Finally, he is a 'pretender
of the stamp of those, who think that there is no reason why
they should not do all that others can, and a great deal more
into the bargain.'

Thus much for his personal character. As to his writings;
—'We like his sermons best—his criticisms less—his politics least of all.' It would seem from other passages, that
the best is bad enough. Even as a preacher, his 'style is
tedious, and his arguments trite.' 'He is prolix without
suspecting it—lays a solemn stress on the merest trifles—
repeats truisms and apologises for them as startling discoveries—plays the sophist, and conceives that he is performing a sacred duty.' The 'general feature' that distinguishes

his works is 'ambitious commonplace.' 'He takes up the
newest and most plausible opinion at the turn of the tide, or
just as it is getting into vogue, and would fain arrogate both
the singularity and the popularity of it to himself.' 'His account of Milton is a mere imitation or amplification of what
has been said by others,' which others are, as we have
seen, afterwards explained to be the critic himself. 'His
style is good, though in general too labored, formal, and
constrained. All is brought equally forward—nothing is left
to tell for itself. In the attempt to be copious, he is tauto-
logical—in striving to explain every thing, he overloads and
obscures his meaning. The fault is the uniform desire to
produce effect, and the supposition that this is to be done by
main force.' 'His politics are borrowed from others, and
are grounded on misrepresentations and falsehoods.' The
'ugly mask,' which once concealed from the world the true
character of Bonaparte, has, it seems, been 'taken off in
England,' but Dr. Channing chooses to lecture on the 'mask
in preference to the head.'

Now we must assume that every journal of the character
and pretensions of the Edinburgh Review, has for its object,
in profession at least, if not in practice and reality, to promote good taste in letters, and good principles in the conduct
of life. This being supposed, we would venture to ask whether the prevalence of good taste is promoted by a studied
depreciation of the merits of the best writers of the time,
or that of good principles by treating the ministers of religion and the most enlightened, active, and ardent friends of
humanity with open insult, merely because they happen to
reside in a foreign country. It is not our purpose to attempt
to fix on this occasion the precise value of the literary labors of the distinguished persons alluded to, and we shall
therefore not undertake to examine whether there be or be
not any real foundation for some or all of the charges here
made against them. They doubtless have, like all other men,
their weak points, and this critic would have proved himself
to be as stupid, as he is malignant, which is not exactly the
case, if he had not selected these as the basis of some at
least of his caricatures. Others, as we shall presently see,

are so entirely destitute of any resemblance to the features
of the originals, that they must necessarily pass for mere
fancy-pieces. But without pretending to refute, or even examine in detail any of these objections—without wishing to
exempt these writers from the full severity of a just and
legitimate criticism,—we confine our view at present entirely to the tone and temper of the article,—about which, after
the extracts we have given, the reader will perceive that
there can be no dispute,—and we ask again what advantage
results to the cause of good taste and good morals from as-
sailing the best writers and the best men with wanton outrage? Is it fair, just, grateful, or honorable to reward in
this way, the labors, the studies, the privations of every
kind, which are incident to the literary profession? The
principle of genius is a keen sensibility, which renders its
possessor uncommonly susceptible to all impressions, and
incapacitates him, as it were, from bearing up with equa-
nimity under the toils and troubles that enter so largely into
even the common lot of humanity,—and are those whose
occupation it is to cultivate and encourage letters, to add to
these troubles the 'slings and arrows' of unprovoked calumny? The delicate texture of a poetical imagination is not
proof against such treatment, which has often been fatal to
the peace, the happiness, the life itself of those who have
suffered it. It was said by Racine, that he had received
more pain from a single unjust criticism, than pleasure
from all the praise that had ever been bestowed upon him;
and it is commonly reported, that he died of the effects of a
reprimand from his sovereign. A modern critic remarks,
that it was a great piece of folly in so wise a man, to allow
himself to be so much affected by so slight a cause; but he
did not recollect that if Racine had been so constituted as to
support with indifference the attacks of critics and the dis-
pleasure of Louis XIV, he could not possibly have written his
exquisite tragedies. Did our reviewer remember when he
aimed at the probity of Mr. Irving, the false and wanton in-
sinuations, or rather assertions, which we have quoted
above, that, coming from such a quarter, they would necessarily poison for a time the peace of one of the purest and

most amiable, as well as ingenious men now living? Was
this a natural return for the pleasure which he has given to
us all—including his cynical calumniator—by the charming
creations, with which his fine genius has for so many years
peopled the monotonous pathway of every-day life? Or even
if we choose to consider the whole business of polite literature as mere sport, and those who cultivate it, as voluntarily exposing themselves to be treated with a wanton and
insolent levity, which they are to receive as mere pleasantry, and requite in kind, what shall we say of the taste and
principles of those who sport in the same way with the sacred subject of religion and its teachers? These may be
supposed indeed to be comparatively indifferent to unjust attacks. Their objects are of a loftier and purer kind than
those of the merely literary man, and raise them above the
sphere of popular applause and censure, in which the other
lives, and moves, and has his being,—above the ordinary
accidents of life. Like their sublime Master, when fixed to
the cross in the fatal hour of his last agony, they can pray
for their spiteful and malignant persecutors, as mistaken
wretches, who know not what they do. But the same reasons,
which render the minister of religion, who truly feels the
spirit of his calling, superior to the influence of calumny,
impose upon others with tenfold force the duty of treating
him in the interest of society with marked respect. We are
willing to believe, and do in fact think it probable, that the
critic was not aware of the extraordinary purity and excellence of the character of Dr. Channing, when he ventured to
assault him in this unmanly style, but it is obvious that the
reverence, which is habitually cherished by all right-mind-
ed persons for every thing connected with religion, in the
absence of any more particular motive, ought to, and would,
if he had felt it, have restrained his petulance.

It is not our intention, as we remarked above, to discuss
in detail the objections that are made to the literary and
moral characters of our distinguished countrymen in the article before us, but we will here barely mention, without
enlarging upon them, one or two very extraordinary incon-

sistencies between the statements of the critic, and the real
facts of the case.

Mr. Irving is represented as entirely deficient in images
and feelings of American origin—'he brought with him no
new earth, no sprig of laurel gathered in the wilderness, no
red bird's wing, no gleam from crystal lake, or new-
discovered fountain, neither grace nor grandeur plucked
from the bosom of this Eden state, like that which belongs
to cradled infancy—but he brought us rifacciamentos of our
own thoughts—copies of our favorite authors.' Now all this,
which is prettily, though somewhat affectedly, expressed,
happens to be exactly the reverse of the truth. The best
parts of Mr. Irving's works are those in which he has
drawn his inspiration wholly from American sources, and
those of which the scene is laid abroad, though often beautiful, are uniformly feebler than the former. Such has been
and is the general opinion of competent judges, and, what
our critic will consider as more to the point, of the writers
in the Edinburgh Review. In a very favorable notice of the
Sketch Book, which appeared in that journal, some articles
were recommended, and in part quoted, as more particularly interesting, of which the prominent one was Rip Van
Winkle. It appears, therefore, that the first bouquet which
Mr. Irving presented to the British public, contained a
'sprig of laurel,' which he had brought with him from home,
and which was pronounced at once by these fastidious critics, to be the prettiest thing in the bunch. In their notices of
his subsequent works, the passages founded on American
scenery and manners, have always been selected as the
most striking and spirited. So obvious indeed is the superiority of these to the rest, that we have no hesitation in
regarding them as the life of the collections in which they
appear, the attic salt as it were, that gave vitality, freshness, and taste to the otherwise somewhat insipid compound.
Mr. Irving had gathered on his native soil, and before he
ever saw Europe, not merely 'sprigs of laurel,' but gar-
lands far more healthy and more likely to endure than those
which he afterwards plucked in the conservatories of England. His Knickerbocker, on the whole the most powerful

and original of all his productions, is wholly American. Every line of it is 'new earth and red bird's wing.' In Salmagundi there were occasionally imitations of Addison and Goldsmith, and the plan was copied from that of the Spectator, but even here the best things are of native origin. The Little Man in Black is not, as far as we recollect, described in 'our stock-books of a century ago,' nor have we seen any account of the American logocracy, the Tunisian ambassador's wardrobe, or the pleasures of a tour to Saratoga Springs by 'the wits of Queen Anne.' When Mr. Irving went to Europe, he carried with him, as we have just seen, sundry sprigs of laurel, a little nursery, in fact, of wild flowers, which he mingled in somewhat sparing proportions with those of foreign growth, that he collected on his way, but which were constantly noticed as the pride of his nosegay. The red bird's wing was always the most conspicuous plume in his bonnet. But we did not find him putting forth all his power until he employed himself again in his Columbus upon a subject exclusively and strictly American. Does our critic find no 'gleam of crystal lake, or new-discovered fountain, neither grace nor grandeur plucked from the bosom of an Eden state, like that of cradled infancy,' in the charming descriptions which Mr. Irving has given us of the indolent, luxurious Paradise of the natives of Haïti? Why, this very writer, or one of his fraternity, employed, but a short time since, almost the same language in telling us what Mr. Irving's style is, that he now employs with the insertion of a negative in telling us what it is not. This is really too bad. Mr. Irving's sketches in England are, as we have hinted above, comparatively feeble. By affecting to represent these as the only things which he has done that are worth attention, and throwing out of view the whole of his best and most spirited productions, the reviewer is able to make him out a mere tame copyist of the British classics, with some degree of plausibility; with how much candor, we leave it for our readers to judge.

An inconsistency with fact, not less glaring than that which we have just noticed, occurs in the account of Dr. Channing, the prominent trait in whose character, according to this writer, is a disposition to 'trim to all opinions, and keep well with all parties at the same time.' Such is the picture; but how stands the fact? Dr. Channing, as our readers are generally aware, is the acknowledged leader of the Unitarian sect, as far as there can be leaders in a communion of which the officiating clergymen are all on a footing of perfect equality. Far from making a secret of his opinions, he habitually declares them with a degree of fearlessness, which some of his friends consider imprudent. Now the Unitarian sect—although it includes perhaps, in proportion to its numbers, as large a share of the talent, virtue, and respectability of the country as any other,—is doubtless among them all the one, which has the least pretensions to popularity. It is in fact one, which, as all who are capable of looking at the subject philosophically well know, from the nature of its tenets never can be popular. It is one which scrutinizes texts—estimates the value of manuscripts and editions—balances the authority of conflicting passages, and consequently addresses itself to a very limited portion of the community: for such a portion only have the means and leisure to pursue these inquiries. We may go further, and affirm with safety, not only that the Unitarians are not a popular sect, but that they are decidedly the most unpopular of all. They are habitually denounced, both here and in England, by those who respect and love them individually, as unbelievers, deists, and sometimes atheists. The state of the case is therefore simply this: Dr. Channing stands forth openly and fearlessly before the world as the leading champion of a decried, suspected, and unpopular class of Christians. It is no part of our business to inquire into the justice of the suspicions entertained of the Unitarians, which may or may not have a reasonable foundation. The fact is undoubtedly as we have stated it. What, then, does the reviewer mean,—what can he mean,—by representing Dr. Channing as a time-server, who trims to all opinions, and keeps well with all parties? Is it trimming to all opinions to espouse a particular one, and maintain it with so much energy, eloquence, and consistency, as to be considered the leader and champion of those who hold it? Is it

keeping well with all parties to oppose and defy them all except a particular one, and that the smallest and most unpopular among them? In his controversial writings, Dr. Channing has no doubt uniformly observed the decorum, which
belongs to his character and feelings, as well as to his position, and has treated his opponents with perfect liberality;
but we venture to hope that the observance of the ordinary
courtesies of life does not make a man out to be a time-
server and a trimmer. If it did, by the bye, we think we
could safely assure the writer of the article before us, that
he would never be considered as obnoxious to those qualifications. In short, the charges here made against Dr. Channing are so obviously and palpably at variance with his position in the world, they attribute to him a character so
entirely the reverse of that which he notoriously bears, that
it is somewhat difficult to imagine how the idea of them
could have gained admission into the reviewer's mind in
connexion with his name. The making of them supposes, no
doubt, an almost complete ignorance of the reputation and
standing of the author whose works he undertook to cut up,
as well as a criminal readiness to scoff at things and persons which all good men regard with reverence; but it also
supposes, we think, the existence of some particular motive
which operated in this case, to give a bias to the mind of the
reviewer, which, under other circumstances, it could not
well have taken.

It appears, in fact, from the tenor of the article, that
there was such a motive, the nature of which is indicated
with sufficient clearness in the closing sentence of the extracts given above. The 'ugly mask' which for a time concealed from the world the character of Bonaparte, has, it
seems, been taken off in England; but 'Dr. Channing continues to lecture on the mask in preference to the head.'
Dr. Channing, has published, under the form of a review of
Scott's Napoleon, a powerful analysis of the intellectual and
moral character of that personage, which, according to the
notions of the reviewer, is not sufficiently favorable to the
'Man of Destiny.' The supposed injustice done to his favorite hero, seems to be the source of the particular disgust

which the reviewer has taken towards our distinguished
countryman; and the supposed inconsistency between a love
of liberty and a dislike of Bonaparte, appears to be the real
foundation for the charge made upon him, of trimming between opposite opinions, and keeping well with all parties.

Now, supposing even that Dr. Channing had in some degree mistaken the character of Bonaparte, we cannot admit
that this would at all justify the critic in his outrageous attack; but, independently of this consideration, we must also
remark, that, according to our judgment, the mistake on
this subject, if there be any, is on the other side. We cannot
perceive that any material injustice is done to the celebrated
Corsican in the Doctor's article. We greatly doubt the fact,
so positively affirmed by the reviewer, that the 'ugly mask,'
which was formerly supposed to be the face of Bonaparte,
has been taken off in England. We have seen no authentic
account of any such operation. The meaning of this language
in plain English—if it mean any thing—is, that Napoleon was
at one time considered as a tyrant, a usurper, and an enemy
of liberty, but that the public opinion on this subject has
been since changed, and that he is now better thought of,
perhaps approved, lamented, and admired; for we are not
informed how far the reviewer means to proceed in his
hero's apotheosis. Now we are free to confess, as respects
ourselves, that we have no knowledge of any such revolution
in the public opinion upon this subject, and we believe that
we may say the same for most of our countrymen. On this
side the water, Napoleon is still the same tyrant, usurper,
and enemy of liberty, that he always was; and Dr. Channing,
in representing him under this point of view, has expressed
the feeling of the great mass of his fellow-citizens, as well
as his own. We know that a mask was removed from his
character some time before his death—not, however, by any
means an ugly mask, but, on the contrary, a brilliant and
dazzling one, like the silver veil of the Prophet in Moore's
poem—we mean the false glare, the prestige, to use an ex-
pressive French word, with which the possession of imperial
power and unbounded wealth had so long surrounded him in
the imagination of the world. When this was removed, he

did not,—such at least is our impression,—rise in the public estimation, but on the contrary was thought to have lost
much of his heroism, without gaining a great deal on the
score of humanity. When we saw the conqueror in fifty
pitched battles—the modern Charlemagne—forgetting the
real, in a vain concern for the imaginary and conventional,
dignity of his character, and disputing with a paltry colonial
governor about the style in which he was to be addressed,
and the number of bottles of claret he was to be allowed for
dinner, with as much apparent interest as he had before
contended with Alexander for the empire of Europe, our es-
timate of his qualities was in some degree lowered, and we
recollected Rousseau's well known ode,

> Le masque tombe—l'homme reste,—
> Et le héros s'évanouit.[10]

Since that time, and especially since the death of Bonaparte, we have had in rapid succession a series of publications, filled with the most minute, curious, and instructive
information respecting his character and opinions, prepared
in general by friendly hands, and compiled, in part, under
his own direction and even dictation. We have had the scientific and military details of his campaigns by himself and his
favorite generals; the diffuse memoranda of his conversations in exile by the Count de Las Cases, and now within a
few months the authentic narrative of his private life while
in power, by his favorite secretary, of which we hope in a
future number to lay some notice before our readers. In addition to this, we have had a hundred collections of memoirs, some of them in the highest degree curious and interesting, by various personages, who figured in his armies or
at his court, from his brother to his butler: and we may
safely say, that there is now, as the Spanish proverb runs,
very little at the bottom of the inkstand. The strain of most
of these works is on the whole decidedly panegyrical, as
might naturally be expected, when we recollect that they
were almost all written by creatures and dependants of the
Ex-Emperor, who looked back to the period of his reign as
the golden age, which for them no doubt it was. Every thing

has been said that could be said, to exalt, embellish, explain, justify, excuse, or palliate, according to the nature
of the particular passage of his life under consideration. His
encomiasts endeavor to make him out the 'wisest, virtuous-
est, discreetest, best' of men, as well as the most enter-
prising, skilful, and successful of commanders. We have
been told how he pinched the Abbé de Pradt's ears, extem-
porised love-tales for the entertainment of the Empress and
her ladies, and played bob-cherry with the King of Rome.
All this may be true, although we must own that we receive
it in part with some grains of allowance. But supposing it to
be all true, it does not much affect the political and moral
character of the personage, who, we fear, must still remain
what he was before—sedet aeternumque sedebit[11]—a usurper,
a tyrant, and an enemy to liberty.

Our critic takes it very much amiss that Dr. Channing
should elevate Milton, Bacon, and Shakspeare in the order
of intellectual precedency above Wellington, Nelson, and
Napoleon, and in general should consider philosophy and
poetry as higher applications of talent than the business of
practical life even in its highest departments, which policy
and war undoubtedly are. He affirms that the latent object of
the Doctor in making this division, is no other than to place
himself at the top among those who talk about things, and
commanders at the bottom among those who only do them.
Now this, which is doubtless in the opinion of the reviewer
very excellent pleasantry, is unquestionably very inaccurate, and we must add, very unfair when considered as a
statement of the theory of our countryman. Dr. Channing
does not place himself, but Milton, Bacon, and Shakspeare
at the top, and he does not place the great commanders,
such as Napoleon, Wellington, and Nelson, at the bottom,
but only below the very few persons who have exercised
equal or greater powers in a still more comprehensive and
general way. The difference between these two versions of
his theory, however unimportant the critic may consider it
for other purposes, is at least very material to the reputation of Dr. Channing for modesty—a quality which is more
valued on this side the water than—to judge by the practice

of the reviewer—we should suppose it to be in Scotland. As respects the principle, we incline to think that it will bear examination, and do not consider it so much at variance with the common opinion of the world as this writer evidently does. If he had not treated it as a paradox, we should have been rather disposed to regard it as a truism. 'In Europe,' it seems, 'we think that Caesar, Alexander, and Charlemagne were no babies.' Has Dr. Channing, then, intimated that he considered Napoleon as a baby? Is every man a baby who could not have written the Paradise Lost, the Novum Organon [sic] or King Lear? If the reviewer's object be caricature, we can understand what he means; but his representation, or rather misrepresentation, is obviously wholly foreign to the merits of the question. 'We think in Europe that to move the great masses of power, and to bind opinions in a spell, is as difficult as the turning a period, or the winding up a homily.' Does the reviewer then mean to tell us that it is the commander, military or naval, who moves the great masses of power and binds opinions in a spell? Is it not perfectly obvious, that no individual, by a direct application of even the highest talent to practical business, can produce any very extensive effects, excepting so far as he may have the advantage of a favorable state of opinion, prepared, 'spell-bound,' as the reviewer is pleased to say, beforehand? No illustration of this remark can be more complete and conclusive than that which is furnished by the example of Napoleon himself. The conqueror of Arcole, Austerlitz, and Jena, undoubtedly possessed a military genius of the first class; but what would he have been under other circumstances—had he lived, for example, fifty years earlier than he did? He would have been under Louis XV. what Dumouriez—a person of much the same character—was, a brigadier-general at forty, with the reputation of a mauvaise tête, and alive at this day. The principle of his great success lay in the fact of his appearance at a critical epoch. The revolution had electrified public opinion, and thrown the great living masses of power, not only into motion, but into convulsions. Bonaparte, with his prodigious military talent, electrified himself by the same

causes that acted upon all the rest, was able, under the favor of circumstances, to give these masses for a time a
direction towards any particular object which he happened to
prefer. Here was a golden opportunity for displaying the
very highest order, not of intellectual, but, what is a still
nobler quality, moral greatness; and had Napoleon done justice to it, he would undoubtedly have placed his name above
those of Milton, Shakspeare, or any other that is named
among men, excepting only that of Washington. To what object then—having as he had the full liberty of choice—did he
direct the almost boundless power which was placed at his
disposal? The good of the world—the service of truth, virtue,
and liberty—the welfare of his country? Oh no! All these
might have been promoted together, and by the same efforts;
but these noble objects, and with them the lives and happiness of millions of his contemporaries, were sacrificed to
a direct regard for his own <u>paltry self</u>, as the reviewer has
it. When the universe was all in alarm, ready for any thing,
and thrown by accident under his command, he could think of
nothing better to employ it upon than the mighty adventure
of changing the style, title, and mode of living of a little
French corporal and his family. Such were his pretensions
to moral greatness; and where a man is deficient in this
particular, there is much reason to fear that his mind is not
of the highest order. 'The heart,' says Vauvenargues, 'is
the true source of intellectual power.' <u>Toutes les grandes
pensées viennent du coeur</u>. But to return to the question, as
stated by the reviewer himself—Who electrified public opinion, and set in motion the great masses of power, which
Napoleon so shamefully mismanaged? Obviously the authors
of the French revolution. And who were the authors of the
French revolution? The military, we know, were the last
portion of the community who had any concern in it. Those
who gave the impulse and carried on the work to its comple-
tion at the taking of the Bastille, were the orators, thinkers,
and writers—to go no higher—of the two preceding centuries,
from Luther to Mirabeau. How did they effect their object?
Precisely by the means which the reviewer speaks of with
so much contempt—'by turning periods' and 'winding up

homilies.' An obscure Augustine monk, by his powerful
preaching, wrought in such a way upon the feelings of his
contemporaries, that they burst all bounds—rent in twain
the sacred veil that had before concealed from the public the
mysteries of religious belief, and commenced a series of
wars that lasted a century and a half, and opened an epoch
in the history of Europe. But as Luther only 'wound up homilies' he was of course, in the opinion of our critic, a very
small man. Calvin and he were mere pigmies in comparison
with Gustavus Adolphus and Wallenstein, who did the things,
which they only talked about. Locke, Montesquieu, Voltaire,
Rousseau, and the rest, by their powerful speculations in
moral and political philosophy, effected the change in the
public opinion of Europe, which immediately determined the
occurrence of the French revolution, and thus unsettled all,
and overthrew the greater part of the governments before
existing in the civilized world. But as these persons only
'turned periods,' their agency was, of course, a very secondary one, and they are not to be named for importance on
the same day with Dumouriez, Pichegru, Moreau, and, finally, Napoleon and his generals, who actually did what they
only talked about. Such is the system of the reviewer. We in
America—very foolishly perhaps—consider the 'kingly-
crowned head' and the 'counsellor heart,' as nobler members of the body, whether politic or natural, than 'our steed
the leg,' or 'the arm our soldier.' Without pretending to
depreciate the importance of the functions of a military or
naval commander, which are among the noblest that belong
to practical life, we conceive that the philosopher occupies
the same situation in the great action of human affairs, and
in relation to the whole human race, that the general does
on the field of battle in reference to his own army. The skilful commander, who knows his business, does not place
himself in the front rank, and lay about him with his own
hands. He takes his station on a neighboring height with a
telescope by his side, and gives his orders to his aids, who
in turn convey them to the inferior officers, until they reach
the subalterns and privates. These are the persons who actually cut down the enemy. They do what the commander-in-

chief and the superior officers only <u>talk</u> about, and on the
system of our critic are the real heroes of the day. In the
same way, the philosopher takes his stand on the intellectual
elevation of superior talent, and talks to the few who are able
to hear him—$\varphi\omega\nu\hat{\alpha}\nu\tau\alpha$ $\sigma\upsilon\nu\epsilon\tau\hat{o}\iota\sigma\iota\nu$.[12] By them his judgments of men and things are communicated to the many, and
having thus wrought out a change in public opinion, begin at
last to exhibit their practical effects, whether for good or
evil, by determining a new order of political events. Thus
far all is done by talking, and the talk is entirely upon general principles. At this period, a new scene opens in the
progress of the action, and a new set of characters make
their appearance. The practical statesman and commander
are now the prominent persons, but still, as before, all is
done by talking. The only difference is, that the conversation, instead of turning upon general principles, now turns
upon the application of them to the business of the world.
The representative and diplomatist talk in Congress and in
Parliament—the commander talks and writes in his cabinet
or at the head of his army—and they thus produce effects
upon a somewhat inferior, but still very extensive scale,
until, finally, the merely passive mortal machine begins to
perform its functions. The tax-gatherer, the soldier, the
sheriff, the surgeon, the attorney, the cultivator, get into motion. Sword and lancet, pill and cartridge-box, plea, plough,
and printing-press are set to work: the talk is over, and the
real action, as our critic considers it, is at last in progress. It is needless, of course, after what we have said, to
dwell any further on the nature of his mistake, which is obviously the vulgar one of considering 'the pride, pomp, and
circumstance,' the 'sound and fury, signifying nothing,'
which attend the appearance of a certain class of the per-
formers in this great drama, as proofs of their superior
importance in comparison with the rest. A man who wears
a laced coat with epaulettes on his shoulders, occupies the
largest house in the city, is attended, when he goes out, by
a multitude of others, and perhaps saluted by the discharge
of a hundred pieces of artillery, is obviously a much greater
character than another who merely sits down in his morning-

gown, to write by his fire-side. The plausibility of the statement, so far as it has any, lies in confounding the faculty of
writing and speaking with grammatical correctness and rhetorical elegance, with the intellectual power which is required for writing and speaking with effect. In the former
sense the art of turning a period or winding up a homily is
undoubtedly a very trifling accomplishment, although we
could wish that, trifling as it is, it were not quite so much
neglected by some of our great men. But to turn a period or
wind up a homily with effect, requires, in addition to all that
Lowth and Blair can supply, a head—with good effect—a
heart; and these are tools which, whatever the reviewer may
think of it, are not to be found in every man's workshop. As
respects the latter, at least, we believe that his own stock
would not be the worse for a little mending.

The reviewer appears to consider the opinion entertained
by Dr. Channing of the character of Napoleon, as not only
unjust and incorrect in itself, but as entirely inconsistent
with the liberal principles, which our countryman professes
in regard to other matters. This supposed inconsistency is,
as we remarked above, the real foundation of the charge
made upon him by the critic of trimming between opposite
parties. It is impossible according to this authority, to love
liberty without loving Bonaparte, and one who pretends to
love liberty, and at the same time to hate Bonaparte, must
necessarily be a hypocrite and a time-server. 'We are surprised, that staunch republicans, who complain that the
world bow to rank and birth alone, should turn with redoubled rage against intellect, the moment it became a match
for pride and prejudice, and was the only thing that could be
opposed to them with success, or could extort a moment's
fear or awe for human genius or human nature!'

Now we must needs say, at the risk of appearing to be ac-
tuated by a spirit of indiscriminate censure, that the inconsistency here, as the error before, seems to us to be on the
side of the reviewer, and not of Dr. Channing. We really
cannot discern the identity between the cause of Bonaparte,
and that of well-ordered and rational liberty, which is so
perfectly obvious and palpable to the sharp optics of this

Scottish seer. We in our turn are surprised that staunch
whigs, nurtured in the principles of Sydney and Russell,
brought up at the feet of Fox, enemies by creed, feeling, habit, and inheritance, of the slightest approach to arbitrary
forms of government, should deem it consistent with their
character to grovel at the footstool of a despot, and kiss the
rod of iron oppression, simply because it is wielded by the
hand of one who rose from the lower walks of life, possessed
great talents, and had once been, or pretended to be, a
friend of liberty. Does tyranny lose its proper character,
and cease to be odious, because the tyrant happens to be also a usurper, an apostate, and an upstart? If the situation
and disposition of a ruler be such, that he will certainly do
me all the injury in his power, is it a rational source of satisfaction to me, that he possesses great talents, and that his
power to injure me will of course be nearly co-extensive
with his will? Can I be blamed for turning with 'redoubled
rage,' if the reviewer like the expression, upon intellect,
when the only use that is made of this intellect is to invent
and put in practice new and more effectual methods of de-
priving me by force or fraud of all I hold dear? Did the Romans of the time of Caesar, who, as Cassius tells us in the
play, were compelled to

> Walk under his <u>huge legs</u>, and peep about
> To find themselves dishonorable graves,

feel much pride in the large dimensions of the political man-
mountain, that was trampling them down in the dust? For
ourselves we are devotedly attached to liberty, and would
make any sacrifice to escape from oppression; but if we
must submit to it, we have no hesitation in saying that we
should much prefer a good, easy, hereditary, gouty despot,
who would ask for nothing but a skilful cook, and a well-
stocked deer-park, to a fiery usurper of first-rate talent,
who would be always on horseback, wasting the blood and
treasure of his people in vain attempts to gratify his wild
and wanton ambition. Tyrant for tyrant, we should certainly
prefer King Log to King Stork, Louis to Napoleon; and we
consider this preference as not only not inconsistent with,

but as the natural and necessary result of a love of liberty. We must even venture to suggest to this critic, with all the deference due to so high an authority, that the intelligent friends of liberty on this side the water have not been edified by the tone of adulation which has generally distinguished the speculations of the Edinburgh Review on the character of Bonaparte. We have seen with regret, and a sort of indignation, the journal which claims to be, and may perhaps be fairly considered as being in Europe, the leading periodical organ of sound political principles, lavishing its warmest expressions of applause and admiration upon the bitterest and most effective enemy to such principles that has yet appeared. We cannot admit as a sufficient excuse for this, that the Edinburgh Review is or was, as respects the party divisions that prevail in Great Britain, an opposition journal; and that it was necessary to defend at all hazards, and with every sacrifice of consistency and principle, the chief of a nation with which the ministry were at war. This might answer as an apology for a humbler class of writers, who profess no other rule of conduct than attachment to their party; but can hardly be received as a good plea in behalf of the Edinburgh Review. Or even if we consent to allow to this consideration somewhat more weight than it is fairly entitled to, what propriety is there in expecting that we in this country, who are not under the influence of the same party feelings, should give way to the same real or affected delusion upon this subject? Because the British whigs deem it politic to rush through thick and thin in pursuit of what they no doubt regard as patriotic objects, are the citizens of the United States, who have no immediate concern with those objects, to affirm that black is white, and sanction the wildest excesses in conduct, and the grossest errors in principle, merely for the sake of keeping them company? We can assure the reviewer, that it is as much as our consciences will bear us out in, to follow up the hue and cry of our own parties, without intermeddling in those of other countries a thousand leagues off. In short, if the critic will but coolly consider these things, he cannot avoid seeing, that the inconsistency complained of is really on his side, and not on

that of Dr. Channing; that the friends of liberty are not, as
such, bound in honor and conscience to bow down before the
brazen image of a ruthless and bloody military despotism;
and that if he, the reviewer, had thought proper to bestow a
little of his friendly feeling upon the young, flourishing,
growing, glorious, English republic of the United States, instead of wasting it all upon an Italian soldier, merely because he was a man of talent, he would have acted much
more consistently with his professed principles, and done
himself a great deal more honor in the opinion of judicious
men.

The general result seems to be, that the attack of the reviewer upon the literary and moral reputation of Dr. Channing, and our other distinguished countrymen, is not less
unjust than it is indecorous. We had intended, after replying
to the article immediately before us, to have alluded to
some other attacks, which have recently been levelled by
the British press against this country, but have only room
at present to notice the manner in which one of the more respectable weekly journals has been pleased to comment upon
our own labors. We shall first quote entire the article to
which we allude, and which appeared in the Edinburgh Scotsman of December 5th, under the title of North American Review, No. 65, for October, 1829.

'We have no great respect for this periodical, of which
a casual number now and then strays into our hands. We
give the writers credit for considerable industry, talent,
and extent of information, and for a large portion of that
worldly shrewdness which disposes prudent men to sail
with the tide, and keep to windward of all doctrines which
are not already in general favor; but they are woefully
deficient in intellectual courage, in profound and original
views, in lofty aims, and in that love of truth and of mankind, which atones for many errors, and sanctifies the
best efforts of the understanding. The journal wants true
American feeling; it wants heart and it wants soul. The
writers creep in the train of our reviewers, and take upon
their shoulders from choice, the load of prejudice and

sophistry which is forcibly entailed upon us by our old establishments, and the feelings and interests which have
grown out of them. There is but one absolutely clear stage
in the world for the discussion of every question that interests mankind; and that, owing to a happy combination
of circumstances, exists in North America. But the periodical writers of the first class there, voluntarily re-
nounce the high functions which thus devolve upon them,
and, instead of heading the tide of liberal speculation,
and boldly proclaiming truths which must either be suppressed in the old world, or uttered in whispers, send us
back a feeble echo of the false doctrines and antiquated
opinions, which are, or were current among ourselves.
For any thing that appears in it on politics, morals, law,
religion, or philosophy, this review might be edited under
the censorship of a Burgomaster of Frankfort, or an
Amtman of Carlsruhe! If it was (were) published in either
of these towns, we should say it was a respectable journal; but as the organ of opinion in free republican America, nothing can be more pitiful. It is as innocent of giving
countenance to innovation, as if Prince Metternich were
the editor! Indeed, it gives shelter and protection to many
errors and prejudices, of which enlightened men in Europe are beginning to be ashamed. The writers have not
the slightest conception that their country exemplifies a
new and happier order of society, which ought to become
a source of light to the world. Were Locke and Sydney
living in our day, they would regard the American government as a beautiful and successful experiment, which has
solved difficulties that had perplexed the wisest of men
from the beginning of time, and unfolded truths of incalculable value to mankind. Not so the sages of the North
American Review. In their eyes, the republican institutions of their country are merely one of the accidental
modes or fashions of government to which the varieties of
national taste and genius give birth, having much in common with the pauper-loaded and priest-ridden systems of
the old world! To transplant its forms, or apply its principles to any state of continental Europe, would, in their

opinion, be a presumptuous and visionary attempt, fit only
for the Radicals of England, or the Tugenbundists of Germany! As men shave their heads in one country—their
chins in another—and wear both their hair and their beard
in a third—so there is a diversity of taste and usage
among nations upon the subject of government, which no
wise man should disturb! The American loves to make his
own laws, assess his own taxes, and appoint his own par-
sons and magistrates. The Englishman's pleasure is to
grumble at the aristocracy, to whom he commits these
functions; the Spaniard rejoices in the dominion of his
rey absoluto and his priests; the Turk is delighted with
the bow-string of his sublime Lord, and the conscience of
the Russian is satisfied provided his back is well flayed
with the knout! All these are equally happy under their
several systems! To transfer the institutions of one of
these nations, in whole or in part, to any of the others,
would unsettle old associations and venerable usages, as
Burke sagaciously observes, and be in fact like an attempt
to fit the jacket of the Laplander upon the shoulders of the
gigantic Patagonian! We assure our readers, that in giving this account of their doctrines, though we cannot quote
words or passages, we are not intentionally caricaturing
the American reviewers, but describing what we honestly
believe to be the scope of their principles; and our opinion
is formed after perusing, at one time or another, a considerable portion of their lucubrations. It does indeed
rouse our indignation to see them, with such unequalled
means of doing good, play false to the cause of mankind,
and lend their aid to prop up the most pernicious errors
and the worst dogmas of the old world.

'Let him who doubts our statement, try the American
reviewers by "any constant question." Let him examine
their opinions as to the effect of church establishments,
the utility of classical literature as a part of general education, the value of the English unpaid magistracy, and of
the technicalities, cumbrousness, and expensiveness of
the English law, the advantages of codification, &c. On all
these points he will find the reviewers ranging themselves

on the side of old opinions, and sailing in the wake of
those writers in this country, who are distinguished as
the enemies of every rational reform, and the upholders
of every old abuse. Though living in a country where improvement is advancing at the gallop, "on the car of
time," they have no faith in the future fortunes of our
race, nor indulge in any aspirations after unattained but
possible good. Such as man has been, such they think he
ever will be, a poor, benighted animal, groping his way
from one error to another, the prey of priests, and the
victim of tyrants, abusing liberty where he has it, and
often more happy as a slave than as a freeman! The weight
of their authority, such as it is, is employed to inculcate
political maxims, which are shallow and grovelling. Their
labors tend to repress true independence of thought, to
bring derision on a generous and enlarged philanthropy,
and to teach the Americans to undervalue those institutions which constitute their chief glory. Fortunately, the
course of things is too strong for the efforts of any knot of
literary men. Truth in our days has, like the ocean, ten
thousand avenues, and its course can be but little impeded
by closing up one or two of them. America will produce
men who can appreciate the moral grandeur of her institutions, and when these appear, her literature will become
a fountain of light to the world.

'In a literary point of view, the present number is respectable. It contains twelve articles, the last and longest
of which is a review of Captain Hall's Travels. We have
seen a writer cut up in a more masterly style, but the
critic does exert no contemptible degree of skill, in showing up the Captain's prejudice, rashness, and inconsistency, and he has imitated the subject of his criticism in
combining the suaviter in modo with the fortiter in re.[13]
So much of the discussion, however, is devoted to special
points, that we cannot find a passage fit for quotation. Of
the other articles, there are not many calculated to interest readers in this country; but we insert an extract from
an article on Modern Greek Literature, for the sake of the
information it contains.'

It is plain, from the tenor of this article, that the mind of
the writer has been severely exercised by something which
he has met with in some preceding number of this journal,
but with the aid of the little light which he has thought proper
to throw upon the subject, we are rather at a loss to conjecture what particular part of our speculations it is, by which
we have been so unfortunate as to give him offence. To the
charges of ignorance and dulness, we of course, plead guilty
with great cheerfulness. Independently of the general presumption against us, which results from the well-known de-
generacy of the race on this side the water, we are quite
aware of our personal incapacity to carry into effect to any
considerable extent, our very honest intentions to entertain
and instruct our readers. We know, that in both these respects, they are too often compelled to take the will for the
deed. We also fully acquit the worthy editor of any intention
to caricature or misrepresent our doctrines. His positive
denial of any such intention would of course be quite sufficient; independently of which, the honor he has done us by
reading the 'casual numbers of our journal that now and then
stray into his hands,' or, as he is afterwards pleased to
explain himself, by 'perusing at one time or another a considerable portion of our lucubrations,' is an ample guarantee that he bears us no ill-will. When, therefore, we find
him asserting that we are 'woefully deficient in intellectual
courage—profound and original views—lofty aims—love of
truth and mankind—heart—soul—and true American feeling,'
—that we 'take upon ourselves from choice a load of prejudice and sophistry,' — 'send back to the old world a feeble
echo of the false and antiquated doctrines that are or were
current there,'—that we 'play false to the cause of man,'—
that 'as an organ of opinion for republican America, nothing
can be more pitiful' than our journal—and finally, that we
'creep in the train of our reviewers,'—with the other gentil-
lesses of the same description, which the reader will have
met with in the above extract, we are bound to presume that
all these pretty compliments are in the nature of confes-
sions, reluctantly extorted by the force of truth from a
warm and real friend, and if the manner appear to be some-

what unceremonious, it must be owing to a want of taste in
us, and not of good breeding in the Scotsman, who is, of
course, thoroughly imbued with the national politeness of
his country.

But even if we allow to this writer all the credit which he
seems disposed to claim for a friendly and respectful feeling
towards us, as well as for a strict observance of the forms
of civility usual among gentlemen, to which his pretensions
are equally well founded; and if we also concede to him the
general inferiority of every product of cisatlantic origin to
the corresponding one of European, and especially of Scottish growth, we may still venture to intimate that, as respects some of the more serious offences with which he
charges us, there may possibly be a mistake in fact. While
assuring his readers that he has no intention to caricature
us, he candidly admits that he cannot quote words and passages in support of his view of our doctrines. Here, then,
is a book, in thirty volumes, lying open before him, and,
according to his account, full of the most dangerous and heretical principles, written—within and without—like the roll
in Ezekiel, with lamentation and mourning and woe; but
when he comes to file his bill of exceptions, he cannot, by
his own admission, quote an objectionable passage—no, not
so much as a single offensive word. This, we confess, does
seem to us a little extraordinary—but let it pass; for we
have not room to treat the subject in detail. In defect of evidence to support his charges, our accuser undertakes to
bring us to confession, forgetting the humane rule of the
common law, which declares that no person shall be held to
criminate himself. He proposes, in his own phrase, 'to try
us by any constant question,' and accordingly suggests two
or three, which we are expected to answer. Independently
of the rather inquisitorial character of this method, we must
be permitted to remark, that the Scotsman is a little unfortunate in his application of it. Of the problems which he
states, all, that are of any importance, have already been
solved in this journal, in a manner which would probably be
satisfactory to him. As to the unpaid magistracy, and the
value of classical literature, they are matters of compara-

tively trifling consequence, on which, if we recollect rightly,
we have not had much occasion to descant: but as respects
the weightier subjects of codification and an established
church, we have repeatedly expressed opinions decidedly in
favor of the former, and against the latter, so that we really
do not know what this writer means by accusing us of heresy
on these points. In treating the question of codification, we
have not even stated before, what we now honestly confess,
that, whatever may be the value of the thing, we heartily
detest and despise the name, which, though patronised by
the Edinburgh Review and the Scotsman, ought, as we conceive, to be utterly eschewed, with all the other abominable
inventions of the same author, by every lover of pure English. Supposing, however, that we had in fact said somewhat
less upon the subjects of the established church and codification, than the opposition journals in England habitually do,
does not the critic perceive, that our position in these respects is entirely different from theirs? We in America have
no church establishment, nor are we embarrassed with 'the
technicalities, cumbrousness, and expensiveness of the
English law.' We have given, long ago, the best and most
decisive evidence of our sentiments on these points, by sim-
plifying the law, and avoiding altogether the plan of an established church. The battle is fought and won. What merit
would there be in railing at the enemy after he is fairly
beaten, and has cried quarter? The thing which the Scotsman
wishes us to be always talking about, we have already done:
and this, according to his neighbor of the Review, is by far
the more important part of the business. He has fallen into
a similar error in charging us with a disinclination to innovate. We deny that we have ever shown any indisposition to
real improvements of any kind; but the Scotsman should remember that we have already attained most of the objects
which the friends of liberty in Europe regard as desirable.
He tells us himself, that 'our country exemplifies a new and
happier order of society, which ought to become a source of
light to the world; that if Locke and Sydney were living in
our day, they would regard the American government as a
beautiful and successful experiment, which has solved diffi-

culties that had perplexed the wisest of men from the beginning of time, and unfolded truths of incalculable value to
mankind.' Such is his opinion of our institutions; and, although he has thought proper to add in the same passage,
that 'the sages of the North American Review have not the
slightest conception of all this,' we can assure him that he
is quite mistaken, and that our opinion upon the subject is
exactly the same with his. But since he has been pleased to
put us to the question, we would venture to ask him in turn,
why, if our government be already perfect, we are called
upon to encourage innovation? Does not he recollect the old
Italian epitaph, I was well, I wanted to be better, and here
I am? We are well—we do not want to be better—we conceive that the best thing that can happen to us is to remain
as we are; and this being the case, we can have no motive
for wishing to innovate. Does our Scotch friend think that,
after reaching the top of the hill, we ought to descend rather
than not keep moving? Does he wish us to change for the
worse, rather than not change at all? Or does he—as is
more probable—only wish to find fault?

Charges, which cannot be supported by words or passages, must of course be of a very loose and general character. When the Scotsman has endeavored to present those
which he prefers against us in a shape at all tangible, he has
failed of giving them the least appearance of plausibility. He
tells us, for example, that we want true American feeling.
On this point, we must refer him again to his neighbors of
the Edinburgh Review, who, at an early stage in our progress, pronounced that we were 'abundantly national,' and
that 'there was no want of patriotic feeling.' The intimation
evidently was, that there was a slight, perhaps excusable,
excess of this quality; and we think we may affirm, without
the danger of being contradicted, that there has been no
diminution since. Again, we 'creep in the train of our reviewers.' As a full defence against this count in the indict-
ment, we appeal with confidence to the articles which we
have had occasion, at various times, from the commencement of our editorial labors up to the present day, to address to 'our reviewers' in reply to their strictures upon

the United States. However feebly executed in other respects,
our readers will do us the justice to allow, that they have
not exhibited any disposition on our part to truckle to foreign
arrogance, or kiss the rod of unjust criticism. We defy the
Scotsman to produce a single sentence in which we have
shown an inclination to court the favor of the British press,
or of any other portion of the British public. We are quite
aware, on the contrary, that the tone we have uniformly
maintained in this respect, is not fitted to conciliate the
good will of our transatlantic brethren; and if this were the
object we had in view, we should of course adopt a different
one. A few compliments to their national pride—a few sacri-
fices to their national interest—and we should soon cease to
be 'a pitiful organ of republican America.' We have lately
seen one of our countrymen raise himself to the rank of 'the
highest existing authorities in political economy,' by saying
that the British have eight million tons of shipping employed
in the coasting trade. Had he carried his calculation up to
ten or twelve millions, he would have equalled the fame of
Adam Smith. For ourselves, we look exclusively for encouragement and support to the home market. We court no
favor from foreigners, and our only ambition is to merit the
approval of our own intelligent countrymen. Far from creep-
ing in the train of 'our reviewers,' we have always regarded it as being, in the present state of the intercourse between the two countries, one of the most interesting branches of our editorial duty, to repel the attacks, and to guard
our fellow-citizens against the misrepresentations of the
British journals; and we have uniformly acted, and shall
continue to act—as far as occasion may appear to require—
on this principle.

As the charges of the Scotsman, whenever they assume a
tangible shape, are thus palpably, and even ludicrously inconsistent with fact, the general accusation which he deduces
from them of lukewarmness in the cause of liberty and a
disposition to sustain exploded errors and abuses, of course
falls of itself. The truth is, that it is very difficult for us in
this country to give satisfaction to our transatlantic brethren, whatever bias we may happen to take. Nothing will

answer but direct homage to their grossest prejudices, and
even then, we must expect to be told that their approbation
of us is merely the result of the national politeness. The re-
proach which has heretofore been generally made against
the American press, is that of a tendency to exaggeration in
the expression of sentiments favorable to liberty. We have
been told that we confounded monarchy with slavery, that
our notions of government were narrow and intolerant, and
that we could see nothing good or great out of the circle of
our own institutions. We have been charged, in short, with
being ultra-democratic in our political opinions, and this
heresy is undoubtedly much more common among us than the
opposite one. But if it happen by accident that a journal
which appears at long intervals of time, and is or ought to
be prepared with more reflection, expresses the same opinions in a rather more deliberate form than the rest, our
censors forthwith attack us with 'redoubled rage,' for the
want of the same quality, of which we were before re-
proached with the excess. So delicate is their taste, that it
is next to impossible not to offend them in one way or another. If violent, we are blind and bigoted democrats—if considerate, we are lukewarm in the cause of liberty—at all
events, we are always in the wrong. This kind of criticism
is so easily seen through, that it would be superfluous to ex-
pose the injustice of it. We yield to none, as we have already
remarked, in attachment to liberty; but we are also aware,
with every body else of the least reflection, that liberty,
like other good things, may be abused, and that the name is
often assumed by false pretenders for unworthy purposes.
We may remark here, since the occasion presents itself,
that we cannot agree in all the principles that are set forth
from time to time upon this subject on respectable authority
in the mother country. We are told for example, in the article of the Edinburgh Review, upon the prose writings of
Milton, to which we have once before alluded, that liberty,
like a certain beautiful fairy in the poem of Ariosto, sometimes 'puts on the form of a hateful reptile—that she grov-
els, and hisses, and stings; but that we must admire and
cherish her in this degraded and frightful shape, if we mean

to be rewarded by her in the time of her beauty and glory.'
All this means, if it mean any thing, that the real friends of
liberty are not only bound to approve, to concur in, and to
sympathise with the rational and well-directed exertions of
the honest and intelligent laborers in her cause, but also to
applaud and aid every charlatan, who chooses for any purpose, however vile, to wear her mask. But a few moments
since we were invited, as friends of liberty, to grovel at the
footstool of Bonaparte, and we are now called upon, always
in the same character, to take counsel with Robespierre—
to yell with Marat for two hundred thousand heads—to listen
with delighted attention to the 'orator of the human race,'
and to bow with reverential awe at the shrine of the unveiled
Goddess of Reason. However highly we may value the approbation of the Edinburgh Review and the Scotsman, we have
no hesitation in saying distinctly, that we shall not purchase
it at such a price; and since these writers express their
opinion with so much freedom upon our conduct, we would
ask them in turn how it happens that they do not set us the
example as well as give us the precept? How happens it that
they pay no court themselves to their goddess, in her grovelling, hissing, stinging shape? Why is it that we do not find
them clamoring with Hunt and Cobbett—blaspheming with
Carlile,—and outraging decency with Mary Wollstonecraft
and Fanny Wright? All this and more they are bound to do on
their own system, but of all this we see little or nothing in
their writings, to judge at least from the 'casual numbers
of the Scotsman that accidentally stray into our hands,' and
from 'perusing at one time or another a considerable portion of the lucubrations' of the Edinburgh Reviewers. The
simple truth appears at last to be, that at the very moment
when they are ridiculing and abusing us for lukewarmness
in the cause of liberty, their own language is much less liberal than ours. So much for the consistency and decency of
these would-be dictators in the republic of letters. As respects the system they recommend to us, and the allegory
by which it is illustrated, we may add, that they involve a
mistake in fact, which was long ago pointed out by the great
English apostle of the rights of man. The degraded and

frightful shape, which in days of trouble has often appeared under the name and character of <u>Liberty</u>, is not, as we are told by Milton, the sweet mountain-nymph herself in disguise, but a ghastly counterfeit of her charming appearance, animated by the foul spirit of <u>License</u>—a malignant demon, tormented by a continual thirst for human blood. Like the Vampyre Bride in Goethe's poem, this loathsome figure puts on specious looks, and uses honied words—wears perhaps upon her brow the golden round of military triumph, or the red cap of deliverance from bondage; but her only delight is to suck out the life of her victims. Her touch is fatal; there is no remedy for it; those who take her to their bosoms shall surely die.

Notes

The text is based on the <u>North American Review</u>, 31 (July, 1830), 26-66: "Art. II.—<u>American Literature</u>. An Article in the 99th Number of the <u>Edinburgh Review</u>." The running head of Everett's article furnishes the title given here.

1. [Original footnote:] The writer of a late article in Blackwood's Magazine, entitled 'Wellington at Cadiz,' containing an account of an entertainment given to his hero upon a visit to that city, goes out of his way to introduce the following episode, which we extract as a specimen of the tone of that journal in regard to the United States. We hardly know whether to admire most the elegance and correctness of the language, or the liberality of the sentiments.
'The British Consul was honored with fifty cards, to be filled up with the names of such of the respectable merchants and their families as he should select. The Portuguese, Sicilian, and other foreign consuls, were complimented with tickets for their families; but in this liberal distribution of favors, by some oversight, the Consul for the United States

was unluckily forgotten. The Republican Eagle was all in a
flutter, at the unintentional indignity. On a representation to
the committee by the Consul, an apology was made for the
omission, and cards of invitation, in blank, to the number of
twenty, were immediately placed in his hands as the 'amende
honorable'—but Jonathan made it quite a 'national' affair;
insisting on an equal number of cards as were bestowed on
the Consul of Great Britain. We were just then on the eve of
a war with the States of stripes and stars, (and slavery.)
Some private discussions took place, during which it is be-
lieved the wishes of the hero of the fête were consulted, and
which ended, for the sake of harmony, in complying with the
American Consul's requisition, (rather than request,) and
fifty cards were officially, or at least more ceremoniously
than cordially presented. This concession (which was, I believe, the subject of a report to the States,) had the effect
of introducing a mob of sleek-headed gentlemen from the
Western world, (chiefly captains and supercargoes from
Philadelphia and New York,) in long skirted coats, and nan-
keen breeches—all redolent of tar and tobacco—among the
embroidered crowd! But even their Republican vanity must
have quailed under the mortifying sneers of the noble Seño-
ras, who appeared to loath the touch of their tanned and un-
gloved paws.'
   The article is written throughout with a great outpouring
of the heart, and seems to be a sort of sentimental prose
poem, the author of which introduces himself as a witness
of the scenes he describes. Should he be disposed to indite
another work of this description in honor of the conqueror of
Waterloo, we would venture to suggest to him, that as the
nearest connexions of his hero have condescended to select
their wives from the families of some of us sleek-headed
gentlemen of the West, it is hardly agreeable to the rules of
the art to make us the villains of the plot. It would also not
be amiss, should the scene be laid in Spain, to consult the
court calendar, so far as to ascertain the title of the Duch-
ess of Benavente; and we would further express our doubts,
whether the kind of triumph, which the hero is represented
as achieving over the Duke of Frias and the Prince of Ang-
lona, be well suited to form the catastrophe of a sentimental

poem to appear in a loyal and religious magazine. A denoue-
ment of this kind, if resorted to at all, can only be employed
with safety in works of a comic order; and even in those,
the example of Pope's Afra has not been considered by the
best modern writers as furnishing a standard for general
imitation.

2. [Original footnote:] This journal, as is well known, is
a mere puffing machine in the hands of the booksellers, conducted, we believe, by a worthless creature named Jerdan.
It has lately signalized itself by an attack upon Washington,
whom the wildest of our foreign traducers had hitherto respected, but on whom this miserable tool undertakes to fas-
ten the foul and odious charge of irreligion. We take for
granted that this proceeding will have its proper effect upon
the circulation of the work in the United States.

3. William Ellery Channing (1780-1842). "Remarks on the
Character and Writings of John Milton" (1826), "Remarks on
the Life and Character of Napoleon Bonaparte" (1827-1828),
"Essay on the Character and Writings of Fénelon" (1829).

4. If published before the Revolution, as Everett states,
the Letters are those of John Dickinson (1767), although the
subsequent discussion may imply that Everett actually has
in mind the Letters of J. Hector St. John (1782; 1784).

5. Nathaniel Bowditch (1773-1838), American mathema-
tician and astronomer.

6. Fisher Ames (1758-1808), American statesman, orator, and essayist.

7. Robert Walsh (1784-1859). Established the American
Quarterly Review in 1827.

8. Joseph Stevens Buckminster (1784-1813), famous
minister of Boston's Brattle Street Church.

9. "Behold—another witticism that I am delighted to have
uttered."

10. "The mask falls—the man remains—and the hero van-
ishes."

11. "He remains fixed and will remain fixed eternally."

12. "Speaking to intelligent people." Everett's spelling
may be correct dialect spelling; the circumflex accent
should be over iota rather than omicron.

13. "Agreeably in manner . . . strongly in matter."

Irving's Columbus

This is one of those works, which are at the same time the
delight of readers and the despair of critics. It is as nearly
perfect in its kind, as any work well can be; and there is
therefore little or nothing left for the reviewer, but to write
at the bottom of every page, as Voltaire said he should be
obliged to do, if he published a commentary on Racine,
Pulchrè! bene! optimè! And as the reputation of the author
is so well established, that he does not stand in need of our
recommendation as a passport to the public favor, it may
appear, and in fact is, almost superfluous to pretend to give
a formal review of his book. Nevertheless, we cannot refuse ourselves the satisfaction of adding the mite of our
poor applause to the ample and well-deserved harvest of
fame, that has already rewarded the labors of our ingenious,
excellent, and amiable fellow-citizen; nor would it, as we
conceive, be proper to omit noticing in this journal, a work,
however well known to the public, which we consider as being, on the whole, more honorable to the literature of the
country, than any one that has hitherto appeared among us.
Before we proceed to give our opinion in detail of the 'History of the Life and Voyages of Columbus,' we shall offer
a few remarks on the character and merit of Mr. Irving's
other works, premising that we write under the influence of
the feelings that naturally result from a good deal of friendly
personal intercourse with this gentleman. If any reader
shall suspect, that we judge Mr. Irving too favorably because we know him too well, he is quite at liberty to make
any deductions from the sum total of our commendation,

that he may on this account deem in candor to be necessary.

Mr. Irving shares, in some degree, the merit and the glory that belong to the industrious hero of his present work, that of leading the way in a previously unexplored and untrodden path of intellectual labor. He is the first writer of purely Cisatlantic origin and education, who succeeded in establishing a high and undisputed reputation, founded entirely on literary talent and success. This was the opinion expressed by a very judicious and discerning writer in the Edinburgh Review, upon the first publication of the 'Sketch Book'; and it is, as we conceive, a substantially correct one. In saying this, we are perfectly aware that there have been found among us, at every period during the two centuries of our history, individuals highly distinguished, both at home and abroad, by important and useful labors in various branches of art and science. We mean not to detract, in the least, from their well-earned fame, which we cherish, on the contrary, as the richest treasure that belongs to their posterity, and would do everything in our power to establish and enlarge. We say not that Mr. Irving is the first or the greatest man that ever handled a pen in the United States, Vixêre fortes ante Agamemnona.[1] Our pilgrim fathers were accomplished scholars and powerful writers, according to the taste and learning of the times. One of their immediate successors, the pride and ornament in his day of a highly respectable college, is justly placed on an equality with the most profound and acute metaphysicians of Europe. The state papers of the revolution have been pronounced by the first orators and statesmen of the mother country, to equal or surpass the noblest efforts of antiquity of the same description. In the exact sciences we have contributed as much as our share, or more, to the common stock of discovery and improvement, from the time of the first settlement of the colonies up to the present day. But our success in the department of polite literature and poetry (which are essentially one and the same thing) had not, until a very recent period, corresponded with our progress in most others. After all that had been done by the Trumbulls,[2] the Hopkinsons,[3] the Dwights,[4] the Barlows,[5] the Humphreyses,[6]—

Arcadians all, —all animated with a fine spirit and by no
means laboring without effect, but yet rather as amateurs
than as artists; —after all that had been done by these and
various others of equal or hardly inferior merit, we still
wanted the 'sacred poet.' We had no name distinguished by
repeated triumphs on the field of polite learning, too brilliant to be overlooked, too generally acknowledged abroad
and at home to be gainsaid or controverted, which we could
present to friend and foe as a proof of our capacity for these
delightful pursuits; no series of elegant and highly finished
works of this class in verse or prose, to exhibit as specimens of what we could accomplish.

The reasons of this deficiency are too obvious in themselves, and have been too often published in good and ill nature, to be now questionable. It was not owing to want of
genius. That divine gift has been as liberally imparted in the
goodness of Providence to this nation as to any other, that
ever flourished on the face of the earth; and the English
race, to which we belong, has always been preëminently
distinguished in both the great branches, Saxon and Norman,
that combine to form its mingled stock, by the favor of the
Muses. Nor yet did the difficulty lie in want of patronage,
the presence or absence of which has little or nothing to do
with the development of genuine excellence. The real cause,
as has been very generally felt by judicious observers, was
the condition of the country, which created an urgent and
continual demand for talent in the various walks of active
life. A vast continent was to be subdued and cultivated; all
the branches of mechanical industry (as far as the mother
country would permit us to exercise them) to be commenced.
Here was business enough for the mass of the people. For
minds of an elevated stamp, the liberal professions, education, public and private, and the high functions of government, opened fields of action, into which such minds could
not hesitate to enter. The desk, the bench, the professor's
chair, the principal political and military offices, were not
with us the patrimony of particular families, but the acknowledged property of merit and talent, which, as soon as
they showed themselves, were summoned, by the loud and

unanimous acclaim of the public, to enter in and take possession. Had our fathers been insensible to this high vocation, they would have shown that they were unworthy of it,
and incapable of excellence in anything. Our Ovids and Mar-
tials were therefore lost in Franklins, Adamses, and Jef-
fersons, as were those of England in Murrays and Pulte-
neys; and the loss, we may well add, was exceeding gain.

It was not then the absence of talent or poetical inspiration, but the more imperious and urgent, —let us not be unjust to our ancestors, —the nobler and loftier nature of the
call for active labor in the moral and political service of the
public, that checked for a time the cultivation of the finer
arts. The shepherd in Virgil, who was compelled to abandon
at once his country and his favorite amusements, beheld
with admiration, if not with envy, his comrade playing on
his rustic pipe, under the shade of the accustomed beech
tree. Our fathers, if they felt any emotions of regret, at
quitting their literary and poetical pursuits, could at least
console themselves with the reflection, that they made the
sacrifice, not to quit but to serve their country; and in
obedience to her sacred voice, sprang with alacrity and
pleasure into the walks of active life. We had men enough
among us, who were 'smit with the love of sacred song':
who in earlier life exhibited splendid proofs that their love
was by no means an unrequited passion; and who, had they
devoted themselves exclusively to letters, would have carried off the most brilliant honors in any department which
they might have selected. Such were the persons, whose
names we mentioned above honoris causâ; but they too fell
under the general rule, and could not withstand those induce-
ments to engage, in one way or another, in the public service, that wrought with irresistible force upon every generous soul. They were all, as is well known, employed in the
highest, the gravest, the most absorbing political, moral,
or military affairs; and we possess in their literary effusions either the unripe fruits of their youth, or the hasty
and casual recreations, that amused the few leisure hours
of their maturer years. Mr. Barlow, for example, was
originally a poet of great promise. His 'Vision of Colum-

bus,' written at a very early age, and which has not been
improved by his subsequent labors upon it, exhibited a talent, which, if properly cultivated by persevering study and
assiduous exercise, would have produced works of a very
high, if not of the highest order; but he was hurried away,
like the rest, by the animating movement of everything about
him, and swept at once into active life, where the serious
affairs in which he was engaged, gradually diverted his mind
from his earlier pursuits, and diminished his capacity to
excel in them; so that when he came back to them at a later
period, for the purpose of publishing a corrected edition of
his poem, he had lost a part of his power, and his verse had
not quite the same freshness and vigor, that distinguished it
before. It is pleasing, however, to see in these productions,
though of somewhat inferior poetical merit, how fondly his
thoughts reverted, from amidst the busy scenes in which he
was engaged, to the happy period of his youth, and dwelt, in
fond recollection, on the rocky hills of New England, and
the beautiful valley of the Connecticut, in which he had his
birth. Thus we find him, while accompanying the French army as a representative of the Convention on the first invasion of Piedmont, so strongly excited by the view of the
maize which grows in abundance in that country, though little
cultivated in most parts of Europe, that he wrote, upon the
spur of the moment, amid the tumults of the campaign, one
of his prettiest and most lively poems. Mr. Barlow's case
was that of all the rest. General Humphreys was a military
officer of high rank, and a foreign minister. He wrote most
of his poems in the tent of the commander-in-chief, which,
in the nature of things, could not well in this case have been
pitched on the summits of Pindus, or in the classic valley
of Aonian Aganippe. Considering the circumstances under
which they are written, his poems are far from wanting
merit, and are equal to the similar productions of the most
celebrated geniuses of Europe. They are quite as good, for
instance, as the poems of Frederick the Great, most of
which were also written in the camp, and some of them on
the eve of the most critical and dangerous battles. The works
of both belong to the class of amateur productions, which,

as such, can never reach the highest degree of excellence;
for this can only be attained, in any department of intellectual labor, by the exclusive and persevering devotion of a
whole mind, for a whole life. Dr. Dwight, in like manner,
who possessed a naturally powerful and highly poetical intellect, with a fund of activity and industry, which would have
carried him to the first rank in any profession, as it did in
that which he pursued, after offering his youthful vows at
the shrine of the Muses in 'Greenfield Hill' and the 'Conquest of Canaan,' gave up his riper years to the serious labors of his sacred calling, and of public instructions; in
which he shone beyond comparison the brightest name of his
day; while he published writings analogous to these occupations, that are justly esteemed as among the most valuable
of their class.

Active life, in short, absorbed the whole talent of the
country. It is of little importance to the general truth of
these remarks, whether there be or be not one or two
names, in the course of the two centuries to which our history extends, that can fairly be cited as exceptions. If there
be such, the men who bore them were isolated beings, who
belonged to another world and a future age. They formed no
school, they left no intellectual progeny to perpetuate their
fame; the public taste was not prepared to feel and appreciate their merit, and they lived and died almost unknown
to their contemporaries. If the Muses did in fact carve the
name of Philenia upon every laurel in the grove of fame, as
one of her admirers assures us, this same grove was at that
time so little frequented as a public walk, that the circumstance passed almost without notice. Dr. Franklin is entitled to the praise of a first-rate writer; but he has no pretensions to the poetical garland, which he voluntarily relin-
quished, like the other persons we have mentioned, for the
purpose of devoting himself to the public service and the
cultivation of science. Charles Brockden Brown has perhaps
the best claim to rank as an exception from the general rule,
and to assert the character of a really powerful and original
writer in the department of polite literature. His works
still retain their hold upon the public attention, and have

rather risen than declined in reputation since his death. And his case singularly exemplifies the observations made above, in regard to the few persons who might be viewed as exceptions to our remarks. He lived, as it were, unknown to the public. His works were widely circulated and read; but, as we are told, generally received as of foreign origin. Finally, when he had at last fought his way into some degree of notoriety at home, and begun of course to partake the feelings of the world around him, he seems like the rest to have been swept away from his original bias towards letters and poetry, into the large stream of active life. The last of his productions was a political journal entitled 'The American Register,' and had his days been prolonged, he probably would have devoted the rest of them to the party controversies of the time. Dennie, another natural poet, published, under the name of a literary journal, only a more refined and elegant political newspaper; and our townsman Paine, singularly gifted as he was with all the elements necessary to the constitution of a real poet, generally devoted the few intervals, which he could spare from his pleasures for labor of any kind, to the establishment of a new newspaper. Such, up to the close of the last century, was the all-absorbing influence of the attractions of active life upon the whole mass of mind existing among us. The period when the three last writers lived, approached, however, so nearly to the present, that had any one of them possessed the vigorous moral constitution, which is indispensable to the full activity and effect of literary talent under any circumstances, and especially when a new course is to be struck out, he would probably have seized the palm that was reserved for another brow, and marked the opening of our western school of polite literature. But these three gifted spirits, all of celestial mould, were like the falcon in Shakspeare, hawked at and killed, while towering in their pride of flight, by the devil of sensual indulgence, and thus failed of accomplishing their high vocation. Their immature and unfinished productions, though glowing at times with life and energy, can only be viewed as the first faint streaks of light, that preceded and announced the approach of day.

Finally, however, in the rapid progress of our population, wealth, and literary advantages, the period arrived when the calls of business no longer absorbed all the cultivated intellect existing in the country; when, after these were fully satisfied, there remained a portion of taste, zeal, and talent to be employed in purely literary and scientific pursuits; when the public mind was prepared to acknowledge and appreciate any really superior merit, that might present itself, in those departments; when in fact the nation, having been somewhat galled by the continual sneers of a set of heartless and senseless foreigners upon our want of literary talent, was rather anxious to possess some positive facts, which could be offered as evidence to the contrary, and was prepared of course to hail the appearance of a writer of undoubted talent, with a kind of patriotic enthusiasm; when finally, for all these reasons, the first example of success, that should be given in this way, would naturally be followed by an extensive development of the same sort of activity, throughout the country, in the persons of a host of literary aspirants, sometimes directly imitating their prototype, and always inspired and encouraged by his good fortune, who would make up together the front rank of what is commonly called a school of polite literature. To set this example was the brilliant part reserved, in the course of our literary history, for Mr. Washington Irving. His universal popularity among readers of all classes, on both sides of the Atlantic, resting exclusively on the purely literary merit of his productions, wholly independent of extraneous or interested motives, attested by repeated successes, in various forms of composition, and stamped by the concurrence and approbation of the most acute, judicious, and unsparing critics, justifies, beyond a shadow of doubt, his pretension to be viewed as the valorous knight, who was called, in the order of destiny, to break the spell which appeared, at least to our good-natured European brethren, to be thrown over us in this respect; to achieve the great and hitherto unaccomplished adventure of establishing a purely American literary reputation of the first order; and demonstrate the capacity of his countrymen to excel in the elegant, as they had before

done in all the useful and solid branches of learning. To have
done this is a singular title of honor, and will always remain
such, whatever laurels of a different kind may hereafter be
won by other pretenders. Thoroughly labored and highly finished as they all are, Mr. Irving's works will hardly be
surpassed in their way. Other writers may no doubt arise,
in the course of time, who will exhibit in verse or prose a
more commanding talent, and soar a still loftier flight in the
empyrean sky of glory. Some western Homer, Shakspeare,
Milton, Corneille, or Calderon, may irradiate our literary
world with a flood of splendor, that shall throw all other
greatness into the shade. This, or something like it may or
may not happen; but even if it should, it can never be disputed that the mild and beautiful genius of Mr. Irving was
the Morning-Star that led up the march of our heavenly host;
and that he has a fair right, much fairer certainly than the
great Mantuan, to assume the proud device, Primus ego in
patriam.[7] To have done this, we repeat, is a singular triumph, far higher than that of merely adding another name
to a long list of illustrious predecessors, who flourished in
the same country. It implies not merely taste and talent,
but originality, the quality which forms the real distinction,
if there be one, between what we call genius, and every
other degree of intellectual power; the quality, in comparison with which, as Sir Walter Scott justly observes, all
other literary accomplishments are as dust in the balance.
It implies moreover the possession of high and honorable
moral qualities; the bold and daring resolution, that plans
with vigor and decision; the unyielding firmness of purpose,
that never tires or falters in the task of execution. These
qualities, which are obviously necessary to such success as
that of Mr. Irving, have also, as exemplified in his writings, been carefully kept within bounds, and have not only
been prevented from running into their kindred excesses,
but, on the contrary, have been judiciously and gracefully
veiled from the public eye, by the outward forms that rather
belong to a character of an opposite cast; a modesty, that
has never deserted him under all his popularity, and a scrupulous regard for decorum and propriety as well as the

higher principles of morals, from which the dazzling success, that has unfortunately attended a different line of conduct in some contemporary writers, has never for a moment
induced him to deviate. This combination of estimable and
in some respects almost contradictory moral qualities, with
a high intellectual power and fine taste, tends to render the
influence of Mr. Irving's example not less favorable to the
country, in a moral point of view, than it is in a purely literary one.

The great effect which it has produced, in this latter respect, is sufficiently evident already, in the number of good
writers, in various forms of elegant literature, who have
sprung up among us within the few years which have elapsed
since the appearance of Mr. Irving, and who justify our preceding remark, that he may fairly be considered as the
founder of a school. We have already a novelist of extraordinary power and facility, decidedly original, although in
form an imitator; and second only in popularity, among contemporary writers of his class, to his celebrated model.
We have a second novelist of gentler mien, as beseems her
sex, whose rapid and constantly progressive improvement
seems to indicate, that she is destined one day to approach,
if not to equal or surpass, the merit of her amiable sister
of the Emerald Isle. We have several youthful poets, who
have already earned, by the best and purest arts, an early
reputation, which the labors of their riper age will no doubt
extend and enlarge. To these distinguished examples might
be added a long list of other aspirants of various, in some
instances perhaps, not inferior degrees of excellence; and
when we take into view, at the same time, the remarkable
development of literary taste, the increased demand for
books and journals, the improvements in the modes and
means of education, and the augmented attention which is
given, in every way, to science and letters, we have a full
right to assume that a decided change has taken place, in
this respect, in the state of the country within the last fifteen or twenty years. We mean not of course to say, that
this change is entirely owing to the example and success of
Mr. Irving. We have on the contrary already explained, in

sufficient detail, that his appearance was in itself one of the results of the same general causes, that produced the other effects to which we have alluded. We only intend to intimate, that he has the peculiar merit and fortune of having taken the lead, under the influence of these causes, in a course, in which he could not but be followed and sustained by numerous successors, who would of necessity be more or less affected by the form and character of his productions. The fact that several of the more distinguished writers, who have since appeared, are from his own state, —while it is partly accounted for by the vast extent, population, wealth, and generally thriving situation of that 'empire in embryo,' New York; circumstances which all tend very strongly to stimulate every form of intellectual activity, —must nevertheless be regarded, in part, as a proof of the direct operation of the success of Mr. Irving.

Having thus noticed the circumstances that attended the appearance of this writer in the literary career, we shall now offer a few observations on the character and value of his works. We trust that, in treating this subject somewhat fully, we shall not be considered by our readers as giving it a disproportionate importance. Independently of the fact, that discussions of a purely literary character form an agreeable variety in a journal intended for readers of various descriptions, and are perhaps (as far as respects the topic) not less acceptable to many than the essays on the graver themes that generally occupy our pages, we may add that their real importance is not to be measured by the extent of their influence on passing events. Science and letters touch the secret springs that regulate the whole complicated movement of the political machine; while the business of administration, with all its bustle and parade, and in all its different departments of war-making, peace-making, speech-making, tax laying and gathering, office seeking and holding, and so forth, can only terminate at best in winding up the said machine and keeping it in action. Hence it is, that in civilized periods, the literature of one age determines in a great degree the history of the next. Voltaire, said his friend Condorcet at the hottest epoch of the French

revolution, n'a pas vu tout ce qu'il a fait, mais il a fait tout
ce que nous voyons.[8] The nature of the operation of the writings of one generation on the form and spirit of society in
the next, depends very much on the manner in which they
are received as merely literary productions by contemporaries. Literary and critical discussions are not, therefore,
as some suppose, merely valuable as the elegant recreations of opulent leisure, but are essentially connected with
interests of deep and lasting importance.

If we examine the works of Mr. Irving, with reference to
the usual division of manner and substance, we may remark,
in the first place, that his style is undoubtedly one of the
most finished and agreeable forms, in which the English
language has ever been presented. Lord Byron has some-
where spoken of him, as the second prose writer of the day,
considering Sir Walter Scott as the first; but with due deference to his lordship's judgment, which was far from being
infallible in criticism or anything else, we cannot but consider Mr. Irving, as respects mere style, decidedly superior to Sir Walter. The latter, no doubt, has exhibited a
greater vigor and fertility of imagination, which, with his
talent for versification, entitle him to a higher rank in the
world of letters; but viewing him merely as a prose writer,
his style, when not sustained by the interest of a connected
narrative, will be found to possess no particular merit, and
in some of his later writings is negligent and incorrect to an
extent, that places it below mediocrity. That of Mr. Irving,
on the contrary, is, in all his works, uniformly of the first
order. Its peculiar characteristic is a continual and sustained elegance, the result of the union of a naturally fine
taste, with conscientious and unwearied industry. His language is not remarkable for energy, nor have we often noticed in it any extraordinary happiness or brilliancy of mere
expression. Though generally pure and correct, it is not
uniformly so; and there are one or two unauthorized forms,
which will be found by a nice observer to recur pretty often.
Its attraction lies, as we have said, in the charm of finished
elegance, which it never loses. The most harmonious and
poetical words are carefully selected. Every period is

measured and harmonized with nice precision. The length of
the sentences is judiciously varied; and the tout ensemble
produces on the ear an effect very little, if at all, inferior
to that of the finest versification. Indeed such prose, while
it is from the nature of the topics substantially poetry, does
not appear to us, when viewed merely as a form of language,
to differ essentially from verse. The distinction between
verse and prose evidently does not lie in rhyme, taking the
word in its modern sense, or in any particular species of
rhythm, as it was understood by the ancients. Rhyme, however pleasing to accustomed ears (and we 'own the soft im-
peachment' of relishing it as much as others,) is, we fear,
but too evidently a remnant of the false taste of a barbarous
age; and of rhythm there are a thousand varieties in the
poetry of every cultivated language, which agree in nothing,
but that they are all harmonious arrangements of words.
If then we mean by rhythm or verse merely the form of poetry, and not any particular measure or set of measures to
which we are accustomed, it seems to imply nothing but such
a disposition of words and sentences, as shall strike the ear
with a regular melodious flow; and elegant prose, like that
of Mr. Irving, for instance, comes clearly within the defini-
tion. Nor are we quite sure that this delicate species of
rhythm ought to be regarded as inferior in beauty to the
more artificial ones. The latter, which are obvious and, as
it were, coarse methods of arrangement, are perhaps natural to the ruder periods of language, and are absolutely necessary in poems intended for music; but for every other
purpose it would seem, that the most perfect melody is that,
which is most completely unfettered, and in which the traces
of art are best concealed. There is something more exquisitely sweet in the natural strains of the Aeolian harp, as they
swell and fall upon the ear, under the inspiration of a gentle
breeze, on a fine moonlight evening, than in the measured
flow of any artificial music. But we must leave these con-
siderations, which would admit of some development, and
return to our author.

If the elegant prose of Mr. Irving be, as we think it is,
but little inferior in beauty to the finest verse, and at all

events one of the most finished forms of the English language, the character and the substance of his writings is also entirely and exclusively poetical. It is evident enough
that 'divine Philosophy' has no part nor lot in his affections.
Shakspeare, though he was willing to 'hang up philosophy,'
out of compliment to the charming Juliet, when he chose to
take it down again, could put the Seven Sages of Greece to
the blush. But such is not the taste of Mr. Irving. His aim
is always to please; and never to instruct, at least by general truths. If he ever teaches, he confines himself to plain
matter of fact. He even goes farther, and with the partiality
of a true lover, who can see no beauty except in the eyes of
his own mistress, he at times deals rather rudely with
philosophy, and more than insinuates that she is a sort of
prosing mad-cap, who babbles eternally without ever knowing what she is talking of. Now we hold this doctrine to be
clearly heretical. We conceive that the universe is not less
worthy of being studied as an expression of the pure and
glorious ideas or images that dwell eternally in the Supreme
mind, than when viewed merely as a pleasing and varied
panorama, or moving picture; and that it even acquires, in
the former case, a sublimity and beauty, of which it is not
susceptible in the latter, and which, in all ages, have ex-
alted and ravished the souls of the best and greatest men,
the Platos and Ciceros of the olden time, and the Miltons
and Newtons of the modern. But though we think Mr. Irving
heretical on this head, we can hardly say that we like him
the less for it, being always pleased to see a man put his
heart and soul into his business, whatever it may be, even
though he may, by so doing, (as often happens) generate in
himself a sort of hatred and contempt for every other.
Within the domain of poetry, taking this word in its large
sense, to which he religiously confines himself, Mr. Irving's range is somewhat extensive. He does not attempt the
sublime, but he is often successful in the tender, and dis-
ports himself at his ease in the comic. Humor is obviously
his forte, and his best touches of pathos are those which are
thrown in casually to break the continuity of a train of melancholy thoughts, when they sparkle in part by the effect of

contrast, like diamonds on a black mantle. But it is when
employed on humorous subjects, that he puts forth the vigor
of a really inventive genius, and proves himself substantially a poet. 'Knickerbocker,' for example, is a true original
creation. His purely pathetic essays, though occasionally
pleasing, are more generally somewhat tame and spiritless.
As a writer of serious biography and history he possesses
the merit of plain and elegant narrative, but does not aspire
to the higher palm of just and deep thought in the investigation of causes and effects, that constitutes the distinction of
the real historian, and supposes the taste for philosophical
research, which, as we have said before, is foreign to the
temper of our author.

Such, as we conceive, are the general characteristics of
the style and substance of the works of Mr. Irving. We notice their deficiencies and beauties with equal freedom, for
such is our duty as public critics, and we have too much respect for our friend to suppose that his appetite for fame
requires to be gratified by unqualified praise. This can never, in any case, be merited, and is therefore always worthless; while the favorable effect of just and candid criticism
is heightened by a discriminating notice of the weak points,
that are of course to be found in all productions. We shall
now proceed to offer a few more particular observations
upon the separate works, dividing them, for this purpose,
into the two classes of those that were written before and
after the author's departure for Europe. Although the general characteristics, which we have pointed out, are common to both these classes, there are some differences of
manner between them, that are worth attention. The 'Life of
Columbus,' again, varies materially from any of the preceding publications, and will naturally be considered by itself, as the immediate subject of this article.

The former class comprehends Salmagundi and the History
of New York, besides some smaller and less important productions. These exhibit the talent of the author in the full
perfection of its power, developing itself with a freshness
and freedom that have not perhaps been surpassed, or even
equalled, in any of his subsequent writings, but directed,

on the other hand, by a somewhat less sure and cultivated
taste. There is a good deal of inequality in 'Salmagundi,'
owing probably in part to a mixture of contributions by other
hands; but the better pieces are written in Mr. Irving's
best manner. Take it altogether, it was certainly a production of extraordinary merit, and was instantaneously and
universally recognized as such by the public. It wants of
course the graver merits of the modern British collections
of Essays; but for spirit, effect, and actual literary value,
we doubt whether any publication of the class since 'The
Spectator,' upon which it is directly modelled, can fairly be
put in competition with it. We well remember the eagerness
with which the periodical return of the merry little yellow
dwarf was anticipated by all classes of readers, and the
hearty good will with which he was welcomed.

> 'Sport, that wrinkled care derides,
> And Laughter, holding both his sides,'

uniformly followed in his train. So irresistibly attractive
and amusing were the quips and cranks of the odd group of
mummers that moved under his management, that our
grave, business-loving, and somewhat disputatious citizens
were taken, like Silence in the play, ere they were aware:
and when the show was over, were surprised, and in some
cases rather chagrined, to find that they had been diverted
from their habitual meditations on the Orders in Council
and the New England Platform, by the unprofitable fooleries
of the Cockloft family and the Little Man in Black, the state
of the Tunisian ambassador's wardrobe, and the tragical
fate of poor Aunt Charity, who died of a Frenchman. Mr.
Irving appears to have had no other object in view but that
of making a sprightly book and laughing at everything laugh-
able; but the work necessarily assumed, to a certain extent,
the shape of a satire on the abuses of popular government;
since the administration of the public affairs is the great
scene of action upon which the attention of the community is
always fixed, and which must be treated, in jest or earnest,
by all who mean to have an audience. The vices and follies
that most easily beset our practical statesmen, their endless

prolixity in debate, their rage for the bloodless glory of
heading the militia in a sham fight, their habitual waste of
dollars in attempting to economize cents, are hit off in a
very happy manner; but as the satire is always general, and
the malice at bottom good-natured and harmless, nobody
took offence, and we all laughed honestly and heartily; each,
as he supposed, at the expense of his neighbor. Nor are we
to conclude that because Mr. Irving has made the abuses of
popular government, and the weaknesses incident to those
who administer such a system, the objects of his satire,
that he is a political heretic and a secret foe to liberty. The
best human institutions are of course imperfect, and there
is quite as much advantage to be derived from a just and
good-humored exposition of the weak points of our own government, as from a continued fulsome and exaggerated pan-
egyric on its merits. Mr. Irving, we may add, was probably directed in the choice of the subjects on which to exercise his pleasantry, by the mere force of the circumstances
under which he wrote, and not by any general views of the
theory of government.

The decided success and universal popularity of his first
attempt naturally encouraged him to repeat it, and 'Salmagundi' was pretty soon followed by the <u>History of New York</u>.
This we consider as equal to the best, and in some respects
perhaps superior to any other of our author's productions.
It is the one which exhibits most distinctly the stamp of real
inventive power, the true test, as we have hinted, of genius.
The plan, though simple enough, and when hit upon, sufficiently obvious, is entirely original. In most other works
of the same general class of political satire, such as those
of Rabelais and Swift, the object of the work is effected by
presenting real events and characters of dignity and importance in low and ludicrous shapes. 'Knickerbocker' re-
verses this plan, and produces effect by dressing up a mean
and trifling fund of real history, in a garb of fictitious and
burlesque gravity. The conception is akin, no doubt, to the
general notion of the mock heroic, as exemplified, for instance, in Pope's 'Rape of the Lock,' but the particular
form, in which it is applied by the learned and ingenious

Diedrich, is not only unusually happy, but wholly new; and the work possesses of course, a character of complete originality, which does not belong to any of the others. The Stout Gentleman is a second application of the same principle, still more exquisitely wrought up and only inferior in the comparative smallness of the canvass. The execution of 'Knickerbocker' corresponds in felicity with the merit of the plan. The graphic distinctness, with which the three Dutch governors, whom nobody ever heard of before, are made to pass before us, each endowed with his appropriate intellectual, moral, and personal habits and qualities, is quite admirable; and the political satire is conveyed with great effect, and at the same time in a very fine and delicate manner, through the medium of these remote characters of the old world. There are some ineffectual attempts at wit in particular passages, and here and there a little indelicacy, which is the more objectionable, as it is inconsistent with the plan of the mock heroic, and in place, if admitted at all, only in the travestie. There is also a somewhat uncouth display of commonplace historical learning in the first book, where the author, while in the act of ridiculing pedantry, as he supposes it to be exemplified in the person of the worthy 'Diedrich,' betrays, we fear, a slight shade of the same quality in himself. But notwithstanding these blemishes, which are indeed so trifling, that we are almost ashamed to have mentioned them, the execution of the 'History of New York' is in the main completely successful. If we were called on to give a preference to any one of our author's productions over all the rest, we should with little hesitation assign the palm to this.

These, with some smaller pieces to which we shall briefly advert hereafter, are all the works, which were published by Mr. Irving before his departure for Europe, and which belong to what may be called his first manner. Soon after their appearance, he visited England, where, and in other parts of Europe, he has resided ever since; and we heard nothing of him for several years, until at length he brought out the Sketch Book, which first made him known to the literary world abroad. In the long interval which had elapsed

since the appearance of his former productions, 'a change
had come over the spirit of his dream.' Advancing years
had probably a little moderated the exuberant flow of his
youthful spirits, and the natural effect of time had, we fear,
been increased by other causes; if it be true, as we have
reason to suppose, that our amiable countryman had in the
interim taken some lessons in the school of that 'rugged
nurse of virtue,' so beautifully celebrated by Gray, who has
in all ages been but too much accustomed to extend the benefit of her tuition to the votaries of polite learning. Whether
under the influence of these causes, aided perhaps by the
wholesome terror, which an American candidate for European favor might be expected to feel of the iron rod of the
ruling critics, or for whatever other reason, certain it is,
that the genius of Mr. Irving appeared to be a little rebuked
at this his second apparition, and spoke in a partially subdued tone. The characteristics of the 'Sketch Book' are essentially the same with those of the preceding works; but,
with somewhat more polish and elegance, it has somewhat
less vivacity, freshness, and power. This difference constitutes the distinction between Mr. Irving's first and second
manner, the latter of which is preserved in all his subsequent publications, excepting the one now immediately before us. Of these two manners the one or the other may
perhaps be preferred by different readers, according to
their different tastes. We incline ourselves to the former,
conceiving that spirit and vigor are the highest qualities of
style, and that the loss of any merit of this description is
but poorly compensated by a little additional finish. The
change would have been however of less importance, had it
appeared only in the language, but it is also displayed in the
substance of the second series of publications; and it is here
particularly, that we discover what we deem the unpropi-
tious influence of a residence abroad on our author's talent.
Not only is his language less free and sparkling, but the
reach of his inventive power seems to be reduced. The
Crayons and Bracebridges, including Master Simon, are
Sketches indeed, and in water colors, compared with the
living roaring group of Cockloft Hall; and although we find

occasional returns of the author's best manner in 'The Stout
Gentleman,' 'Rip Van Winkle,' 'Sleepy Hollow,' 'The Mon-
ey-diggers,' and so forth, the rich material employed in
these pieces is not, as before, the staple of the work, but a
passing refreshment, that serves excellently well to remind
us of what we wanted, but from the smallness of its quantity
rather awakens than satisfies the appetite.

As it is difficult or rather impossible to suppose any actual diminution of power in the author, we must take for
granted, that the difference in question is owing to the
change in the general character of his subject. Humor and
satire are, as we said before, evidently his forte, and these
compose the substance of the preceding works. There is but
little attempt at the pathos in 'Salmagundi,' and none in
'Knickerbocker.' The subjects of satire are principally the
abuses of government and the follies of leading characters
and classes; and hence these works, though light in form,
have an elevated object, which gives them dignity and solid
value. Looking at them in a literary point of view, the circumstances of writing upon subjects actually before his eyes
gives his pictures the truth to nature, which is the chief element of all excellence in art. Had the author proceeded on
the same plan in his latter publications, he would have taken
for his subject the abuses of government and the follies of
leading classes and characters, as exemplified in the old
countries. This again would have opened a field for the exercise of his peculiar talent, still more rich and various than
the former one. Into this, however, whether from a terror
of criticism, a wish to conciliate all parties alike, a natural
modesty, a want of acquaintance with foreign manners and
institutions, or for whatever reason, he did not choose to
enter. Indeed the task of satirizing the manners and institutions of a country, in which one is at the time residing as a
guest, is so ungracious, that we can neither wonder nor regret, that Mr. Irving should have shrunk from it with in-
stinctive disgust. It is nevertheless certain, that the subjects alluded to are the best, indeed almost the only good
ones, for lively and pungent satire; and that in voluntarily
resigning them, our author was compelled to deprive himself

almost wholly of the use of his favorite and most efficient
instrument. He still, it is true, exercises it with no little
skill and success, upon subjects afforded by the fund of vice
and folly common to all nations, as in the story of the Lambs
and the Trotters, but we think with less effect, than when
following his original instinct, and laughing con amore at the
peculiar foibles of his own dear countrymen. Conscious
probably that the field for satire, which he felt himself at
liberty to explore, was less rich and productive than he
could have wished, he calls in the aid of the pathetic and
sentimental; in which departments, though, as we have said
before, occasionally successful, he is seldom eminently
so, —seldom exhibits the bright, sharp, true expression of
nature, which we see in his best comic pictures. In other
portions of these works, such as the whole description of
Bracebridge Hall, as it appears in the 'Sketch Book,' and
the work of that name, the tone wavers between the sentimental and the comic, and we hardly know whether the author meant to ridicule or eulogize the manners he describes;
which, however, are in either case evidently manners of his
own creation, having no prototype in this or any other period of English history. Bracebridge Hall, with its Christmas
sports and its Rookery, its antiquarian Squire, and its Master Simon, is as much a castle of fairy land, as the one in
which the Fata Morgana held entranced for six hundred
years the redoubtable champion of Denmark. The British
country squire is now as he ever was, and probably ever
will be, either a fox-hunter or a politician. Western and
Allworthy are the only two varieties of the species; and the
squire of Mr. Irving, with his indifference to politics, and
his taste for black-letter lore, is as completely a fancy-
piece, as the Centaurs and Harpies of the ancient poets.
These castles in Spain occupy a considerable portion of the
second series of works; and we really cannot but wonder
how Mr. Irving, generally so just and acute an observer of
nature, should have failed so completely in seizing the true
aspect of rural life in England, or why, if he saw it as it is,
he should have given us an unreal mockery of it instead of a
correct picture. It is refreshing and delightful to find how,

under all the disadvantages of writing on domestic subjects
in a foreign land, he recovers his wonted power, and dis-
ports himself with his pristine grace and sprightliness, the
moment that he lays the scene of his fable at home. No
sooner does he catch a glimpse of the venerable Kaatskill,
lifting his shaggy head above his white ruff of ambient
clouds, and frowning on the glorious Hudson as it rolls below; no sooner do the antique gable-roofed domes of the
Manhattoes, and Albany, and the classic shade of Communi-
paw rise upon his fancy, than 'his foot is on his native heath
and his name is M'Gregor.' When we think of this, although
we rejoice that Mr. Irving has been able, as he might not
otherwise have been, to levy a large and liberal golden contribution from the superfluity of the mother country, this
being, as it were, a spoiling of the Egyptians, we sometimes regret, for his own fame, that he ever left America.
There was a fund of truth, as well as ill nature, in the remark of one of the paltry, scandal-mongering novelists of
the day, that Mr. Irving would have done better to stay at
home, and pass his life among the beavers.

We have stated above, that the sentiment, which probably
induced Mr. Irving to refrain from exercising his satirical
talent upon the institutions and public characters of Great
Britain, was a natural and highly laudable one; but we cannot conscientiously speak with the same approbation of his
apparent disposition to represent the British aristocracy
under a favorable point of view, as compared with the other
classes of the people. If this representation were true, we
should not object to it, although the sort of complacency,
with which it is put forward, would still, in a foreigner and
a republican, be somewhat ungraceful. But the worst of it
is, that it is obviously and notoriously the reverse of the
truth. Let us take as an example the account given in the
'Sketch Book' of the author's attendance on public worship
at a village church, where he met with the family of a nobleman and that of a wealthy merchant. The former, especially
the young men and women, were all attention, candor, simplicity, and true moral dignity; the latter, all bad taste,
affectation, and vulgarity. Now every one, who has seen

anything of Europe, knows perfectly well, and Mr. Irving
certainly by this time, whatever he may have done when he
wrote the 'Sketch Book,' better than anybody, that if there
be a class of persons in that part of the world, who as a
class may be said to be more deficient than any other in
simplicity, candor, and a correct notion of true moral dignity, it is precisely this very British aristocracy, especially
in its younger branches, to which our author attributes these
virtues. We should say no more than might be inferred from
that portion of the popular literature of the day, in England,
which illustrates the manners and morals of fashionable life,
did we assert, that, if there be, in the known world, an animal, who by the general consent of all who are acquainted
with his habits, realizes the idea of complete puppyism, and
is in the strict sense of the term insupportable, it is the
young Englishman of rank and fortune. His candor, simplicity, and notion of moral dignity are exhibited in a drawling,
affected pronunciation; a foppish dress; manners at once
awkward and impertinent; the habitual use of the grossest
and most profane language; an ignorant and contemptuous
disregard for religion and morality, for the noble pursuits
of philosophy, literature, science, and the elegant arts,
even for politics, the regular occupation of his order; and
an exclusive devotion to coarse and rude sports, gaming,
and licentious indulgence of the lowest and foulest kind, for
he has not even elevation enough to be refined in his vices.
We know that there are honorable exceptions to this remark.
Such was the late amiable and excellent Earl of Guildford,
the founder of the University of Corfu. Such were the four
young gentlemen, members of parliament, who lately honored this country with their presence. Such have been, and
are several others of those, who have visited this country
on official errands, being, naturally, gentlemen selected for
their talent, industry, and capacity for business. But such,
as we have stated, is the character of the class. It was lately held up, in bold relief, to the horror and disgust of the
world, by Lord Byron, who combined a genius of his own
with some of the moral qualities of his order. Such is the
generation which Mr. Irving represents as models of sim-

plicity, candor, and moral dignity. On the other hand, the
wealthy merchants of England and other parts of Europe,
with their families, afford perhaps on the whole, the most
favorable specimen that could be selected from the educated
classes, of those very virtues, with which our author compliments the aristocracy at their expense. They are distinguished by intelligence, information, activity, application to
business, and as a natural consequence, correct and deco-
rous habits; and if not a deep sense of the importance of
religion and morality, an external regard, at least, for their
practical injunctions. These valuable qualities are often
united with a love for polite literature and the fine arts, as
in the case of Mr. Roscoe,[9] or a successful cultivation of
the more solid branches of science, as in the honorable example of the late Mr. Ricardo.[10] The vulgar, purse-proud,
ignorant merchant of Mr. Irving, is an exception or a fancy-
piece, probably in him a reminiscence of the false tone, on
this subject, that pervaded the polite literature of England
a century or two ago; and his candid young nobleman is
merely a little Sir Charles Grandison, in a blue frock and
white pantaloons, at whose formal manners, and patriarchal
ignorance of the world, the real dandy of the present day
would be the first to shrug up his shoulders with ineffable
contempt, and a perfect conviction of [his] own superiority.

While we have felt it a duty to point out this error in the
tone and spirit of Mr. Irving's later works, we must add,
that we do not, as some have done, attribute it to any hank-
ering in him after the aristocratic institutions and habits of
Europe. We acquit him entirely, as we have said before, of
political heresy; and without supposing him to be deeply
versed in the theory of government, we have no doubt that he
is strongly and sincerely attached to the republican institutions and forms established in his country. Neither do we
believe, that he was influenced in making this representation, by an interested wish to conciliate the British aristocracy, for the purpose of obtaining their patronage as a writer, or admission into their circles as a gentleman. We have
too high an opinion of Mr. Irving's independence, delicacy,
and elevation of mind, to suspect him for a moment of such

baseness. We think it probable, that he wrote the parts of
his work to which we now allude, under the influence of an
illusion, resulting naturally from his former situation and
literary habits. Without having studied the subject of government very deeply in the abstract, or possessing probably
any very precise general notions respecting it, he was led
by the original bent of his mind and his local and social
position, to employ himself, for several years, in ridiculing
the abuses of popular institutions, and the peculiar follies
and weaknesses of republican statesmen. Thus far he kept
himself within the line of truth and nature; for popular governments, however valuable, certainly have their defects,
and republican statesmen, like all other mortals, their be-
setting sins and characteristic foibles. Now, although it
does by no means follow from this, that monarchy is a perfect system, or an established aristocracy ex officio a corps
of Lord Orvilles and Sir Charles Grandisons, it was perhaps
not unnatural, that Mr. Irving, habitually gathering his impressions more from impulse than argument, should, by
constantly looking at the ridiculous features of one form, be
led to take up a too flattering idea of the other. Some such
mental operation as this appears to have been the source of
the illusion under which, as we conceive, he was at one
time laboring; and when he wrote the 'Sketch Book,' where
the error in question is most apparent, he probably had not
had much opportunity to bring his ideal picture to the test of
comparison with real life, for it was not, we believe, until
he had acquired a high reputation in England, by the publication of this work, that he frequented very intimately the circles of the British aristocracy. We have reason to suppose
that he has since reformed his theory on this subject, and
we mention the fact with pleasure, as a proof that the opportunities he has had for actual observation, have not been lost
upon his naturally acute and sagacious, as well as sensitive
mind.

Having thus cleared our consciences (we trust without
doing injustice to our author) by pointing out certain particulars, in which we consider his European manner inferior
to his American one, we return with pleasure to the remark

we made before, that the former has somewhat more of elegance and polish than the latter; that the characteristics of
both are (with the deductions we have specified) substantially the same; that all his productions are among the most
agreeable and attractive, as they certainly have been among
the most popular of the time; that they do the highest honor
to himself and through him to his country; and that he has
already secured and will permanently maintain, in our literary annals, the brilliant position of the harbinger and founder of the American school of polite learning.

We come now to the 'History of the Life and Voyages of
Columbus,' which has furnished the immediate subject and
occasion of the present article. This work differs essentially
in manner, as we have already said, from any of the preceding. It exemplifies on a larger scale, and in a more complete and finished way, the plan of the short biographical
sketches, which the author published before his departure
for Europe, principally of contemporary officers of the
navy. We shall first endeavor to ascertain the class of historical writing to which it belongs, and then make a few remarks upon the merit of the execution and the general value
of the work.

The great division of this department of literature is into
the two classes of philosophical and purely narrative history. They are not, it is true, separated by a very strict
line, but on the contrary run into each other, each possessing to a certain extent the peculiar characteristics of both;
but the distinction is nevertheless real, and whenever a
writer has talent enough to give his work a marked character, it is evident at once to which of the two classes it belongs. The object of philosophical history is to set forth, by
a record of real events, the general principles which regulate the march of political affairs; that of purely narrative
history to give a correct and lively picture of the same
events, as they pass before the eye of the world, but with
little or no reference to their causes or effects. It is obvious
that these two sorts of history are not only essentially different, but that they belong respectively to two very different
and in some respects opposite departments of literature.

The distinction between them is the same as that between
Laplace's 'Exposition of the System of the Universe,' and a
description in words of the various constellations and plan-
ets that are laid down in the charts of the celestial sphere,
as they appear in the blue vault of heaven to the ordinary observer. The same facts undoubtedly form the groundwork of
both, but the object, the mode of execution, the peculiar
capacity and disposition respectively supposed in the authors
of each, and the pleasure afforded by each, when the plan is
executed with talent and success, are very different; and
that to such a degree, that the two works appertain to the
adverse domains of philosophy and poetry. History, therefore, which Lord Bacon describes as a third department of
learning, entirely separate from the two just mentioned,
seems to be in fact a divided empire, situated between the
others, and acknowledging, in the part bordering upon each,
the jurisdiction of its more independent neighbor. Philosophical history is properly a branch of philosophy, since its
purpose is to teach general truths in the form of narrative;
while purely narrative history, which merely offers a picture of the outside of passing or past events, is, when properly written, substantially poetry. To inquire which of these
two sorts of history has the superior rank, would be in one
respect to compare things which admit of no comparison.
Who can pretend to say whether a brilliant thought is more
beautiful than a bright eye, or whether Newton's 'Principia'
is a greater work than the Iliad? Nevertheless, as history
occupies a middle region between the two great adverse
realms of learning, and partakes, in some degree, of the
characters of both, we may, in this instance, institute such
a comparison with less impropriety, and the palm would
perhaps be assigned, without much hesitation, to the philosophical over the merely narrative historian; for the poet,
by restricting himself within the limits of real facts, loses
for the time the use of his highest attribute, and that which
properly gives him his name, original creation or invention,
and thus voluntarily places himself on a secondary line in
the scale of his own art; while philosophy, when 'teaching
by example,' without abandoning any of her peculiar advan-

tages, borrows for the occasion the airs and graces of her more attractive sister, since the facts which she relates, with whatever purpose of instruction, may and must be told with elegance and spirit. In other words, a first-rate philosophical history can only be written by a person who combines most of the essential talents and accomplishments of the philosopher and the poet; while a purely narrative history of corresponding merit in its way, might be produced by a poet of a secondary order who had no tincture of philosophy. The former, taken in the abstract, must therefore be considered, on the whole, as the decidedly superior form of writing.

Mr. Irving's present work, if technically classed according to the general principles just stated, belongs to the lower species of history, and is so described by himself in his preface. 'In the execution of this work,' he remarks, 'I have avoided indulging in mere speculations or general reflections, excepting such as naturally arose out of the subject, preferring to give a minute and circumstantial narrative, omitting no particular that appeared characteristic of the persons, the events, or the times; and endeavoring to place every fact under such a point of view, that the reader might perceive its merits, and draw his own maxims and conclusions.' The omission of all general speculation is indeed a good deal more complete than this preliminary declaration would have necessarily led us to suppose it, since the exception of 'such reflections as naturally arise out of the subject' would admit almost any degree of latitude in this respect. In point of fact, there is no political speculation whatever, the very few reflections that are interspersed being on matters of ordinary private morality. In giving this color to his work, Mr. Irving doubtless followed instinctively the natural bent of his genius, which does not incline him, as we have repeatedly observed, to philosophical researches; but he has thereby produced a much more valuable literary monument, than with his peculiar taste and talent, he could have done in a different way. In estimating the positive worth of particular works, we must take into view the merit of the execution, as well as the dignity of the class to

which they belong; and if the latter be, in the present instance, of a secondary order (though still secondary only as
compared with the very highest and most glorious exercises
of intellect,) yet such have been the good taste and felicity
of our author, in the selection of his subject, such his dili-
gence, research, and perseverance in collecting and em-
ploying his materials; and such his care in giving the highest
finish and perfection to the style; that he has been able to
bring out a work, which will rank with the very best histories of any age or nation, which will take a permanent place
in the classical literature of the language, which is, in fact,
one of the most agreeable, instructive, and really valuable
productions to be met with anywhere, and one that, as we
remarked above, does, on the whole, more honor to the
learning of our country, than any previous work written on
this side the Atlantic.

For the particular kind of historical writing, in which Mr.
Irving is fitted to labor and excel, the 'Life of Columbus' is
undoubtedly one of the best, perhaps we might say without
the fear of mistake, the very best subject afforded by the
annals of the world. While his discoveries possess the importance belonging to political events of the first magnitude,
the generous elevation of his mind, the various fortunes that
checquered his course, and the singularity, the uniquity
rather, if we may be allowed to coin a word, of his achievements, throw a sort of poetical and romantic coloring over
his adventures, and render him of all others the fittest hero
for a work of this description, which, as we have shown
above, is essentially a poem. The only objection that could
possibly be made to the choice of the subject would be, that
it was before exhausted; and this has in fact been said by
some of the newspaper critics of the mother country. The
assertion is however quite groundless. Before the publication of the work before us, there was no satisfactory account
of Columbus in any language. The one given by his son is, as
is well known, merely a brief and imperfect sketch; and the
portion of Robertson's 'America' which is devoted to him,
though as large as it could be with propriety, considering
the author's plan, did not allow a detailed and accurate

investigation of the events of his life. Into this and other
general histories, Columbus enters partially as one of the
leading personages of the age, and is treated in connection
with the rest; but the singular splendor and prodigious permanent importance of his actions, as well as the moral
grandeur and sublimity of his character, entitled him fully
to the honor of a separate and detailed biography. How much
finer and loftier a subject is he, than his contemporary
Charles the Fifth, who has yet furnished a theme for one of
the best histories in the language! The materials, printed
and manuscript, were ample, but not accessible in their
full extent, excepting to a person resident, for the time, in
the capital of Spain. We consider it therefore as a singularly fortunate circumstance, that Mr. Irving should have been
led, in the course of his pilgrimage abroad, to visit this,
on some accounts, unattractive part of Europe. Thus favorably situated, and possessed of all the talent and industry
necessary for the purpose, he has at length filled up the void
that before existed, in this respect, in the literature of the
world, and produced a work, which will fully satisfy the
public, and supersede the necessity of any future labors in
the same field. While we venture to predict that the adventures of Columbus will hereafter be read only in the works
of Mr. Irving, we cannot but think it a beautiful coincidence,
that the task of duly celebrating the achievements of the
discoverer of our continent, should have been reserved for
one of its inhabitants; and that the earliest professed author
of first-rate talent, who appeared among us, should have
devoted one of his most important and finished works to this
pious purpose.

> 'Such honors Ilion to her hero paid,
> And peaceful slept the mighty Hector's shade.'

In treating this happy and splendid subject, Mr. Irving has
brought out the full force of his genius as far as a just regard for the principles of historical writing would admit.
This kind of history, although it belongs essentially to the
department of poetry, does not of course afford any room
for the display of the creative power in the invention of facts

or characters; but, in this case, the real facts and characters far surpass in brilliancy any possible creation of mere
fancy, and in the other requisites of fine poetry, a judicious
selection and disposition of the materials, a correct, striking, and discriminating picture of the different personages,
a just and elevated tone of moral feeling, and above all, the
charm of an elegant, perspicuous, and flowing style, Mr.
Irving leaves us nothing to desire, and with all, who can
look beyond mere forms and names into the substance of
things, sustains his right, which he had before established,
to the fame of a real poet. To say that this work is superior
to any professed poem, that has yet been published, on the
life of Columbus, would be giving it but poor praise; since
the subject, although attempted by bards of no slight pretensions, has not yet been treated in verse with eminent
success. We would go farther than this, and express the
opinion, that Mr. Irving's production may be justly ranked
with the fine narrative or epic poems of the highest reputation. A polished and civilized age may well be supposed to
prefer, especially in a long composition, the delicate melody of flowing prose, setting forth a spirited and elegant picture of actual life, to the 'specious wonders' of Olympus or
fairy land, expressed in artificial measures, strains and
subjects that seem more naturally adapted to a yet unformed,
than to a mature and perfect taste. Hence a fine history and
a fine novel may perhaps with propriety be viewed as the
greater and lesser epic (to use the technical terms) of a
cultivated period, when verse is better reserved for short
poems accompanied by music. But however this may be, and
with whatever class of compositions we may rank the work
before us, its execution entirely corresponds, as we have
said before, with the beauty of the subject, and leaves of
course but little room for the labor of the critic. The interest of the narrative is completely sustained from the beginning to the conclusion, and is equal throughout, for any
mature mind, to that of the best romance. Instinctively pursuing the bent of his genius, the author has everywhere
brought out into full relief the most poetical features of the
story. He dwells, for instance, with peculiar pleasure on

the golden age of innocence and happiness, that reigned
among the natives of Haiti before the arrival of the Spaniards. The careless and luxurious indulgence, in which they
passed their peaceful hours beneath 'the odorous shade of
their boundless forests,' under the amiable sway of a beautiful queen, who is represented as charming their leisure
with her own sweet poetry, seems to realize the notion of
an earthly elysium; and if there be, as there probably is,
some little exaggeration in the coloring of the picture, it
must be viewed as a natural effect of the just indignation
and horror, with which we contemplate the devilish malice
which afterwards carried death and destruction through
these bowers of simple bliss. The two leading personages
are happily contrasted, not by labored parallels, but indirectly by the mere progress of the story. The towering sublimity and bold creative genius of the Admiral; the sagacity,
activity, and dauntless courage of the Adelantado; the faithful and tender attachment with which they stood by each
other, through a long life of labor, danger, and suffering;
these are moral traits, that furnish out another picture, not
less beautiful and even more edifying, than that of the Indian
Paradise.

We are grateful to Mr. Irving, for bringing particularly
into view the high religious feeling, which uniformly governed the mind of Columbus, which led him to consider himself as an agent, expressly selected by Providence for the
accomplishment of great and glorious objects,—and how, but
by a poor quibble upon words, can we refuse him that character?—which induced him finally to look forward to the recovery of the Holy Sepulchre, as the last labor of his life,
to be undertaken after the complete accomplishment of all
his projects in the New World. If there be any error in the
passages, which treat of this particular, it consists in un-
derrating the merit of this conception of Columbus, which
appears to be viewed by Mr. Irving as the effect of an amiable, but somewhat visionary and mistaken enthusiasm. The
plan was no doubt, as entertained by Columbus, the result
of a high religious enthusiasm, and so was that of his grand
discovery; but this feeling acted, in both cases, under the

direction of an extraordinar[il]y sound and acute judgment,
and with the aid of all the learning of the age. The recovery
of Palestine was a project not only dear to every Christian
heart as such, but recommended by the strongest motives of
state policy, at a time when the Ottoman Power was developing itself in the plenitude of life and vigor; already over-
shadowing Christian Europe, and from year to year menac-
ing its whole commonwealth of nations, with complete
subjugation. Let it be remembered, that it was not till half
a century after the death of Columbus, that the sea-fight of
Lepanto broke the naval power of the Turks; that as lately as
the year 1688, their armies invested Vienna, which would
undoubtedly have fallen and left the road open to Paris, had
not the siege been raised by the timely arrival of the king of
Poland; let these facts, we say, be remembered, and we
shall not probably consider the scheme of the Admiral so
visionary, as it might be thought upon a merely superficial
view of the present state of the world. The religious enthusiasm, which has more or less inspired the Europeans in their
wars against the Turks, has in fact, from the commencement of these wars up to the present day, coincided with the
suggestions, not so much of good policy, as of strict self-
defence. The Mahometans have been throughout the aggres-
sors. They subdued the whole of Christian Asia and Africa
(which they still retain in brutal oppression and debase-
ment,) subdued some of the fairest portions of Christian
Europe, such as Spain, Greece, and parts of Italy, and had
pushed their arms into the very heart of France, when they
received the first check, from Charles Martel, at the battle
of Tours. All these aggressions on the Christians were entirely unprovoked. When the tide of invasion was once
checked, the only skilful and scientific plan of conducting the
war was, of course, to carry it back into the enemy's territory, in which Palestine, from its central position, was
the proper point of attack. Such was the principle of the long
series of wars denominated Crusades, which occupy two or
three centuries of the history of Europe; nor, although the
danger of any farther progress on the part of the Turks has
for some time past disappeared, will they ever cease to be

regarded as public and permanent enemies, until the present
or some future generation shall have completely recovered
from them the lost domains of Christendom, and planted the
standard of our religion on every fortress from the Indus to
the Senegal.

It would give us pleasure to expatiate at greater length
upon the merit of the beautiful and valuable work before us;
but we perceive that we have reached the proper limit of an
article, and must here close our remarks. We cannot however refrain from expressing our satisfaction, at the very
favorable manner with which Mr. Irving's 'Life of Columbus' compares with one or two works of a similar kind,
that were published about the same time by the best writers
of the mother country. The 'Life of Napoleon,' by Sir Walter
Scott, and the 'Life of Sheridan,' by Moore, particularly
the former, resemble it so nearly in plan and form, that,
coming out, as they all did, about the same time, they exhibit in a manner a trial of skill between three of the most
elegant writers of the day. We feel a good deal of pride as
Americans in adding, that our countryman appears to have
retired from this dangerous contest with a very decided advantage, we think we might say a complete victory, over
both his competitors. We mean not to deprive these illustrious transatlantic bards of any fame, to which they may be
justly entitled, by the productions in question; nor do we
mean to represent Mr. Irving's general reputation as at
present superior or equal to theirs. We simply state the fact
as it is, considering it to be one highly honorable to our
countryman and our country. We shall even go farther,
being in a patriotic vein, and while we freely admit that Mr.
Irving's fame is and ought to be at present inferior to that
of the two British poets above-mentioned, we shall take the
liberty of adding, that we are not quite sure whether it will
always remain so. Moore and Scott have already done their
best, and from the character of their productions for some
years past, as compared with those of earlier date, it is
evident that they will not hereafter excel or perhaps equal
their past efforts. Mr. Irving's talent seems to us, on the
contrary, to be in a state of progress; for although his

second manner be, as we think, inferior, on the whole, to
his first, the difference is not, as we have already expressly stated, owing to any decay of genius, but to an unfavorable change of scene and subject; and in this first specimen
of a <u>third</u> series of publications, we recognize, though under
a somewhat graver form, a development of power superior
to that which is displayed by any of the preceding ones, even
should the 'History of New York,' as a bold original creation, be considered as belonging to a higher class of writings. We also recognize in the selection of the subject, the
persevering industry with which the work has been executed,
and the high tone of moral feeling that runs through the
whole of it, the symptoms of a noble spirit, on which the
intoxicating cup of public applause acts as a stimulant rather
than an opiate. Mr. Irving is still in the vigor of life and
health; and when we see him advancing in his course in this
way, with renovated courage and redoubled talent at an age
when too many hearts begin to wax prematurely faint, we
are induced to anticipate the happiest results from his future
labors; and are far from being certain, as we said above,
that he may not in the end eclipse the most illustrious of his
present contemporaries and rivals. We rejoice to find,
from the selection of the subject of the work now before us,
that though long a wanderer, his thoughts are still bent on
the land of his birth. Although we wish not to hasten his return before the period when he shall himself deem it expedient, we indulge the hope that he will sooner or later fix his
residence among us, and can assure him that whenever he
may think proper to do so, he will be welcomed by his countrymen as a well-deserving citizen and a public benefactor.
When he shall be seated again upon his native soil, among
his beavers, if Mr. D'Israeli pleases, when he shall again
apply to those subjects of strictly native origin, in which his
genius seems to take most delight, the force of his mature
talent, and the lights of his long and varied experience, we
think we may expect with reason a <u>fourth</u> series of publications, that shall surpass in value all the preceding ones,
including even that, which he has now so honorably opened
with the work before us.

Notes

The text is based on Critical and Miscellaneous Essays, Second Series (Boston: James Monroe and Co., 1846), 145-184. Subtitle in the source: "[North American Review, January, 1829.]." Footnote to the source's title: "A History of the Life and Voyages of Christopher Columbus. By WASHINGTON IRVING. 3 vols. 8vo. New York, and London, 1828."

1. "Brave men have conquered before Agamemnon."
2. John Trumbull (1750-1831), the most talented of the poets known as the "Connecticut Wits."
3. Francis Hopkinson (1737-1791). "The Battle of the Kegs" is his best-remembered poem.
4. Timothy Dwight (1752-1817). The Conquest of Canaan (1785), Greenfield Hill (1794).
5. Joel Barlow (1754-1812). The Vision of Columbus (1787).
6. David Humphreys (1752-1818), officer on Washington's staff and poet of timely and patriotic subjects.
7. "I am first in the country."
8. "Voltaire . . . did not see all that he did, but he did all that we see."
9. William Roscoe (1753-1831), historian and cultivator of the arts.
10. David Ricardo (1772-1823), economist.

Lord Vapourcourt; or, A November Day in London

Lord Vapourcourt was the lineal representative of an English family of rank and fortune; and to this accidental advantage he united the natural gifts of a good person, a vigorous constitution, and respectable intellectual endowments. The last had been cultivated by the process usually employed in the education of a British nobleman of the present day. His Lordship had devoted his regular seven years to the study of Greek and Latin prosody at Eton College, and by virtue of his privilege, had taken the usual degrees at Oxford without keeping his terms. After quitting the university, he had passed three years in making the grand tour upon the Continent, and had brought back from his travels a competent knowledge of French cookery, and a correct notion of the comparative merits of Champagne and Rhenish. His father, the old Earl, had died during his absence, and the son was called home rather suddenly, to assist in arranging the succession, and to take his seat in the House of Peers. As the estate was wholly unincumbered, the necessary forms were soon despatched, and his Lordship entered quietly into possession of a clear income of ten thousand pounds a year. Such was the situation of this young nobleman at his first appearance upon the stage of active life, at the age of five and twenty; and his friends and connections, as may well be supposed, formed the most brilliant anticipations of his

future success, and of the figure that he would make in the
world.

It was soon perceived, however, with surprise, that Lord
Vapourcourt took but little interest in the occupations and
amusements that ordinarily engage the attention of a young
British Peer. He did not show himself above once or twice
at the Fives Court, and was never known to assist at a regular set-to. He had a capital stud of horses, and a famous
pack of hounds, but seldom took them out; and was not a
regular attendant upon the races, either at Ascot or New-
market. What was still more extraordinary, he frequented
none of the fashionable gaming houses, rarely betted, and
when he did, not more than four or five hundred guineas at a
time. These circumstances gave his character a strong tinge
of singularity; and that part of the public whose business
consists in attending to that of other people, were pretty
soon in deep speculation upon the causes of this strange
conduct. It was conjectured at first, that his Lordship was
in love; but this supposition proved to be erroneous. It was
speedily ascertained that he never saw any female society,
and had kept himself wholly aloof from the overtures of sundry mammas, who had indirectly laid siege to him soon
after he came to his title. Finding this theory untenable, a
few persons took upon them to imagine, that Vapourcourt
had come to the resolution of attending to business or to
study; and that he would turn out a politician, a poet, or
some other odd animal of the same genus. But here again
speculation appeared to be at fault, for it was pretty soon
discovered, that his Lordship had never been in the House of
Peers, excepting to take his seat, and that he had not opened
a book since he left Eton College.

While these different and groundless rumors succeeded
each other, respecting the causes of Lord Vapourcourt's uncommon mode of life, the real truth after a while came out;
and it was at length generally known in the circle of his
friends and connections, that his Lordship was violently attacked with the spleen. It was then recollected that this
malady was hereditary in the family. The same anxious persons who had before been so active in discovering the nature

of the disease, were now equally busy in recommending
remedies. A young clergyman, connected with the family,
who had just taken orders, and was dying to see the world,
advised a repetition of the grand tour, under the direction of
a lively and intelligent tutor; and offered his services in this
capacity. A leading ministerial Peer attributed his Lordship's illness to want of occupation, and intimated that there
would be no great difficulty in procuring for him a respectable appointment in one of the Departments of State or foreign Embassies, it being understood that his Lordship's four
votes in the house of Commons should in that case regularly
strengthen the hands of His Majesty's ministers. Lady Look-
about, who had a pretty, marriageable daughter on her
hands, extolled the happy effects that had resulted in various
cases of this description, from the free use of curtain lectures; and earnestly recommended a loquacious and spirited
young wife.

Vapourcourt, as the reader will easily imagine, gave no
heed to any of these good-natured hints, and grew gradually
worse from year to year, until he might be said at last to
vegetate, rather than live. The malady finally reached such
a height, that in the year 18—, after yawning away the summer at the old family castle in the country, he resolved,
from mere fatigue, not to stay for the Christmas holidays,
and returned to town about the last of October, when the cold
weather was just setting in, and the hunting season opening
in all its beauty. The neighboring gentry considered this desperate measure, as a certain proof that his Lordship's com-
plaint had now reached a degree of intensity, which was
equivalent to actual madness; and concluded unanimously
that it must soon terminate in a crisis of one kind or another. Having settled this point, with various others of equal
importance, one night over the bottle, a company of thirty
or forty of them, all in high and buoyant spirits, took the
field the next morning at daylight, superbly mounted, and
uniformly dressed in scarlet coats and jockey caps, the
hounds in full cry, the weather clear, fresh, and frosty,
and scoured the country for thirty miles round in quest of a
fox. Meanwhile Lord Vapourcourt, at about the same hour,

got into his travelling chariot, drawn by four post horses, where he soon fell into a languid and uneasy sort of slumber, and hardly opened his eyes wide enough to take notice of anything without the carriage, until it stopped, late at night, at the door of his house in Pall-Mall.

The next morning, Lord Vapourcourt rang for his <u>valet-de-chambre</u> at about half past eleven, having slept somewhat later than usual, in consequence of the fatigue of the preceding day's journey. The servant made his appearance, and proceeded to open the shutters; but the rays of the sun showed little or no disposition to take advantage of the circumstances. The air was filled with one of those murky and impenetrable fogs, which sometimes envelop the city of London, and which can be distinctly imagined by those only who have seen and felt them. A sort of dim and smothered twilight gleamed faintly through the windows, but was not sufficient for the usual operations of domestic life, and the servant had accordingly brought in lights to aid his master in the business of dressing.

'What's this?' exclaimed the Peer, struck with astonishment at the unusual circumstances, and terrified at the thought that he had rung four or five hours too soon. 'What o'clock is it, Johnson?'

'Half past eleven, my Lord,' replied the servant; 'but the fog is so thick that your Lordship would not be able to see to dress, and I thought it best to bring in lights.'

A deep sigh, succeeded by a wide and almost interminable yawn, expressed the feelings of Vapourcourt, whose habitual malady weighed down his spirits with more than usual oppressiveness, at this piece of news. The disgust occasioned by the state of the weather, was, however, slightly tempered by a gleam of satisfaction, at the idea that the day was further advanced than he had feared; and after a few more long yawns, his Lordship at last determined to rise. The servant assisted him in dressing, and then withdrew to order his master's breakfast, having placed lights in a small adjoining cabinet, where Lord Vapourcourt usually passed the morning.

There are few things more oppressive to feeble nerves,

than the effect of artificial light in the daytime. There is
something rich and cheerful in the clear flame of a wax tap-
er, or a well ordered lamp, when we see them in the evening, illuminating a group of happy faces collected around
them; but, in the daytime, they produce a different impression. Their little paltry glare, placing itself in comparison
with the clear, transparent beauty of the solar rays, has a
sombre, and, in the language of Shakspeare, an 'ineffectual'
aspect. The morbid feelings of Vapourcourt sickened at the
view, and on entering his cabinet he moved instinctively
towards the window, in the hope of discovering something
more attractive. The prospect without corresponded completely with the gloomy appearance of the apartment. A
dense and dingy mass of vapor brooded heavily over the tops
of the houses; and although it was now high noon, the rays
of the sun produced no other effect upon the fog, than to give
it a sort of brassy hue, and to design through it, in a dim
and uncertain manner, the outlines of the objects it covered.
Another long and dreary yawn indicated the sensations of the
hypocondriac Peer, at this enlivening spectacle. It was difficult to say whether the aspect of things without, or within,
was the more inviting. In the uncertainty which he felt upon
this question, Vapourcourt remained for several minutes
gazing listlessly at the movements of the fog, which sometimes undulated in large white volumes like the waves of the
sea in a storm, and then cleared away for a moment, and
permitted the sun to exhibit a glimpse of his broad, rayless,
yellow disk, which, from its strange appearance, rather
increased than diminished the gloom while it was visible,
and was scarcely seen before it was clouded in again by new
mountains of vapor, that swelled in successive exhalations
from the river. Fatigued at length with standing, his Lordship mechanically moved towards a well-stuffed sofa, that
was placed near the chimney, and stretching himself upon it
at his length, with his head supported by a couple of large
cushions, he prepared, after another fit of yawning not less
long and dreary than the last, to await the arrival of Johnson
and the tea.

   The servant soon appeared, bringing with him the breakfast apparatus, and the morning paper. In a large family, breakfast is commonly a gay repast. If the spirits are at all elastic, they move with fresh vigor at the opening of a new day. The appetite, after an abstinence of several hours, is keen and active, and the view of a table covered with preparations to satisfy it, diffuses hilarity and sprightliness through the circle. The hissing of the tea urn, a sound not very musical in itself, appears agreeable, when it is felt to be the indication of a refreshing beverage. The hot rolls, the muffins, the sliced ham, the eggs, and the conserves, present an ensemble, which, though not to be compared, in the opinion of an epicure, with a real déjeuner à la fourchette, has no small charm for a plain unsophisticated appetite. The morning papers, in the various articles of intelligence and entertainment which they always contain, furnish innumerable topics of conversation, and open inviting prospects for entertainment or occupation during the day. There is doubtless something more grand and imposing in a regular dinner, but for mere gaiety and light-heartedness, perhaps no meal in the four and twenty hours, can be compared with breakfast, considered in its best and proper state. That of a solitary hypocondriac like Vapourcourt, presented, of course, none of these attractions. The hissing of the tea urn disturbed his nerves; the rolls were burned, the muffins cold, the eggs too much boiled, and the formal countenance of Johnson diffused a sort of tiresome solemnity over the table. Vapourcourt, after drinking two or three cups of tea, sent away the breakfast with a feeling of disgust, and mechanically took up the Morning Chronicle.

The political science and patriotic feeling of Mr. Perry were, however, wholly lost upon our hero, who never looked at any part of the paper but the court news and the movements of the world of fashion. Under the head of arrivals, he remarked the following article.

'At his residence in Pall-Mall, the Right Honorable the Earl of Vapourcourt, from Vapourcourt Castle.'

The least ambitious minds are not wholly insensible to the charms of public notice and attention. Vapourcourt experi-

enced a momentary sentiment of satisfaction, at seeing his
name thus presented to the view of the world, and his movements recorded almost as fast as they were made. But the
feeling was soon chastened, by a recollection of the gloom
that surrounded him. 'Had I known that the morning would
have been so foggy in London,' quoth he, extending his jaws
into another boundless yawn, 'I should have been tempted to
stay another day at the Castle. But what matters it,' he
added, after musing a few moments, 'where life passes?
Town or country, at home or abroad, 'tis all of a piece. We
pass ten or twelve hours in restless and interrupted slumber, rise with a heart-felt languor, and a secret wish that
the day were over, before it is well begun; we sip two or
three cups of weak tea; we read in the papers that the King
went to Brighton yesterday, and that the Duke of York will
hold a levee to-day; we yawn away the morning on the sofa,
ride out at three, and, like a blind mill-horse, go over once
more in the park, the same track which we have gone over
a hundred times before; look in at the coffee-house or the
club, and meet the same originals, engaged for the hun-
dredth time in the same eternal contest whether my Lord A.
or Mr. B. ought to sign the public despatches; dine at the
same hour upon the same dishes, read again in the evening
paper the same news which we had read before in the morning one, and then to bed, to recover strength and spirits to
pursue the same course again the following day. Such, for-
sooth, is life!'

At the close of this philosophical soliloquy, Lord Vapourcourt rose from the couch, and returned to the window, to
look again upon the neighboring streets. The fog was now
still more dense and gloomy than before, and had evidently
settled down for the day upon the city. The volumes of vapor
that rolled over the tops of the houses, were thicker and
more frequent, and their color still more sombre and
brassy than it had been. It was with some difficulty that the
houses on the opposite side of the street, or the carriages
and walkers that passed below, could be discerned at all.
At times, when the mist cleared away a little, they were
seen looming up into more than their usual dimensions from

the effect of the density of the intervening medium, and to an
observer of a livelier fancy, would have offered a scene of
amusing contemplation. A young girl with a white gown and
bonnet, had the look of a schooner-rigged small craft seen
at a distance under full sail; and the black Lincolnshire
horses drawing their loaded carts, appeared like huge ele-
phants, with armed castles towering up from their backs.
But these, and other such imaginary likenesses, were lost
upon Vapourcourt, who perceived nothing but the undiminished gloom of the fog, and was musing with dismay upon the
long and dreary hours that were opening before him. At this
fatal crisis, the weariness of life, which he had so long experienced, pressed upon his mind with a weight which he
had never known before. The whole question seemed to come
to a point at once. To stand at the window and gaze forever
at the fog was evidently impossible; to return to the sofa
and yawn away the rest of the day, was not less so. And yet
the present moment was an epitome of life. Every day,
every hour brought with it, like this, a recurrence of successive alternatives, either side of which was equally intolerable.

Under the influence of these gloomy reflections, the combined result of a morbid state of mind, and an uncommonly
foggy day, it suddenly occurred to our unfortunate hero, that
it was possible to pursue a middle course, which would
clear him at once and forever from both the horns of this
perpetual dilemma. 'Why,' exclaimed he, 'submit to this
insufferable burden, when we are at liberty to shake it off at
any moment? Why not manfully turn at once to the rope or
the river? Why not put a voluntary end to this dreary succession of weary nights and wearier days, called life? Let
others drag it out to the last hour, and drain the cup of _en-
nui_ to the dregs. I have had enough of it already, and will
finish it this very night, in the old Roman fashion.'

Vapourcourt had a naturally vigorous and resolute character, and, with a better education, would have played a
very different part in the world. Such as he was, he was
still capable of acting with promptitude and firmness, when
driven by extraordinary motives, imaginary or real, to feel

the necessity of it. Having taken the violent resolution just
mentioned, he was not deterred from executing it, by any
merely mechanical or constitutional apprehensions. He de-
liberated coolly with himself upon the best manner of carrying it into effect, and finally concluded that the easiest and
least scandalous process, would be to wait till evening, and
then walk quietly down to the bridge, and throw himself into
the river. 'The night,' said he to himself, 'will be dark and
foggy, the thing will not be observed at the moment, may
perhaps never be discovered, and at any rate will create
little or no immediate scandal. If I go to blowing my brains
out à la Werther, the whole street will be in an uproar for
the night, and the old women of the neighborhood will talk
the matter over for at least a month to come.'

Having settled this question, our hero rang the bell, and
ordered dinner at five o'clock, which was three hours earlier than usual. The rigid aspect of Johnson expanded, and his
dull narrow eyes brightened with a gleam of surprise at this
extraordinary command; but accustomed to obey in all cases
without explanation, he retired in silence to give the necessary directions. Vapourcourt then proceeded to make some
little arrangements in regard to his affairs, and wrote one
or two short letters of business, after which he proceeded,
very tranquilly, to put on a walking dress, that he might be
ready to go out after dinner, and execute his project. These
preliminary matters being adjusted, he employed himself,
during the short interval of leisure that remained, in traversing his cabinet, and reflecting on the prospect before
him. His spirits were now in a finer flow than they had been
at any time for years preceding. The little occupation in
which he had been engaged, and the vigorous resolution that
had been the fruit of his previous meditations, had given a
stir to the stagnant current of his feelings, and diffused over
them a momentary coloring, not wholly unlike that of cheerfulness. The sun, meanwhile, had partly dissipated the thick
vapor that filled the air in the morning, and poured through
the windows a rich yellow radiance, like the golden lights
in the paintings of Rembrandt, which harmonized finely with
the bright colors of the Turkey carpet. The change of weather

contributed, with his late uncommon exertion, to relieve the
oppression of our hero's spirits. He walked gaily up and
down the room, satisfied with himself, and secretly proud
of the firmness and promptitude with which he had come to
his decision. 'Why this,' said he, 'is as it should be. As
Kean says, "Richard's himself again." I now feel the truth
of a remark which I met with at Eton, in an old Latin book
called Seneca, purporting that a man of sense is always the
master of his own fortune. It is but showing a little firmness, and you may put to flight an army of blue devils, were
they as numerous as those which beset St. Anthony. What
says the poet?

> "Throw but a stone—the giant dies."

My tormenter is half frightened to death, before I have well
taken up the pebble; a few hours more, and I finish him forever.'

  Could his Lordship have pursued this train of lively reflection for any length of time, he might perhaps have realized the truth of the poet's assurance in a more rational
way, than that which he now contemplated. But the short November day was now drawing fast to a close; the sun set before five, and the fog collected again, and hung with deeper
gloom than before upon the city. Johnson now appeared to
announce that dinner was on the table, and Vapourcourt repaired to the dining room to enjoy for the last time his
splendid, though solitary repast. Under the excitement of
the moment, he ate with more than ordinary appetite; and
the attendants, connecting this circumstance with that of the
uncommonly early hour, concluded that some event of a singular, but highly agreeable kind, had occurred to enliven
the languid tenor of their master's life. They all anticipated
that the close of dinner would be followed by an order for
the carriage, and that his Lordship would go out upon some
important and interesting expedition. Johnson, with the political feeling natural to a freeborn British subject, thought
it probable, that his master meant to make his début in the
house of Peers, where there was to be that evening a debate
upon the foreign policy of the country. A French footman

decided that Vapourcourt was going to the opera, where
Catalani was to make her first appearance for the winter;
and a young jockey, fresh from the country, who had not yet
had opportunity to gratify his curiosity in regard to the wonders of the metropolis, was sure that our hero intended to
indulge himself with the spectacle of the feeding of the wild
beasts at Exeter Change, which is regularly exhibited every
night at nine o'clock. To the surprise of all, Lord Vapourcourt, after eating heartily of various dishes, drinking a
bottle of Bordeaux, and reading with uncommon care and
attention the fashionable news in the Courier, rang for his
hat and cloak, and left the house on foot and alone, for the
first time that he had done such a thing of an evening, since
he came to his title. The servants looked on for a time in
mute astonishment, and then, after agreeing that their lord
was a queer one, sagely added, that it was after all none of
their business whether he went out on foot, or in the carriage, and adjourned, by unanimous vote, to dinner.

Lord Vapourcourt, bent on his gloomy purpose, took his
way, upon leaving his house, towards Westminster Bridge.
The fog, which, as I remarked above, had been dissipated
for an hour or two during the warmest part of the day, had
collected again, and assumed a still greater degree of density than before. It was now of such a consistency that it
might almost, in the common phrase, have been cut with a
knife. Immense masses of a dank, unwholesome mixture of
coal-smoke, and heavy exhalations from the river, filled up
the streets, and made it impossible to discern objects at the
smallest distance, or to recognize the most familiar places.
The lamps were lighted, but produced little or no effect,
their rays being choked up within a foot or two of the flame;
and they presented the appearance of nebulous stars twink-
ling feebly through the mist, but affording no means of dis-
tinguishing the objects and persons below them. As it was
still early in the evening, the streets were full of carriages
and walkers, and the noise and tumult which naturally ensued, were truly terrible. With all the care and circum-
spection of the guides, who moved along as slowly as they
could, the wheels of the different vehicles were continually

interlocking with a tremendous crash, which was regularly
followed by an explosion of oaths and curses from the drivers, and agonizing shrieks of terror from the women and
children within, whose lives were endangered by the accident. The confused trampling of horses and creaking of carriages, were mingled with the hurried exclamations of the
unwary walkers who had come unluckily within the vortex of
the whirlpool. The side-walks presented a spectacle somewhat less dangerous, but still unpleasant and tiresome
enough in its way. Here elbows contended with elbows, and
canes and umbrellas essayed strength with each other.
Every now and then was heard the doleful groan of some unwary wight, who had dashed his nose against the projecting
casement of a window, or the stifled imprecation of some
unusually sensitive traveller, who regarded the violent contact of a foreign toe with the hinder part of his person as
wounding, not only his feelings, but in some degree his
honor. In the midst of this mingled uproar of human voices,
were heard the various cries of the different animals who
had in one shape or another, become entangled in the melée;
dogs barking and howling; cats mewing and spitting; horses
neighing; asses braying; cows lowing; monkeys mowing;
children bawling; nurses squalling. The whole scene, in
short, reminded one of Smithfield on a market-day, or the
door of Westminster Abbey at the Duke of York's funeral.

  Vapourcourt made his way slowly and painfully through
this scene of confusion. The annoying interruptions of every
kind, which continually checked his progress, would have
been sufficient of themselves to prevent him from thinking
too deeply on the plan he was about to execute, or from feeling any compunctious visitings of conscience in regard to its
consistency with policy or principle. The minor miseries
which he now encountered, were indeed substantially of the
same nature with those which originally determined him to
take the resolution, and tended strongly of course to confirm
it. As he went on, therefore, he became every moment
more and more satisfied, that a world of ennui within doors,
and fog without, was not fit for an honorable man to live in.
It was accordingly with a feeling of real relief, that he

finally reached the bridge, where he mounted at once upon
the parapet, and, without stopping for any further reflection,
prepared to take the decisive leap.

The fog that covered the bridge was so thick, that it was
impossible to distinguish objects at arm's length; but at this
critical moment a sudden gust of wind swept it off temporarily from the spot where our hero stood, and he perceived, at
a distance from him of less than three yards, another person evidently bent on the same object with himself. The
stranger had already given his body an impulse, which had
shifted the centre of gravity from within the base, and
thrown the line of direction into an angle of about forty-five
degrees with the horizon. The delay of another second, would
have made it perpendicular on the opposite side, and would
probably have been fatal. Vapourcourt, seeing the movement, started aside by a sudden impulse, and grasping the
other firmly by the upper part of the arm, drew him rapidly
backward. The body oscillated from side to side for an in-
stant, during which the final result was doubtful. The centre
of gravity then returned within the base, and the man resumed his upright position on the parapet.

Vapourcourt gazed, with a mixture of surprise and curiosity, upon an individual whose fortunes appeared to coincide
in so singular a manner with his own, but there was nothing
attractive or remarkable in his outward appearance. He was,
on the contrary, rather below the middle height, with an
awkward person and a coarse expression of countenance.
His cheeks were pale and wan, his eyes haggard, his fore-
head ploughed with furrows; and his black uncombed hair,
staring out loosely in all directions, gave him a wild and
ferocious aspect. His dress was of the meanest kind, and his
whole ensemble indicated extreme wretchedness. He made
no attempt to resist the salutary violence offered by Vapourcourt; but looked as if he felt that he had been detected in
doing what he knew to be wrong, and had nothing left but to
submit with dogged resignation to his destiny.

A spectator, who in passing accidentally had remarked
the different appearance of these two persons thus standing
together on the parapet, would have hardly imagined, that

they had mounted it for the same purpose. In the hurry and
excitement of the moment, the circumstance had also apparently escaped the attention of Vapourcourt, who, not recol-
lecting that it was hardly his cue to express much astonishment at the sort of proceeding which he had just been the
cause of preventing, addressed the other in the tone of re-
proof and surprise, that any indifferent person would have
naturally employed on the same occasion.

'What ails thee, man? Hast thou nine lives at thy disposal,
that thou dealest thus freely with the one now in thy possession?'

'I have found one,' replied the other, in a low and somewhat sullen voice, 'a burden too heavy to be borne, and
trust that I shall not be condemned, in this world at least, to
sustain the weight of any other.'

'What?' said Vapourcourt, to whose recollection this
reply brought back the thought of his own project, and of the
load of care and weariness that had led him to adopt it,
'what, my friend, have you too experienced, like me, the
intolerable weight of existence, the dreary vacuity of days,
and months, and years, following each other in the same
dull, uninterrupted round, without occupation, without interest, without amusement? Have you passed long and sleepless
nights in tossing and rolling from side to side, on a bed of
down? turned with loathing and satiety, from sumptuous
feasts, and delicious liquors? sunk with stupor at select
conversations, and gay assemblies? perished with fatigue
and ennui at enchanting operas, and interesting debates in
Parliament? If you have experienced this—and I cannot doubt
that you have, for what else but this could have brought a
man to such a pass as that from which I have too hastily
rescued you,—if you have in fact experienced all this, why
then, my friend, I can only say, that I do not blame your
resolution, and that to make amends for the questionable
piece of service that I have done you in keeping you out of
the river, I am now ready to push you into it, and by the
same impulse to follow you myself to the bottom.'

Occupation and excitement were things so unusual with
Vapourcourt, that they acted on his mind like a strong stim-

ulant, and the occurrences of the day had given to his language an energy, which he had hardly ever known before.
The above tirade was, however, in a great measure lost upon
the person to whom it was addressed, who understood but
partially the language and still more imperfectly the train of
thought conveyed by it.

'Alas, sir!' replied he, 'I know not what you mean, and
can hardly imagine how a life of leisure and continual enjoyment, can produce disgust. It has been my lot, sir, to work
constantly, ten or twelve hours every day, in order to gain
a living for myself and my family, and the greatest happiness I have ever known, was that of devoting occasionally a
leisure hour to recreation in their company. You talk of
turning with loathing from sumptuous dinners and tossing
restlessly on a down bed. I have never had the means of enjoying any luxuries of this description; but in better days,
when our table was regularly covered with a sufficiency of
plain and wholesome food, we always eat [sic] it with a good
appetite, and slept, without dreaming, on our comfortable
feather-beds, from night till morning.'

'What then brings thee here?' cried Vapourcourt, in a
rather discontented tone, and relapsing into his habitual
train of ideas, as he heard the other talk of thoughts and
feelings entirely foreign to his own experience. 'If thou art
well and happy at home, in the name of common sense, what
urges thee to throw thyself into the river?'

'Want and misery,' replied the other, bursting into an
agony of tears. 'My poor wife and children are at this moment suffering for a morsel of bread.'

'Bread!' exclaimed Vapourcourt, in a tone of surprise,
and wholly incapable of realizing the existence of actual distress—'want of bread! Why, man, thou must be a dolt indeed, to take on in this way, at so simple an accident. If
the baker did not leave bread enough this morning to last till
to-morrow, why not send to his shop, or make up the deficiency with pastry?'

'Nay, sir,' answered the man, 'do not mock at misfortunes which you never can have felt, and apparently can
hardly think of as possible. I have been, sir, an honest and

a hard-working man; and by keeping steadily to my business,
I continued, as I told you before, to support my family, and
all went well with me. But a few months ago I was seized
with a severe fit of illness, which prevented me from working, and brought my earnings to a stand. Housekeeping,
medicines, and rent, soon swept off our little hoard of previous savings, and we found ourselves reduced to very poor
and scanty fare. We submitted cheerfully to this, as a temporary evil, and as I was fast recovering my health, we all
hoped that I should soon be able to go to work again as usual.
In the mean time, however, the rent of my house, which is
hired by the week, must be regularly paid, for the landlord,
who is a severe man, will not hear of such a thing as giving
a day's credit. Last Saturday night I paid him nearly the
last shilling I had, and during this week, we have lived upon
almost nothing. This evening he called me as usual, and,
finding me unable to settle the account, he declared that if I
did not pay him in the morning, he would seize the furniture,
and turn us all into the street. Exhausted as I was with illness and want, these terrible menaces, which I had no
means of averting, for the moment unsettled my reason; a
temporary fit of madness came over me, and I rushed out of
the house, with the project of throwing myself into the river.
You, sir, have been the instrument of Providence in saving
me from this fatal catastrophe. The delirium has now passed
away, and I see the guilt that I was about to incur, by de-
priving my wife and children of their natural protector. I
shall return home with a feeling of gratitude to God, for his
goodness in rescuing me from the commission of so great a
crime. I shall apply to some charitable neighbor for a temporary relief. I am now nearly well, and shall soon be
strong enough to go to work again. The good Being, who has
thus interposed in our favor, will not desert us; and we
shall, I trust, after a while, be again easy and happy.'

'Nay, man,' said Lord Vapourcourt, whose heart was
naturally kind, and who had been a good deal touched by this
simple story of distress, 'if all thou wantest be some temporary relief, thou needest not to go far to find the charitable neighbor that shall afford it thee. If a little, or even a

good deal of money, will make thee happy, thou shalt not be
long miserable. I will take it on myself to assist thee, were
it only for the singularity of the case; for who ever heard
before, of a family suffering in the heart of London for want
of bread? A hundred pounds, more or less, will make but
little difference in the Vapourcourt property. My heirs will
not miss it. I may as well throw myself into the river two
or three hours hence as now, and if by means of this delay
I can make an industrious family happy for life, I assure
thee, my good friend, that I will submit to it with cheerfulness, and even pleasure, however eager I may be to escape
from this world of fog and ennui. So come along, my friend,
and let us settle this business without more ado.'

So saying, and without waiting to listen to the acknowledgments which his protégé would have poured out from the
fulness of his gratitude in a torrent of thanks and tears,
Vapourcourt leapt lightly from the parapet, where they had
both been standing during this conversation, to the floor of
the bridge, and, accompanied by his new companion, returned with a rapid pace toward his own mansion. The sudden gust of wind, which had been the means of discovering to
him the dangerous situation of the person whom he had thus
rescued from destruction, proved to be the first breathing of
a fresh breeze, which had now in a great measure swept off
the fog, and displayed the bridge, the river, and the streets,
silvered over with a fine yellow moonlight. Whether it was
that the change of weather relieved his spirits, or whether
he found himself agreeably excited by the work of benevo-
lence in which he was now engaged, it is certain that Vapourcourt for several preceding years had rarely felt his blood
circulate so freely, or, as Juliet says,

        His bosom's lord sit lightly on his throne,

as at this moment. He pursued his way through the still
crowded street, without experiencing any inconvenience or
uneasiness from the little accidents that fall to the lot of the
pedestrian traveller. He was conscious of a curiosity about
the condition of his new acquaintance, which he would not
have dreamed of in other circumstances, and which tales of

distress, much deeper than his, generally failed to move.
The man readily communicated the short history of his life,
in which there was nothing in the least remarkable. He was
a tailor, born, bred, and married, in the street in which he
now lived. He had never been out of London, and his longest
excursion was a walk to the Park. He had several children,
the oldest of whom he represented as a fine girl just turned
fifteen, and he dwelt with a parent's partiality on her goodness and beauty. After satisfying the curiosity of Vapourcourt, he inquired, in turn, with due respect, into his benefactor's circumstances, and on hearing his name, burst out
into new effusions of gratitude. The combination of goodness
with high rank, wealth or celebrity, though not unnatural,
nor even rare, is so delightful, that whenever it is perceived
it excites a sort of rapture, especially in the person who is
the object of it. The virtues of the great are like diamonds
polished and fitly set; the gem is substantially the same as
in its natural state, but the increase of lustre and effect is
incalculable.

Upon reaching the house of Vapourcourt, which the tailor
found to be at no great distance from his own, he requested
permission of his Lordship to return home at once, in order
to relieve the anxiety of his family, and to bring his children
with him to join him in offering thanks to their generous
benefactor. Vapourcourt, though not very agreeably struck
with the latter part of the proposal, was now in a humor to
consent to almost anything. He acceded at once to the request, and the tailor went his way, while his Lordship entered the house alone. The servants were rather surprised
to see him come back so early, before he could well have
accomplished either of the several objects, which, as they
respectively supposed, had drawn him out; but passive and
even silent obedience, was the rule of the house. Johnson
made no remark, as he attended his lord with a light to his
cabinet. The latter then took from a secretary, a pocket-
book containing a hundred pounds, which he intended to present to his protégé, and placing it on a table, awaited his
appearance. Though his frame of mind was unusually agreeable, he was nevertheless still bent on his original purpose,

and felt some impatience to be relieved from the engagement
which had thus obstructed its execution.

In about an hour, Johnson made his appearance at the
door of the cabinet, with a look of considerable dismay, to
announce that Mr. Stitchcloth and his children were below,
and desired to speak with his Lordship. A visit of this kind
was a thing so entirely at variance with the long established
usage of the house, that it appeared to Johnson like a sort of
wonder, and although he could not pretend to form any notion of its meaning, it struck him on the whole as an occurrence that boded no good. He confined himself, as was his
mood, to silent reflection, and on receiving the order to
admit the visitors, attended them to the door of his Lordship's cabinet with his ordinary courtesy. The principal
persons in the group were Stitchcloth and his daughter,
mentioned above, the other children being still too young to
attract notice, and their mother having been too much exhausted by her previous distress, and by the sudden shock of
the present happy change in the condition of the family, to
make her appearance. The tailor himself was greatly improved in his exterior since his late début on the bridge. He
had arranged his dress, and his countenance no longer wear-
ing the forlorn and haggard aspect of misery, had put on a
placid and agreeable expression, and the man altogether had
the air of a respectable mechanic, rather above the common
level. His daughter corresponded, with some little deduction
for parental partiality, to the description which he had given
of her. She was a fair and blooming maiden, with the freshness belonging to her age, and although there was nothing
decidedly distinguished either in her face or person, there
was a natural ease in her manner, and sweetness in her
countenance, which struck an observer agreeably, and which
were of course improved on this occasion, by the dominant
feeling of the moment. The whole party crowded eagerly
round their benefactor, and expressed their gratitude in the
various tones and phrases natural to their different periods
of life.

A scene of this kind was entirely new to our hero, and
produced an excitement in his mind which it might not have

done in one more accustomed to offices of kindness. The
heartfelt acknowledgments of the father, and the lively prat-
tling of the children, who partook the general satisfaction
without well knowing what it meant, affected him deeply; but
he was more particularly moved with the animated looks and
gentle tones in which the pretty daughter expressed her
gratitude. Vapourcourt, though for some time past estranged
from the world of fashion, had formerly frequented the most
brilliant of its circles; but whether from habitual apathy, or
some original peculiarity of character, he had not been attracted by any of the reigning coquettes. The natural grace
and beauty of this little damsel produced a stronger effect
upon his feelings than all the artificial airs of the belles, or
the sentimental phrases of the blues. It struck him, that a
kind and gentle companion like this, would enliven his existence, and contribute to his happiness; or rather, without
reasoning at all upon the subject, he felt himself, partly
perhaps in consequence of the extraordinary excitement of
the moment, irresistibly attracted by this seducing object.
Like most other persons of similar habits, Vapourcourt was
much under the influence of impulse, and no sooner had the
notion occurred to him, than, losing sight of the former
project of the morning, he proceeded at once to act upon this
new fancy.

'Stitchcloth,' said he to the father, taking him aside a few
steps, 'Stitchcloth, what say you to a Peer of the Realm for
a son-in-law?'

'Your Lordship is jesting,' replied the astonished tailor—
'I am sure you would not think of dishonoring a family,
which you have so nobly rescued from despair.'

'Jesting!' returned our hero, 'why, man, I was never so
serious in my life. Dishonor your daughter, Stitchcloth! you
mistake me quite. The worst fortune I wish her, is that of
seeing her the true and lawful Countess of Vapourcourt before to-morrow morning. Stitchcloth, I like your daughter;
I am pleased with her appearance and her manners. I find
in her a natural grace and sweetness, which I have looked
for in vain in the fashionable beauties of this metropolis.
I am wholly independent of the world, and have nothing to

consult but my own inclination in the management of my affairs. I have an unincumbered fortune of ten thousand pounds
a year; and if you and your daughter consent, I am ready to
place it this very evening at her disposal. Ay, Stitchcloth,
and I view it in point of fortune as no unequal match, for
your daughter, I see, is a good-humored girl; and a Scotchman, whose name I heard at Oxford, but have since forgotten, says, "that a naturally pleasant humor is equal to an
estate of ten thousand pounds a year." On that score we are,
therefore, precisely on a level.'

To this proposal, there was no objection to be made. The
tailor acquiesced with becoming expressions of thankfulness,
but having a spice of humor in his character, and feeling
himself now a little more at his ease with his future son-in-
law, he ventured to inquire, whether a matrimonial project
would not be in some degree inconsistent with the other resolution of the morning.

'Good God!' exclaimed Vapourcourt, 'I had entirely forgotten. Stitchcloth, no more of that, if you love me; above
all, not a word to the bride. Let us have as little as you
please of the adventure of the bridge, for the honor of us
both. The double suicide, Stitchcloth, would not tell very
well, either upon your shop-board or at my dinner-table.
But, Stitchcloth, instead of indulging in these reflections,
proceed rather, at once, and inform Mrs. Stitchcloth, that
her daughter is to be married this evening, while I despatch
Johnson to procure a license. I will entertain the charming
Elizabeth in your absence, and endeavor to obtain her consent to this sudden connection.'

The reader will easily imagine, that this, like all the
other preliminary points, was settled without much difficulty. The marriage was announced in the Morning Chronicle of
the Monday following, in these terms: —

'Married, at his residence in Pall-Mall, by special
license, on Saturday evening last, the Right Honorable the
Earl of Vapourcourt, to the amiable and accomplished
Miss Elizabeth Stitchcloth, eldest daughter of Solomon
Stitchcloth, Esq., the eminent habit-maker of Thread-

needle Street. This alliance between the great agricultural
and manufacturing interests of the country,—which political causes have for some years past tended to alienate
from each other,—has been long in contemplation, and, as
we fondly anticipate, will be attended with the happiest results. It has not only met the concurrence of the immediate friends of the parties, but has been cordially approved
in the Highest Quarter. His Lordship had been for some
weeks at his family residence in Cumberland, for the purpose of making suitable arrangements for the reception of
his lovely bride, and arrived in town on Friday evening
last, as was announced in our paper of the following day,
to celebrate the union. The happy pair set off yesterday
morning early, in his Lordship's travelling carriage and
four, for Vapourcourt Castle, where they intend to pass
the honey-moon.'

Note

The text is based on Critical and Miscellaneous Essays,
Second Series (Boston: James Monroe and Co., 1846), 452-
475. Subtitle in the source: "[The Token for 1831.]."

An Exhibition
of Pictures

The community are in our opinion deeply indebted to the
proprietors and trustees of the Athenaeum, and especially to
the public-spirited and intelligent gentlemen composing the
committee employed for this purpose, for their unwearied
and very successful exertions to organise an annual exhibition of paintings in this city. A spectacle of this kind, continued for a series of years, and afforded at a price, which
places it within the reach of almost every citizen,—while it
furnishes a cheap, rational and elegant entertainment,—
serves at the same time to refine and exalt the character of
the people. Painting—like eloquence, poetry, and the other
fine arts—is one of the developments and exhibitions of the
higher and better principles of our nature. The cultivation of
the art, and the habit of seeing and admiring its products,
tend in connexion with other causes to raise the mind above
the sordid interests of a merely material life. It has often
been said—and probably with truth—that the peculiar grace
and softness of manner, which distinguish the Parisians of
all classes, have been derived in part from the effect of a
frequent contemplation of the treasures of art contained in
the Gallery of the Louvre. The poet Goethe mentions as one
of the means which he employed for maintaining his taste and
talent in a progressive state, that he had crowded his study
with the finest specimens of sculpture and painting, which he
could procure. Nor is the advantage confined to an ameliora-
tion of the mere external forms of social life or a heightening

108

of the aptitude for excellence in other branches of art. The
taste for Beauty in art and nature is nearly allied to the love
of Good—so nearly indeed, that it has often been doubted
whether Beauty be any thing more than a visible manifesta-
tion of those amiable moral qualities of which the mere idea
fills the heart with delightful emotions, and confers a charm
on every person or thing with which they appear to be associated. However this may be, it is certain from experience,
that a familiar observation of the beautiful forms of nature
and the imitations or expressions of them in works of art,
has the effect of cherishing the benevolent affections, re-
pressing evil passions, and improving the general tone of
moral feeling. In a community like ours, where the disposition to active pursuits, and the selfish views and angry controversies that are naturally connected with them, is perhaps too strong—where the form of the government keeps up
an almost uninterrupted war of political parties—it is highly
important that every principle of a soothing and civilising
tendency should be brought as much as possible into vigorous
action. The cultivation of the arts, if not the most effectual
of these principles,—and we are not disposed to exaggerate
its influence,—nevertheless has its value. It comes in aid of
the great and essential elements of civilisation, which are
found in a judicious system of political and religious institutions, and gives the last polish to the character of men and
nations. Nor is it any objection to the encouragement and
cultivation of the arts, that they may be and have been made
subservient to the purposes of vice. If it were, we should be
obliged to abstain from the use and enjoyment of all the good
gifts of nature. It may also be remarked, that in a young and
progressive community like ours there is very little danger
of such a result. The abuse of art for the purpose of flattering licentious passions is always a symptom of its decline,
and indicates rather than produces a corrupt state of moral
feeling. While the condition of society is healthy, and the
arts are flourishing, the artist is in general found to be endowed with a pure and 'excellent spirit.' Art is then like
the Archangel in Milton's Poem—

Severe in youthful beauty.

She draws her inspirations from the high and holy sources
of religion, and dwells in preference on subjects connected
with serious contemplations. The artists of the age of Leo X.
rarely employed their pencils upon any other than scriptural
scenes; and this very circumstance is doubtless one among
the causes of their extraordinary success. They rejected
with unerring instinct, rather than on fixed principles or
from any calculation of probable effect, every low idea as
inconsistent with the train of their habitual studies, and such
must ever be the case with those who have actually attained
or are capable of rising to real excellence. We may add,
that experience fully confirms the opinion, that in this country there is very little danger of the abuse of art. In painting—and the same may be said of the sister arts of eloquence
and poetry—the prevailing style and the only one which
meets with any public favor is of the severest cast. This
circumstance, independently of its other beneficial effects,
may be looked upon as one of the most flattering prognostics
of the progress which the arts will probably make among us.
The only important exception to the uniformly pure and correct character of all the products of art in this country is
to be found in our theatrical entertainments, which have
hitherto been merely copies of the worst models that are
furnished by the corrupt societies of the old world. If the
managers of these entertainments would try the experiment
of making them—as they might be made—schools of good
feelings and principles, instead of nurseries of vice, they
would soon find in the increased patronage bestowed upon
them, the difference between obeying the just demands of the
public sentiment, and treating them—as they now do—with
continual and systematic outrage.

The exhibition of this year was not perhaps quite equal to
some of the preceding ones. It contained, however, a considerable number of first-rate works of the old masters,
several beautiful copies of originals in Europe, and a variety
of excellent native productions in the different walks of this

enchanting art. We propose to offer a few remarks upon some of the pieces which more particularly attracted our attention. It is impossible in a single article of this kind to exhaust the subject, and we shall not be understood to intimate that other pieces may not be equally or perhaps better entitled to notice. In making a selection, we must of course prefer those in which we felt the deepest interest, although this interest may have been in some cases the effect of accidental and local causes.

Among the works of the old masters exhibited on this occasion, the most remarkable was the <u>Martyrdom of St. Lawrence</u>, by Titian. This large picture, belonging to Mrs. Meade of Philadelphia, is an undoubted original, in the best manner of that great artist, and in a state of complete preservation. It exhibits in full perfection the beauty, mellowness, and perfect truth of coloring, which formed the characteristic excellences of Titian, and in which he has never been surpassed. In the moral expression of his personages—the highest effect of the art—his superiority in this, as in his other works, is less decided. It is even somewhat difficult to determine precisely what expression he intended to give to his principal figure. St. Lawrence—as our readers will of course recollect—suffered martyrdom in the not very poetical form of being broiled to death upon a large gridiron. In the picture of which we are speaking, the Saint is stretched at his length on this instrument of torture over a blazing fire, which two or three executioners are engaged in stirring and feeding with fuel. In the legend the gridiron is said to have been heated red hot before he was placed upon it. In the painting, there is, however, no effect of fire observable, either on the person or drapery of the martyr, and his face is turned upward with a perfectly serene and tranquil expression. It was probably the design of the artist to intimate by this expression, the triumph of religious faith and hope over bodily anguish; but it is hard to conceive that the effect should extend so far as to guarantee the limbs and even the drapery from the action of fire. It would be therefore more natural to imagine that Titian meant to indicate a supernatural interposition in favor of the Saint, like that which is represented as having taken place at the martyrdom of St. Polycarp, when the flames that were kindled at the foot of the stake to which he was attached, retired as they rose from the person of the holy man, and formed a sort of hollow sphere around him, refusing even to singe a hair of his head. But it is hardly probable that Titian would have varied from the legend, which states that St. Lawrence actually suffered death in this form; and we may therefore conjecture that he probably sacrificed the truth of his painting, in order to avoid the exhibition of the disgusting image of mere physical suffering. In other respects, the image of nature is admirably preserved. The ferocious countenances of the executioners contrast finely with the sweet expression of the suffering Saint. The figures are well drawn and grouped, and the painting wears in every part the appearance of a carefully wrought and highly finished production.

This fine picture was purchased in Spain by Mr. Meade, formerly our Consul at Cadiz, and was no doubt painted at Madrid, where Titian resided for several years. Although the subject is in some respects not a very seducing one, he appears to have painted it a number of times. We have had the pleasure of seeing another picture of his on the same subject, though varying a little from this in the details, in the Chapter-House of the Convent of the Escurial, and we are informed that there are two or three more in existence. The first was probably executed for the purpose of being placed in the Escurial, the subject having been selected with a view to this destination. This convent, as our readers are probably aware, was erected in honor of St. Lawrence.—Its proper style and title is the Convent of the Royal St. Lawrence—San Lorenzo el Real—the name Escurial or Escorial, as it is written in Spain, being that of a neighboring village, and, as is generally supposed, a corruption or modification of the word scoriae, which expresses the cinders and rubbish proceeding from a mine that was formerly wrought on this spot. It is well known that Philip II. before going into the battle of St. Quentin—which was fought on St. Lawrence's day—made a vow that if he gained the victory, he would erect a convent in honor of the Saint, and in the shape of the instrument on which he suffered martyrdom. Having in fact won the day, the King, or rather the ingenious and justly celebrated architect Herrera, whom he employed, not only executed this vow to the letter, but contrived at the same time to produce a building, which is justly considered as one of the finest specimens of modern architecture. It would be hard to imagine beforehand how so handsome an edifice could possibly be built upon a model apparently so ill adapted to the purpose; but the architect by a happy exertion of ingenuity, similar to that by which Columbus succeeded in setting his egg upright upon its smaller end, removed at once the principal difficulty, by turning the gridiron upon its back with its legs upwards. The achievement was now comparatively easy, and the building to be erected susceptible of a high degree of architectural beauty. It is constructed of a handsome reddish freestone, in the form of a hollow square, the four sides of which are connected together by several lines of buildings crossing each other at right angles, and enclosing a number of small courts. The four sides represent the frame, and the interior buildings the bars of the machine, while at the points where they intersect each other, and at the four corners of the main edifice are placed towers, which represent the legs. From the side opposite the main entrance projects a wing, which forms the handle. This wing with a part of the side of the main edifice adjoining it, is occupied by the Court when they take up their residence at the Escurial. The remainder of the building consists of the large and truly magnificent church, two libraries, and the public and private apartments appropriated to the use of the monks who inhabit the convent. One of the libraries contains the collection of Arabic Manuscripts, which is considered the richest in Europe. We found on inquiry, that there is at present no person in the convent who reads that language. The exterior of the building is decorated with great taste, and the general appearance is simple, imposing, and on the whole highly satisfactory. It stands on the declivity of a mountain; and at a considerable height above is a stone seat—called Philip's Seat—where the interior courts are distinctly seen, and the gridiron principle of the plan becomes apparent in all its beauty. On this seat the gloomy despot who ordered the construction of the building was accustomed to repose in his solitary walks, and contemplate, no doubt with great satisfaction, the complete success with which he had executed his pious and somewhat singular design. The interior of the convent is adorned throughout with the choicest productions of the pencils of the first artists. The principal stair-case was decorated by Jordaens, and is considered his finest work. The cloisters were painted in fresco by a celebrated Spanish artist, called from his having been dumb, El Mudo. The public apartments are hung with the masterpieces of Raphael, Titian, Rubens, Murillo, Velasquez, and the other principal painters of the Spanish and Italian schools. In the sacristy is to be seen among other beautiful pieces a celebrated Holy Family, by Raphael, which on account of its singular perfection, is commonly called the Pearl, and which was purchased for the King of Spain by his Ambassador at London at the sale of the paintings of Charles I. In the Chapter-House is the Madonna de la Pez, or Virgin with the Fish, by the same great artist, which is reckoned in like manner one of his capital pieces. The subject is singular, and if taken literally involves a good deal of anachronism. The young Tobias of the Apocrypha, holding a fish in his hand by a line, is presented to the Virgin. She is seated as usual with the infant Jesus in her arms, who is eagerly extending one of his hands to grasp the fish, and with the other is playing with the leaves of an open bible, which St. Jerome is perusing on the left. The painting is commonly supposed to be an allegorical representation of the admission of the Apocryphal books into the Canon of Scripture by the Council of Trent. This piece, with the Pearl —the Pasmo di Sicilia, now in the museum at Madrid, by the same artist, which was painted as a companion-piece to the Transfiguration, and is considered next to that as his best production—and a number of other pictures, was transported to Paris during the period of the French ascendency in Spain, and exhibited for several years in the Gallery of the Louvre. They returned after the abdication of Bonaparte, varnished and restored in a way, which has not been thought by competent judges to increase their value. In the same apartment with the <u>Madonna de la Pez</u> is the <u>Martyrdom of St. Lawrence</u>, by Titian, which has led us into this little digression. It is not in so fine a state of preservation as the one which was exhibited at the Athenaeum, having suffered a good deal of late, in common with many of the older pictures in the Escurial, from want of attention. It still, however, produces great effect.

Among the other paintings of Titian preserved at the Escurial, is a remarkable piece commonly called <u>Titian's Glory</u>, which did not obtain the dangerous honor of a transportation to Paris, and consequently exhibits at present the real touches of the masterly author in a state of greater purity than it would have done if it had undergone a reparation by a modern French painter. The hint of this superb picture seems to have been borrowed from the <u>Transfiguration</u> of Raphael, and the general aspect of it is somewhat similar although its subject is wholly different. The painting exhibits the various orders of the heavenly host in the act of adoring the Supreme Being. The three persons of the Holy Trinity, drawn with their usual attributes, dressed in sky-blue drapery and surrounded by a <u>Glory</u>, which gives its name to the painting, occupy the upper part of the canvass. They are nearly in the attitudes of the three principal figures in the <u>Transfiguration</u>. Below are the saints and angels—'Dominations, Princedoms, Virtues, Powers'—gazing upwards with adoring looks at the object of their worship. The subject of this picture is conceived in a loftier tone of thought and feeling than that of any other piece of Titian's, which we have seen, and the execution does it perfect justice. The work, however, does not seem to have been fully appreciated by its present possessors. It now hangs without a frame in a small room, which serves as a sort of passage from one part of the convent to another, but which contains, it is true, some other very fine pieces. It was probably owing to its being kept in this comparatively obscure place that it was not carried to Paris. In the same room is an exquisite <u>St. Catherine</u> by the same artist—a single figure in a green drapery, discovering one leg and foot, which have often been cited as

models of perfection for this part of the female form. There
is a repetition of this charming piece in the museum at Madrid, where there are also a number of other fruits of the
labor of the same indefatigable and prolific genius while in
Spain. We may mention particularly the portrait of Charles
V. on horseback, the Danaë, the Ariadne and the two full
length portraits of the Princess of Eboli, sometimes called
the Venuses, from their being entirely without drapery.
This celebrated favorite of Philip II. figures to more advantage under the pencil of Titian than she does under the pen of
Schiller, who has introduced her as one of the characters in
his tragedy of Don Carlos. It is rather a singular circumstance, that with no recommendation but mere beauty she
should have had the fortune to be handed down to immortality
by the separate labors of these two masters in their respective arts. In all these pieces the art of coloring—especially
in its application to the human body—is carried to the highest perfection which it has ever attained or is probably capable of attaining. We well remember the air of satisfaction
with which the distinguished Scotch artist Wilkie, with whom
we had the pleasure of going through the museum at Madrid,
pointed to the figure of Ariadne, and pronounced it a piece
of real flesh and blood. For this reason the works of Titian
are excellent studies, more especially at a time when the
example of the modern French school has a tendency to
diffuse a false taste in this branch of the art. We are highly
gratified that so fine a work of this great colorist as the one
we have been considering should have been obtained for the
Exhibition, and only regret that the funds of the Athenaeum
were not in such a state as to allow of its purchase. It is
true, that the subject is not so attractive as might be wished;
but it is rare that a first-rate painting by this great master
is for sale even in Europe, and a century may probably
elapse before another opportunity will occur for procuring
one in this country.

Having had occasion to advert to the collections of paintings that are found in Spain, we proceed in this connexion to
mention, as one of the principal ornaments of the Exhibition
at the Athenaeum Gallery, the fine picture, by Murillo, of

the Meeting of Rebecca and Abraham's Servant. This we are
happy to say belongs to the institution, and has of course
appeared at the preceding exhibitions, but is well worthy of
continued notice and attention. It is not indeed by any means
so good a specimen of the manner of Murillo as the Martyrdom of St. Lawrence is of that of Titian; and it also appears
to have suffered some injury, but it is nevertheless an undoubted original, and has much of the sweetness, grace and
truth to nature that characterise the best of the author's
works. Under the head of this picture we find in the Catalogue the following remarks.

'Bartolomeo Esteban Murillo was born in 1613, and died
in 1685. He showed a very early inclination for painting,
and received instruction from his uncle, Juan del Castello,
and afterwards from Velasquez. He was employed by the
King of Spain to paint several historical pictures, but his
favorite subjects were beggar boys in various exercises
and amusements. His coloring is mellow, his tints clear
and skilfully opposed by proper shadows. His pictures
are in great esteem throughout Europe, but few of them
have reached this country. This picture has been much
injured. Its great merit is, however, apparent, and has
been appreciated by the community.'

This brief notice, though in the main correct, and perhaps
as complete as it could be made consistently with the limits
of a Catalogue, hardly does justice to the extraordinary
merit of the great artist in question. Although his works
are, as is remarked in the Catalogue, in great esteem
throughout Europe, they are nevertheless not so generally
known and valued even there as they would be were they
more favorably situated for the observation of artists and
travellers of taste. They were all painted in Spain. Very few
of them have found their way into the other parts of Europe;
and as Spain has been for a century past entirely out of the
regular line of travel, whether for business or pleasure, the
treasures of art, which are contained in the Spanish collections, have been sequestered, as it were, from public view.
Hence the names of Murillo, and his master Velasquez, are

much less familiar to the European public than those of
many Italian and Flemish artists of inferior merit. Several
fine works were, however, carried to Paris by the effect of
the late political movements, and the engravings that have
recently been published at Madrid of the paintings in the
museum have made them better known abroad than they were
formerly. We were informed by Wilkie that the Spanish
painters Murillo and Velasquez were very inadequately appreciated in England, and that he had himself no idea of the
extent and value of their productions until he met at Rome
with the collections of engravings to which we have just
alluded, and which afforded him so much satisfaction that he
immediately determined on a visit to Spain for the express
purpose of seeing the originals. The high expectations he
had formed of them were entirely equalled, if not surpassed,
and his correspondence on the subject with the late President
of the Academy will have contributed much to rectify the
opinions of the British artists on this subject, and to give a
new idea of the merit and richness of the Spanish school.

From the tenor of the above extract it would be natural to
conclude that low life was the favorite walk of Murillo, that
he had deviated into the historical department in compliance
with the wishes of the king, but that his success in this
branch had been less remarkable than in the other. This idea
of the nature of his talent is, however, incorrect. Like all
the artists of his time, he painted principally for churches
and convents, and of course on scriptural subjects, from
which every allusion to low life is necessarily excluded. His
acknowledged master-piece is a large picture in one of the
convents at Seville, on the subject of Moses striking the
Rock. This grand work has been thought by many competent
judges to bear away the palm from the Transfiguration, and
is admitted by all to be one of the noblest efforts of genius
in existence. His taste was, however, undoubtedly for grace
and sweetness rather than sublimity, and he accordingly
excelled in his Holy Families—a favorite subject with him,
as with all the painters of the day. There is one in particular
in the museum at Madrid of pre-eminent beauty, in which
the Virgin is represented as in a sort of extacy, with one

foot resting on the crescent moon,

> 'With eyes upraised, as one inspired,'

robed in a flowing blue and white drapery and surrounded by a glory that fills the back ground of the picture. For truth of drawing, spirit and felicity of composition, and a peculiar brilliancy and charm of coloring, the manner of Murillo in this and his other best pieces could not well be surpassed. His figures have been thought to want in some degree the high intellectual expression that distinguishes those of the great masters of the Italian school, and which is no doubt the loftiest attainment to which genius in the art can aspire. Had he combined this with his other excellences he would probably have excelled most other modern painters. The faces of his Virgins are said to have been copied from that of his daughter. They have a charming simplicity and sweetness of expression, inclining, however, to childish weakness rather than to the poetical elevation, which must naturally be supposed to form the other ingredient in the character. Murillo was uncommonly happy in his delineations of boys, but they were by no means always placed, as might perhaps be imagined from the above extract, in situations connected with common life. His two separate pictures of the <u>Infant Saviour</u> and the <u>Infant Baptist</u>, in the museum at Madrid, are among the most exquisite productions of his pencil, and surpass perhaps any other work on a similar subject, unless we except the <u>Young Samuel</u> of Sir Joshua Reynolds, which seems to realise the idea of absolute perfection. But though the talent of Murillo was not confined to the delineation of common life, it is nevertheless true that he greatly excelled in this as well as in the higher walks of his art. <u>The Pet Kitten</u> of the Exhibition is a specimen of his manner in this line, but, if an original, is not one of his best pieces. In a large picture, in the Academy of the Fine Arts at Madrid, representing the exercise by Isabella, Queen of Castile, of the faculty formerly supposed to be inherent in all royal personages, of curing by the touch certain cutaneous diseases, the artist has combined, injudiciously perhaps, the expressions peculiar respectively to high and vulgar life.

The Queen, surrounded by her court, and with the air of
dignified solemnity and deep interest, which would naturally
accompany the use of her miraculous gift, is washing the
head of one little urchin, while another, who stands by the
side of the basin waiting for his turn, affords himself a
temporary relief by scratching with both hands, and displays
an irresistibly comic expression of countenance. This piece,
though, as we have intimated above, defective in its plan, is
in point of execution one of the most successful and perfect
of Murillo's works.

  It is remarked in the Catalogue that but few of the works
of this artist have reached our country. There are some in
the collection of the Academy of the Arts at New York; but
the best on this side of the Atlantic is probably the Roman
Charity, in the collection of the Academy of the Arts at
Philadelphia. This was purchased by the Academy of our
countryman Mr. Rich, formerly our Consul at Valencia.
While in his possession it had suffered some alteration from
the effects of the rather exaggerated delicacy of a contemporary Spanish artist of considerable merit, named Lopez,
now chief painter to the King of Spain. In the picture, as it
came from the hands of the artist, and into those of Mr.
Rich, the neck and breast of the female figure, who, agreeably to the well-known anecdote, is represented nursing her
father in prison, were discovered. There seems to be little
in such an exhibition at which the purest mind need to be
alarmed. The scrupulous Spaniard, however, took it amiss,
and resorted to a very summary process for abating the
nuisance. He had prevailed on Mr. Rich to lend him the
picture for the purpose of studying it at home, and while he
had it in his possession, without consulting the owner, very
kindly supplied the fair Roman with a handkerchief from his
own pallet. In plain English, he coolly set himself to work
and painted over the bust of the female figure with a sort of
shawl or mantle, apparently without reflecting whether
something were not due to his neighbor's right of property
as well as to what he doubtless considered a just delicacy.
We have not had much opportunity to examine this picture in
detail, but have been informed by Mr. Rich that it is in the

best manner of the artist. Its actual value is perhaps a little diminished by the injudicious <u>reform</u> to which we have alluded; but it will probably attract hereafter more rather than less attention from having been the subject of so curious an anecdote.

Velasquez, the master of Murillo, is less known beyond the limits of his own country, than his great pupil, but is generally regarded by the Spaniards, and by such other persons as have had the opportunity to appreciate his merit, as being, in some respects at least, the superior artist. For truth to nature in drawing and coloring, his works may be considered as approaching the point of actual perfection, and they would form the best possible study for such proficients in the art as were in danger of being seduced by the false brilliancy of the modern French school. We must confess, however, that in our judgment Velasquez errs a little on the other side, and that his coloring, though admirably fresh, distinct, and true, is rather cold. In the Catalogue of the Paintings in the museum at Madrid the manner of this great artist is described in the following terms.

'Velasquez possessed a genius for painting of the very first order. He united a brilliant imagination and a singularly correct judgment with great industry. The beauty and felicity of his drawing are admirable; and his coloring, while it is perfectly true to nature, has a peculiarly seductive grace. What harmony and correctness in his landscapes! The illusion is there so perfect that we can hardly realise, at a little distance, that we are viewing a picture and not the thing itself. No artist ever understood better the effect of light and that aerial perspective which regulates the size and hue of objects according to their distance. In short, he had improved his strong natural talent for the art by the most careful and judicious course of study and practised it with complete success in all its parts. It may be said with safety, that there was more truth in his coloring and more firmness in his drawing than in those of even Titian. The means employed are seen more distinctly on a near examination without the least diminution of the general effect at the proper distance.'

The museum at Madrid is rich in the works of this great
artist, which consist principally of historical pieces and
portraits. Among the latter may be noticed particularly
those of Philip IV. and his Queen Doña Mariana of Austria,
under whom he flourished, and those of their son the Infante
Don Baltazar Carlos, and of the celebrated Count-Duke
Olivares—the two last on horseback. A portrait of one of the
Princesses of the royal family, daughter of Philip IV., is
even more remarkable, and is thus described in the Catalogue.

'This is a portrait of the Infanta Doña Margarita Maria of
Austria, daughter of Philip IV., receiving a glass of water
from one of her ladies. In the list of the spectators is the
artist himself with his pallet in his hand taking the portrait
of the Princess, and on the right are the two dwarfs Nicolas
Pertusano and Maria Barbola, who are endeavoring to
amuse her and are playing with a favorite dog. This picture
is admirable for the correct drawing and ingenious composition, but especially for the wonderful effect of light. The
apartment seems to be filled with a kind of vapor, which
surrounds and removes all the objects that require to be
represented as more distant. It is a singular proof of the
talent of Velasquez, that he succeeded in placing in the middle of the piece an open door, admitting a light so strong
that it brightens the door, the staircase behind it, and the
person who is going out,—the whole executed with perfect
truth and yet without injuring the general effect. This picture is a sort of miracle in the way of perspective, both
aerial and linear. It was called by Giordano the Painter's
Bible, (La Teologia de la Pintura.)'

Among the history pieces of Velasquez in the same collection may be mentioned the Surrender of Breda to the Mar-
quesses of Spinola and Leganes in presence of the armies of
Spain and the Netherlands. 'This,' says the Catalogue, 'is
one of the capital pieces of this artist. The plan is well
conceived, the composition skilful, the drawing correct, the
expression spirited and noble, the coloring rich and true,
and at the same time so bold, that we may safely say that
Velasquez alone could have ventured, as is done here, to

introduce a mass of strong light between the Spanish army
and the escort of the Flemish general. We admire the art
with which he groups together the figures thus separated by
the friendly attitude of the Spanish General throwing his arm
over the shoulder of the Governor of the fort. The horse of
Spinola is painted with extraordinary truth. In the back
ground is a vast plain extending to the horizon. It is a low,
moist country, corresponding with the real character of the
scene of the action, and covered with burning castles and
villages, which show too well the fatal consequences of war.'

A fancy-piece by the same artist, representing the interi-
or of a carpet-manufactory, and commonly called The Spin-
ners, (Las Hilanderas,) is considered one of his happiest
efforts, and is thus described.

'In the back ground are some ladies looking at carpets.
On the front of the picture is a woman spinning and talking
with another, who is drawing a scarlet curtain. At a little
distance is a girl carding wool. On the right of the spectators is a young woman winding yarn, whose features are not
visible, although we may be sure that they are handsome
from the beauty of her shoulder, and another, who has in
her hand a sort of basket. This picture,' says the commen-
tator, 'was painted off-hand, with a bold, free, and playful
pencil. The skill with which the artist has harmonised the
different lights, which he has introduced into it, is truly
marvellous.'

We have been led to make these brief remarks on the
general manner of Murillo and Velasquez for the purpose of
turning the attention of the public to the merit of two great
artists, who are not sufficiently known beyond the limits of
their native land, and in the hope that opportunities may
occur for acquiring a greater number of their works in this
country. We must now proceed, a little more rapidly than
we have thus far done, in our survey of the paintings exhibited at the Athenaeum Gallery.

Of the other original pieces of the old masters, may be
mentioned particularly The Laughing Boy, by Gerardo delle
Notti, which, as a mere specimen of effect in the disposition of light and shade, was undoubtedly by far the most

powerful picture in the Exhibition. The artist, whose real
name was Gerard Honthorst, obtained the one above quoted,
by which he is usually known and which means literally
Gerard of the Nights, or, according to the English idiom,
Gerard Night-Piece, from his extraordinary talent for producing the effect of lamp-light. The two large paintings,
representing respectively the fish of the Bay of Tarentum
and of the Bay of Naples, from the collection of Joseph Bonaparte, though the subjects are not attractive, nevertheless
afforded great pleasure from the spirit and truth to nature,
which distinguish the execution. The Jacob wrestling with the
Angel, by Domenichino, belonging to Mrs. Meade, is a
valuable production of one of the most distinguished Italian
masters. Domenichino, or little Dominic, as he has been
affectionately denominated by the dilettanti of his country,
was less prolific than some of his great predecessors and
contemporaries. The extreme correctness and high finish of
his pictures account in part for the comparative slowness
with which he appears to have wrought. A Seaport, by
Claude Lorraine, a View of the Lake of Thrasymene, by
Vernet, and several landscapes with figures, by Salvator
Rosa, furnished interesting specimens of the manner of
their respective authors. The Vernet, in particular, was a
very beautiful landscape. We may also mention as among
the most remarkable old pictures, the Joseph and his Brethren, by an unknown master, the St. Francis, by Tintoretto,
and the St. Anthony, by Luca Giordano, all large pieces,
from the collection of Mrs. Meade; the Lady drinking, by
Terbourg; the Dying Seneca, by Vandyck; the Views of
Venice, by Canaletti, and the head of a Madonna, by Sasso-
Ferrato. These, with a number of others, to which we cannot now advert, are well entitled to a more detailed notice;
but the space we have already occupied reminds us that we
must leave this branch of the subject and proceed to make
some remarks on a few very highly finished copies of originals in Europe, which formed a part of the Exhibition.

    The most interesting of these was a copy of the celebrated
Descent from the Cross of Rubens, by F. de Brackelaer, a
Flemish artist of great merit. It has recently been imported

from Europe by Colonel Perkins, the distinguished President of the Athenaeum, whose continued exertions and liberal contributions for the promotion of learning and the arts have justly entitled him to the gratitude of the community. The work was executed under very favorable circumstances, the original having been placed in the hands of the artist, on its return from Paris, for the purpose of being prepared for its new position in the Cathedral at Antwerp. The size of the copy is greatly reduced from that of the original, but it gives in other respects a most exact and faithful representation of it, and is itself a very superior picture. It includes the two companion-pieces, which were placed on the right and left of the Descent from the Cross, when it occupied its original place as the altar-piece of the Cathedral, and which represent respectively the Salutation of Mary and Elizabeth and Simeon bearing Christ in his arms.

The Descent from the Cross of Rubens is, as is well known to every lover of the art, the master-piece and pride of the Flemish school, as the Transfiguration of Raphael is of the Italian, and the Moses striking the Rock, by Murillo, of the Spanish. In this noble production the characteristic beauties of the great author, and of the school which he adorned, are exhibited in their highest perfection, and with the least mixture of the defects by which they were accompanied. The richness and beauty of the coloring, the skill displayed in the grouping of the figures, and the truth, with which they exhibit the passions and affections belonging to their respective characters, are really admirable, and we scarcely notice in the midst of so many excellences the slight defects in taste—vestigia ruris—that linger even here round the pencil of the illustrious Fleming and depress his work a little below the complete perfection of the unrivalled Italians. It is remarkable that Sir Joshua Reynolds, who appears from his Lectures to have been hardly satisfied, at least on a first inspection, with the manner of Raphael, bestows the most unqualified commendation on this production of Rubens.

'The Christ'—he remarks, as quoted in the Catalogue—'is one of the finest figures that were ever invented. It is

most correctly drawn, and in an attitude of the utmost difficulty to execute. The hanging of the head on the shoulder,
and the falling of the body on one side give such an appearance of the heaviness of death, that nothing can exceed it.'

On the companion-piece representing Simeon bearing
Christ in his Arms, Sir Joshua remarks that it is 'admirable indeed; the head of the priest more especially, which
nothing can exceed; the expression, drawing, coloring, are
beyond all description, and as fresh as if the piece were
just painted.'

This superb picture was transferred to Paris by the
French when they took possession of the Netherlands, and
remained for several years in the Gallery of the Louvre,
where we had the pleasure of seeing it in 1812. It appeared
to advantage in immediate comparison with the finest works
of the greatest painters of all countries, among which it was
then placed, and was regarded by all as one of the two or
three first, by some as the very first piece in the collection.
It approaches in fact more nearly to perfection in its way,
than perhaps any other picture that could be named, and if it
be inferior to some, it is only because the artist habitually
exhibits in his most successful efforts somewhat less purity
of taste and intellectual, or, as it is often called, ideal
expression, than would be required for the attainment of the
highest degree of excellence. In many of his pieces his
deficiency in these respects is very remarkable, and forms
a singular contrast with his extraordinary success in others.
It is particularly conspicuous in his female figures, which
were evidently copied directly from nature in a climate
where the sex is distinguished for freshness and beauty of
complexion, rather than delicate proportions or graceful
symmetry of form. It is wonderful that Rubens who travelled
much, and visited all parts of Europe, did not learn from
his acquaintance with the fair of other regions, to correct
his original notions of female beauty. His imagination appears to have dwelled with unabated fondness to the last upon
the solid charms of his countrywomen which were probably
endeared to him by the recollections of his youthful loves.
His Three Graces in the museum at Madrid exhibit under a

transparent delicacy of complexion, a largeness of bone and
firmness of muscle, that would do honor to the champion of
England. They form a strange contrast with the slender and
symmetrical brunettes of Titian, that figure in their neighborhood. Complete perfection is, however, not to be expected in any human production; and notwithstanding some very
obvious faults, the works of Rubens will always be viewed
as among the master-pieces of the art. For brilliancy and
richness of coloring and fertility of invention, they perhaps
excel all others, and if they want the ideal expression of the
Italians, they are animated by an admirable spirit and vivacity, which are the best substitutes that could be found for
that still superior quality. As a series of paintings on the
same subject we are acquainted with none in the whole compass of the art to be compared with the twelve on the Marriage of Catherine de Medicis, that are now exhibited in the
Gallery of the Louvre. These splendid pieces compose a sort
of grand epic poem, not inferior in fire, nature, variety of
character, wide range of supernatural machinery, and harmonious disposition of the various parts of a great and
crowded action, to the immortal master-piece of heroic
song. If one of the works of Velasquez alluded to above has
been called the Painter's Bible, this series might be described with equal justice as an Iliad on Canvass; and the
analogy is not the less striking because the artist conceived
and executed his plan without the slightest reminiscence of
Homer, nor because the action represented is in every particular wholly different from the celebrated wars of Troy.
In works of art direct imitation never produces a real resemblance. This can only take place when minds of equal
power and kindred genius, working perhaps, as in this case,
in different lines, but under the influence of the same inspiration, and with the materials supplied by the same common
nature, bring out under great varieties of form, works that
are distinguished by the same general characteristics and
produce the same effects on the imagination and the heart.
There is no resemblance—for example—between the charming Allegro and Penseroso of Milton, and the Pacifico and
Bellicoso of Mason, or twenty other parallels in the same

form, that have been written in imitation of them; but we can easily find one in the delightful painting where the Muses of Tragedy and Comedy—each with her appropriate expression and costume—are struggling for the exclusive possession of their common favorite Garrick, although the idea of Milton and his poem probably never once occurred to the mind of Sir Joshua Reynolds while he was planning and executing the work.

The superiority of the works of Rubens is not more extraordinary than the facility with which he appears to have produced them. The collections of Europe are crowded with his paintings, frequently of large size, and when we consider the length of time which is employed by many artists of great merit upon a single piece, we are disposed to wonder that he was able to execute so much. It is not impossible that in the latter part of his life he availed himself to a considerable extent of the labor of assistants and pupils; but it is well known that he wrought with great facility and threw off many of his admirable works at a single heat. The same was the case with some of the other great masters who lived in the best days of the art, and it seems to be chiefly at a later and less brilliant period that we find their successors adopting a different method, and substituting the slow results of patient and reiterated toil for the first glowing effusions of genius. There is no doubt an aptitude in different minds to proceed by different methods, and a man of merit can commonly work better in the way to which he feels himself naturally disposed than in any other; but it may be doubted whether much is gained in painting, poetry, or any other art, by the long delay and repeated revision by which some persons are accustomed to ripen their productions. An artist who has cultivated his taste by the usual methods, and reached the maturity of his judgment, has acquired all the talent he will ever possess, and the more freely and fearlessly he exercises it, the better in general will be the product. We mean not of course to recommend an inconsiderate precipitancy or to exclude the process of revision and correction within its proper limits; we only mean to say that a work which a man of genius, whether poet, painter, or orator, throws off in a happy moment, and at the height of his talent, is substantially as good when it first comes from his mind, as the nature of his subject, and the extent of his powers will allow him to make it. By reviewing it in a cooler moment, he may remove blemishes—improve the disposition of details—introduce additions of minor importance, and thus give the whole a finished air, which will considerably augment the general effect—but he cannot possibly by any revision or correction change the substance of it for the better. To change the substance of a work is, in other words, to produce a new one on the same subject, and this new one must, in general, in the case supposed, be inferior to the former, because it is produced under circumstances much less favorable to excellence. The want of facility which is experienced by some artists might, we fear, in many cases be more correctly described as a want of the moral courage and generous self-confidence, which are as necessary to success in art as in every other department of action. When we find a poet who was capable at twenty years of age of writing the Pleasures of Hope—the most elegant of all juvenile productions—bringing out nothing else in the course of a long life devoted to poetry, but a few short fragments, we see at once, that for fear of hazarding the reputation he had acquired, he has not exhibited the maturity of his talent, and that his works give us no indication of what he might have done if he had not been prevented by indolence or constitutional timidity from doing his best. Campbell at twenty was a much better poet than Scott at thirty—but the latter by manfully doing as well as he could without fear of criticism, gradually improved his powers by exercise, and in the end has completely overshadowed the other, though possessing a talent originally much superior to his own. The moral is the same with the common proverb—that faint heart never won fair lady—and that a man will never get the credit of doing what he has too little confidence in himself to undertake. Trust yourself, says Goethe, and others will trust you.

Wenn du deiner selbst vertrau'st
Vertrauen dir die andere Seele.[1]

Our readers will perhaps think that there is little danger of
an error on the score of excessive diffidence in a community
where most of the citizens are ready enough to push their
pretensions of all kinds, as far as they ought in reason to be
carried, but we have in our view some cases connected with
the subject of this article, in which the hints we have given
might, we think, be turned to account. It is time, however,
to resume our survey of the Gallery.

The copies, by Meyer of a large and beautiful landscape by
Ruisdael with figures by Berghem, and by our countryman
Fisher of the portraits of Rembrandt and Vandyck by themselves now in the Gallery of the Louvre, were highly interesting, but we have only room to notice that of the Shepherd-
ess Madonna of Raphael, by Subba. This picture represents
the Virgin at full length, in a standing position with a crook
in her hand; the two infants Jesus and John Baptist standing
beside her with their faces turned upwards to hers; the
scene an open country, with hills and woods in the back
ground. The artist appears to have repeated this subject
several times. We have ourselves seen two originals at
Paris, and it is stated in the Catalogue that there is one at
Naples. Of the two which we have seen, one is in the Gallery
of the Louvre, and the other in the possession of our coun-
trÿman, Samuel Williams, Esq. formerly our Consul at
London, and now temporarily resident in Paris. The latter
has been supposed by some of the British connoisseurs to be
a copy by another artist, and for that reason commanded a
comparatively low price at a public sale a few years ago.
Its genuineness is, however, perfectly apparent on its face
to all who are acquainted with the style of the great author,
and its history is so well known that there can be no reasonable doubt upon the subject. It is traced back with certainty
for about two centuries, to the time of Cardinal Mazarin,
who employed it as the altar-piece of his private oratory;
and in his various capacities of Italian, Prince of the
Church, and Viceroy over the Queen of France, was not
likely to be cheated in a painting by Raphael. It remained in
the possession of his representatives till the commencement
of the French revolution, when the property of the family

was confiscated, and the paintings sold at auction. The one
in question was purchased by Colonel Trumbull, who happened to be at Paris at the time, and who, after keeping it
several years, transferred it to Mr. Williams. At the sale
of Mr. Williams's effects, it was offered with the rest, but
brought so low a price that it was bought in for the owner.
From the peculiar circumstances under which it is now
placed, it might probably be obtained for a sum considerably
below its real value, and would form a most important and
interesting addition to any of our collections. The drawing
and coloring are in the best manner of the author, and although the principal figure is rather deficient in expression,
the picture has always been regarded as a capital work. So
far as we are informed, there is no original painting by
Raphael in this country, and we should be highly gratified if
it could be found practicable to improve the present opportunity for placing a very fine one in the Gallery of the Athenaeum.

We come now to that part of the Exhibition which consisted
of the works of our native artists, and we regret that their
number and importance were not such as to authorise us to
devote to the examination of them a larger portion of the
present article. The splendid Sortie from Gibraltar by
Trumbull, which belongs to the Athenaeum, still retains its
place, but it is too well known to the public to require or
admit of a detailed notice. There were also, beside the
Mother and Child, which is the property of the institution,
two very beautiful landscapes by Allston, belonging respectively to Mr. Weeks of New York, and Mr. S. A. Eliot of this
city, a number of valuable works from the pencils of Sully,[2]
Doughty,[3] Fisher,[4] and Salmon,[5] and several interesting
portraits, particularly that of the Chief Justice of the United
States by Harding.[6] Without intending to undervalue the
merit or importance of these productions, we cannot but
remark, that they give a very imperfect notion of the richness and abundance of the recent labors of our native artists.
Few countries have in fact done more within the last half-
century in the way of painting than this. We know of none
that can produce a more respectable list of painters who

have flourished within that period, than is composed by the
names of West,[7] Copley,[8] Trumbull,[9] Allston,[10] Newton,[11]
Leslie,[12] Stuart,[13] and Sully,[14] to which might be added those
of many other younger aspirants of undoubted merit. Several
of these distinguished artists have been and still are the
principal ornaments of the British school, which, for the
time in question, belongs at least as much to the United
States as to the mother-country. England has in fact only
three names of equal pretensions and of native origin to add
to the above list—we mean those of Reynolds, Wilkie, and
Lawrence. The first of these, had he devoted himself exclusively to the higher walks of his art, would have probably
placed himself at the head of modern painters, by which we
mean those of the last century—and even as it is—although
he gave up his pencil almost wholly to portraits—he is perhaps very fairly entitled to that high eminence. Wilkie and
Lawrence are excellent, each in his line—which is not, however, in either case the highest—but the combined merit of
the three, with that of their inferior fellow-laborers—does
not authorise the mother-country to claim more than an
equal share of the glory of the common school. The style of
painting in France during the same period has been decidedly vicious, and although it has obtained a temporary popularity in that country is not approved by competent judges
from any other. In the rest of Europe there has been little
or no activity in this branch of art; so that the United States
—as we remarked above—have done at least as much for
painting during the last half-century, as any other country.
We hope that efforts will be made to procure for the future
Exhibitions a larger number of the choice products of the
native pencil. In the meantime without confining ourselves
to those which were brought forward on this occasion, we
propose to conclude the article with a few general remarks
upon the style and works of some of the eminent American
artists, whose names are recapitulated above.

   That of West is commonly and in some respects deserved-
ly placed at the head of the list. The length of his career—
his conspicuous position at the head of the British Academy
and the indefatigable perseverance with which he pursued

his labors up to the very close of his protracted life—all
these circumstances placed him in full relief before the public, and perhaps raised his reputation a little higher than it
will be maintained by the impartial judgment of posterity.
Perceiving or supposing that his merit was exaggerated, a
certain number of persons were induced, as always happens
in similar cases by a sort of reaction, to depreciate the
value of his works, and even to deny altogether his pretensions to excellence. Without speaking of Peter Pindar, who
attacked him merely because he was patronised by the King,
we may find the feeling to which we allude exhibited in a
quarter where we had a right to look for good taste and
political impartiality. Lord Byron, in one of his poems describes our illustrious countryman as

———'the dotard West,
Europe's worst dauber and poor England's best.'

But even here the noble lord, however opposite may have
been his intention, has borne a sort of involuntary testimony
to the high deserts of the painter. The British school, which
in his wayward humor he represents as the worst in Europe,
was undoubtedly at that time and still is the best, and by
putting West at the head of it he rendered him in fact all the
justice which his warmest friends could possibly have
claimed for him. His real merit was very considerable,
although he may not have risen precisely to the level of the
greatest masters of other times. It was sufficiently evinced
by the great popularity and success of his last and best
pieces the Christ Rejected, and the grand composition of
Death on the Pale Horse. We had the pleasure of seeing
these noble paintings when they were first brought out at
London, and witnessed the enthusiasm which they excited
among the lovers of the arts and the public at large. The
sum of ten thousand pounds was offered for the latter work—
a higher price probably than was ever commanded by any
other picture. As there was nothing meretricious in the
style of West, and as the public of a city like London is not
often very widely mistaken in matters wholly unconnected
with any accidental or temporary interest, it is impossible

to account for this extraordinary vogue without allowing to
the artist a talent of a very high order. His works exhibit in
reality almost all the qualities that designate a first-rate
painting. His walk lay in the highest department of the art.
His subjects were always of a poetical cast, and he treated
them all in a large, free and generous spirit; and while he
possessed the principal requisites of a great painter his
manner was almost wholly free from faults. He had in particular the great merit of avoiding the unnatural style of
coloring which prevailed in the neighboring kingdom and
seemed likely at one time to corrupt the taste of the rest of
Europe. His excellent moral character contributed much to
his talent and still more to his fortune. It kept him steady
to his profession during a period of violent political convulsions, which swept away from their natural occupation
almost all the high and stirring spirits. It recommended him
to the favor of the King, and through that to the Presidency
of the Academy, and it preserved his health and capacity for
constant employment to the last moment of a very long life.
He enjoyed the rare happiness of realising in his lifetime
his full deserts on the score of reputation—perhaps something more—and of laboring with undiminished activity and
a constant increase of fame beyond the ordinary term of
human existence. We had the satisfaction of seeing him frequently in his last days, and have seldom known a more
striking example of a serene and happy old age. He was then
at nearly eighty a healthy, handsome man, busily occupied
upon his last and greatest works, and enjoying the vogue
which they successively obtained on their first exhibition.
The natural simplicity and modesty of his manner were
mingled with a slight air of self-importance and conscious
satisfaction with his recent success, which appeared rather
graceful than otherwise in one so much respected and so far
advanced in years. The freshness and vigor of his mind
were truly remarkable. He was still alive to every means
of improving himself, and when the Athenian marbles were
received in England, he addressed a printed letter to Lord
Elgin, in which he spoke of this event as forming a sort of
epoch in his life, and anticipated the great advantage which

he should derive from the study of these admirable remains of antiquity in the further prosecution of his labors, which, however, were very soon after brought to a close.

We have said above that the manner of West was almost wholly free from faults. His conceptions are noble, his drawing correct, his coloring true, and his composition skilful and spirited. If we miss any thing in his paintings it is, perhaps, the secret indescribable charm of coloring, which, like the curious felicity of language in some writers, seems to be a sort of natural 'grace, beyond the reach of art,' but affording, at the same time, a higher delight than any of those beauties, which can be more distinctly analysed and defined. Of this Sir Joshua Reynolds possessed a larger share than West, and will probably on that account be always ranked above him in the general scale of merit.

The paintings of West, which remained in his possession at his death, were offered for sale soon after, and we have anxiously desired, that the whole or a portion of them should have taken the direction of this country. They would have formed a most interesting and valuable addition to our collections, and would then have reached what may fairly be considered their natural destination, the birth-place and original home of their author. We are not exactly informed what disposition has been made of them, and venture to hope that the expectation we have expressed may still, in part at least, be realized.

The general reputation of Trumbull is hardly equal to that of West, although the Sortie from Gibraltar is perhaps superior in effect to any single production of the latter artist. This noble picture may justly be ranked with the finest productions of the pencil, and would forever secure to its author, had he done nothing else, a rank with the greatest masters of the art. If his success has been on the whole inferior to that of his illustrious contemporary, it is probably because his devotion to his profession has not been so exclusive. The important military and political occupations, in which he was engaged during a considerable portion of the most active part of his life, diverted his attention for the time from painting, and when he afterwards resumed the

pencil he seemed to have lost in some degree the vigor and
freshness of his youthful talent. Hence his reputation has
not continued to increase with his years, and his last works
have not, like those of West, been regarded as his best. The
four great paintings, on subjects connected with the revolutionary war, which he executed for Congress, have, on the
whole, hardly satisfied the public expectation, and for that
reason have perhaps been depreciated below their real
worth. They are all valuable pieces, and the Declaration of
Independence, which we look upon as the best of the series,
is one of a very high order. They derive a great additional
interest from exhibiting portraits, as far as they could be
obtained, of the Signers of the Declaration, and of the other
patriots and warriors, who took a part in the memorable
action of the Revolution. We incline to believe that these
paintings, should the liberality of Congress allow the appro-
priation necessary for keeping them in existence, will gradually gain upon the public opinion, both as works of art and
as historical memorials, and be viewed by the next generation with more interest than they are by the present one.

Of our living native artists, Mr. Allston is the one, to
whose future productions the country looks with reason for
the most brilliant exhibitions of talent, and the most valuable accessions to our public and private collections. Few
painters have ever possessed at his age a higher reputation,
or one acquired by nobler means; and from his character
and habits there is room to suppose that his fame will continue to increase, like that of West, to the last period of his
labors. Inspired by that exclusive and passionate love for
his profession, which is the sure characteristic of a real
genius for it, and by a lofty and generous disinterestedness,
which has prevented him from consecrating his pencil to its
lower and more lucrative departments, he has, under some
discouragements, steadily confined himself to historical,
scriptural and poetical subjects, and has formed his manner
upon the highest standard of excellence. His conceptions are
uniformly happy, and, when the subject requires it, sublime; his taste and skill the mechanical details of his art
complete; and he knows how to give his works the secret

charm to which we alluded before, and which adds the last
finish to every other beauty. If there be any thing to complain of in him, it is that he is not satisfied himself with the
degree of merit, which would satisfy every one else, and
employs in correcting, maturing and repainting a single
piece, not always perhaps with any real accession of effect,
the time and labor which would have been sufficient for completing a dozen. This extreme fastidiousness may have been
at an earlier period of life a virtue, and is probably one of
the qualities, which have enabled the artist to realize the
high idea of excellence, which originally warmed his young
fancy. But, if we might venture to express an opinion on the
subject, we should say that the time has now arrived when
he might throw it off with advantage, and allow himself a
greater rapidity of execution. His manner is formed. He
possesses his talent, whatever it is, and, as we remarked
above, when we treated the same question in general terms,
the more freely and fearlessly he exercises it, the more
natural and spirited, and, on the whole, the better will be
the product. We trust that he will not permit another year to
pass over without putting the last hand to the grand heroic
composition, upon which he has been employed so many, and
that this will be followed by a series of others of equal merit
and of a rather more rapid growth. By this change in his
manner of working we believe that he would gain in ease and
spirit without sacrificing any real beauty, and would labor,
on the whole, with infinitely more satisfaction and profit to
himself and the public than he does now. We offer these
remarks, however, with all the deference that is due from
mere amateurs to an artist of consummate genius, who is
after all the only true judge of effect in his art and of the
best means of producing it.

The two landscapes by Mr. Allston, which were exhibited
this year, were both very beautiful in different ways. The
one belonging to Mr. Eliot is, we think, in the happiest manner. It has the warmth and softness of coloring of Claude,
and is, as far as we are able to judge, in no way inferior to
the fine productions of that artist. The Mother and Child,
which belongs to the institution, is a highly interesting little

piece, upon the merit of which there has been, however, some difference of opinion. If we may venture to offer our sentiments, we should say that the piece is beautifully finished and quite perfect in every thing that belongs to the mechanical details of the art. The coloring of the body of the infant in particular is as true to nature as it could possibly be made, and is fully equal to any that we have seen from the pencil of Titian. The artist does not seem to have been so fortunate in the drawing of the infant, who has too little fulness, as well as too much meaning in his face, for so young a child. The expression of the countenance of the mother is rather uncertain, and her face is thrown into a sort of mysterious shade, for which the spectator is not very well able to account. The piece, however, taken as a whole, is a first-rate work, and forms one of the choicest ornaments of the Athenaeum Gallery.

We regret that a larger number of the paintings of Mr. Allston were not exhibited on this occasion. We should gladly have seen in the Gallery the Valentine of Mr. Ticknor, the Miriam of Mr. Sears, the Jeremiah of Miss Gibbs, and the other fine productions of the same artist, belonging to other gentlemen in this country. These paintings, while they are kept in the houses of their owners, are seen by a very limited number of persons, and it is much to be desired, as well for the improvement of the public taste, as for the mere gratification of the curious, that they should be displayed from time to time in a place where they can be freely examined at leisure by the whole community. The advantage and satisfaction, which the public would derive from such an exhibition, would afford, we are sure, an ample compensation to the liberal proprietors for any trifling sacrifice of their own convenience, that might be required by such an arrangement.

We had intended to offer a few remarks on the style and works of our distinguished countrymen, Newton and Leslie, and also on the landscapes of Doughty, Fisher and Salmon, and some of the portraits that were exhibited on this occasion; but we have already passed the just limits of an article, and must reserve them for a future one. The most

remarkable portrait was undoubtedly that of Chief-Justice
Marshall, painted by Harding for the Athenaeum. It has been
pronounced by those, who are most familiar with the appearance of the illustrious original, to be a striking likeness,
and it certainly does great credit to the painter, who must,
however, make some further advances in his art before he
can aspire to rival the mature fame of Stuart. The landscapes of Fisher as well as his copies from Rembrandt and
Vandyck were very beautiful. Those of Doughty were hardly
less so, and we regret that the sale of them at the present
moment of depression in business has not afforded the artist
the compensation for his labor, which he had a right to expect from the liberality and good taste of the citizens of this
metropolis. The works of Salmon have a more decidedly
characteristic manner, than those of Doughty or Fisher, and
are, we believe, in general greater favorites with the public.
The three artists are all capable of rising by a proper course
of study and practice to a high degree of excellence, and we
trust that they will receive from their countrymen that encouragement, which is absolutely necessary to enable them
to proceed in their labors with spirit and success. A copy,
by Sully, of a female head by Guido, and of a Gipsy from a
French artist, attracted some attention. The Bridal Eve of
Miss Sully, if not in the purest style of coloring, was curious
as a specimen of the French manner, in itself essentially
vicious. The most valuable effort of female genius exhibited
on this occasion was a landscape by Miss Scollay.[15]

It is time, however, to close these remarks. Before we
quit the Gallery we cannot refrain from expressing the
pleasure with which we have viewed the busts in marble of
John Quincy Adams and Mr. Quincy by Greenough,[16] who is
also, we are informed, the inventor of the plan of the
Bunker-Hill Monument. The great merit of this design furnishes itself a strong presumption in favor of the taste and
talent of the author. He is now, we believe, pursuing his
studies at Florence, and we cannot but form very high expectations for the future progress of a career that opens
with so fine a promise.

Notes

The text is based on the North American Review, 31 (October, 1830), 309-337: "Art. III—Catalogue of the Pictures exhibited at the Fourth Exhibition in the Gallery of the Boston Athenaeum. Boston. 1830." The running head of Everett's article furnishes the title given here.

1. "If you have confidence in yourself, other souls will have confidence in you."
2. Thomas Sully (1783-1872), portrait painter.
3. Thomas Doughty (1793-1856), landscape painter.
4. Alvan Fisher (1792-1863), portrait and genre painter.
5. Robert Salmon (c.1775-c.1842), English marine painter who immigrated to Boston in 1829.
6. Chester Harding (1792-1866).
7. Benjamin West (1738-1820).
8. John Singleton Copley (1738-1815).
9. John Trumbull (1756-1843). Painted a famous portrait of Alexander Hamilton.
10. Washington Allston (1779-1843). His best-known paintings include "Belshazzar's Feast."
11. Gilbert Stuart Newton (1795-1835), portrait painter.
12. Charles Robert Leslie (1794-1859).
13. Gilbert Stuart (1755-1828), America's most famous portrait painter.
14. Jane Sully (1807-1877), painter, daughter of Thomas Sully.
15. Catherine Scollay (d.1863), landscapist, figure painter.
16. Horatio Greenough (1805-1852), sculptor.

The Present State
of Polite Learning
in England and America

GENTLEMEN OF THE SOCIETY!

Permit me to express to you how much I feel myself honored and gratified by your kind request to meet you here
upon this occasion. Diffident as I am of my ability to say
any thing to you, that will be either interesting or instructive, it is still a source of the highest satisfaction to me to
have an opportunity of witnessing, in person, the increasing
prosperity of this institution; of meeting in the bosom of
your young and busy community this large and brilliant company, brought together by no other motive than the interest
they feel in the progress of education and letters. On a former occasion of this description, which occurred some five
and twenty years ago, the orator who preceded me and whom
I am happy to call my valued friend, invited you, in the
classical dialect of Greece, to go with him to Athens. *ΙΩΜΕΝ
ΕΙΞ ΑΘΗΝΑΞ*,[1] was the burden of the address; and I well
recollect that one of the chief ornaments of our Massachusetts Alma Mater remarked, after reading it, that the pupils
of Bowdoin were apparently already somewhat nearer to that
celebrated seat of learning than we of Harvard had before,
in the pride of our comparative antiquity, been willing to
admit. Since that time, Gentlemen, great changes have occurred throughout the world. The eye of Greece, as Athens

141

is so beautifully called by Milton, after having been closed
for fifteen hundred years in the death-trance of slavery, is
again opened. The latest accounts from Europe inform us
that the city of Minerva has been fixed upon as the residence
of the new king of Greece, a prince selected from a family
which has long been distinguished for its love of learning
and the arts. Under his enlightened patronage we may confidently hope that the banks of the Ilyssus, and the olive
groves of the Academy, will again be frequented by other
Platos, and that the maids of Athens will no longer be
obliged to wait for an English poet to sing their charms in
the language of their own land. Here too, Gentlemen, in our
favored abode of liberty, much has been done in every part
of the country in the way of intellectual and literary improvement. From the shores of the Atlantic to the utmost
bounds of the far west, there has been throughout the Union
a generous rivalry in efforts to elevate the standard of civilization and learning. Far be it from me to assume the ungracious office of deciding which of these efforts have been
most successful, but I feel myself justified in the remark,
that no where in the United States has the progress been,
upon the whole, more rapid, and at the same time more
secure, than in the State of Maine. Destined as she is to
take, at no distant period, a very conspicuous place among
her sisters, we may confidently trust that her superiority
will not result from her vast material resources alone, and
that she will justify by her eminence in learning and the
arts, as well as in population, wealth and political importance, the proud device and inscription which she bears em-
blazoned on her arms.

To concur within the sphere of our activity, and to the extent of our power, in this great and good work, the intellectual and moral improvement of our country, is the object,
Gentlemen, of our association. In times like the present,
of high political excitement and angry contention, it is
pleasing to find that there are still subjects in which we all
take a common interest;—that for literary purposes, at
least, we can still meet together in large assemblies, and
separate with feelings of unmingled kindness for each other

and for all our fellow-citizens. Let us then, Gentlemen, forget for an hour the engrossing cares of business, the agonizing strife of political controversy, and turn our thoughts
to the pursuits of literature; —to those studies which, in the
elegant language of Cicero, nourish us in youth and form
the recreation and delight of our riper years; which are the
ornament of prosperous, and the solace of adverse fortune;
a source of pleasure, that is always at hand; at home or
abroad; by night or by day; in town, or in the country; and
from which many of us, doubtless, in the lingering hours of
absence in a foreign land, have derived the same consolation
which they formerly afforded in his unmerited exile, to the
illustrious orator who had cultivated them with so much
success.

There are periods in the history of learning, when men
seem to rest contented with the acquisitions and achievements of other ages, —to sleep, as it were, upon the laurels
of their fathers. At such periods it would be natural, on an
occasion like this, to seek for a topic in the vast storehous-
es of ancient learning. But at a time of great intellectual
activity, when, in the community with which we are connected, all the branches of learning are cultivated with extraordinary zeal and talent, it may seem more suitable to consider rather what is going on among and around us. Permit
me then, Gentlemen, to invite your attention to a few general views on the present state of polite learning in England
and America. General they, of course, must be, from the
impossibility of compressing any other than very general
views upon so large a subject into the narrow space of an
address like this; —imperfect and unsatisfactory, on every
account, as I am but too well aware, they will be; —and,
Gentlemen, I can only hope that you will receive them with
the indulgence which your kindness authorizes me to expect,
and which is due, perhaps, to the hasty effort of one much
occupied with other cares and studies.

Let me remark, however, by way of preface, that I propose to consider the state of learning in England and America as merely two branches of one and the same subject.
Whatever may be the character of the political relations

between Great Britain and the United States,—and I am happy to believe that the natural progress of events is daily
rendering them more and more amicable,—but whatever
may be the nature of these relations, the two countries must
always, in a literary view, be regarded as one great community, held together by the indissoluble bond of the same
common language. This condition of our literature, while it
is the unavoidable result of the circumstances in which we
are placed, is also, to every generous mind, a source of
high satisfaction and pride. We glory, as Americans, in the
literary glory of the land of our fathers. The names of
Shakspeare, Milton, Locke, Bacon and Burke are as dear
and sacred to us, as they can be to any native son of the
fast-anchored isle. We read their works with as deep an
interest, as if we had passed our lives in exploring the long-
drawn aisles, and storied vaults of Westminster Abbey, or
in gazing on the silver stream of the soft-flowing Avon.
Perhaps I may even say, that our feelings are of a higher
and more enthusiastic cast; as the inhabitants of the distant
provinces of Palestine, when they came up annually to worship in the temple at Jerusalem, performed their devotions
with greater fervor than those who constantly dwelt in the
Holy City. Nor do we feel this sympathy only in the ancient
glories of the common literature. The names of Scott, and
Byron are household words, on the shores of the Hudson and
the Mississippi, as well as on those of the Tweed and the
Thames. While we strive to emulate the intellectual achievements of our brethren on the other side of the Atlantic, we
feel that the head-quarters of the common literature, still
are, and for some time to come, will remain in the parent
country. You will, therefore, not be surprised, if in speaking to you of the actual state of learning in England and
America, I shall have occasion to enlarge chiefly upon the
former branch of the subject; and, in reference to our own
country, shall be obliged to hold out to you a fair prospect
of future attainment, rather than a great amount of wealth in
present possession.

Literature has been correctly described by an eminent

female writer, as an expression of the state of society. Its
existence indicates a certain degree of advancement in civilization, and its character changes with the changes in the
condition and character of the nations by which it is cultivated. These changes are of course very gradual, but in taking
a survey of the whole literature of almost every country,
which possesses one, we observe three distinct periods,
corresponding with the three principal periods in their political history: —I mean their progress, maturity and decline.
During the first period, while the community is still in a
state of rapid expansion, more busily occupied with great
substantial interests, than with nice distinctions of form and
manner, the basis of literature is a bold and simple expression of the feelings and thoughts, that are first suggested to
the mind by the spectacle of nature, —unpolished in style,
and uninformed by the spirit of philosophy. The general
characteristics of this period are strength, simplicity, and
an imperfect taste. To such a period belong, considered as
literary compositions, the sublime effusions of the Hebrew
prophets; to this belong the gigantic creations of Dante, the
Spanish Drama, and the great but unequal Corneille. Homer,
though seldom deficient in taste, wears the impression of
having flourished in the youth of society, in the absence of
philosophical reflections. The progress of wealth and the
continued cultivation of letters bring in, after a while, a
second period, the leading characteristic of which, as distinguished from the preceding one, is good taste. A nicer
observation of nature in connexion with the works already
produced, enables the artist to avoid the faults of the former
period, and to present his conceptions in pure and correct
forms. This is justly regarded as the most brilliant period
in the history of learning. It was the age of Pericles in
Greece; of Augustus in Rome; of the Medici in Italy; of
Louis XIV. in France. In the beautiful productions that belong to it, the simplicity and vigor of the former period are
still preserved, and the absence of the wild and eccentric
graces which before accompanied these qualities, is more
than compensated by the finished elegance which now as-
sumes their place. Having thus reached its natural maturity,

there is of course no room for further progress, and the
state of learning exhibits, under various modifications of
minor importance, the leading characteristics of the second
period, while the community maintains itself in a vigorous
and flourishing condition. But it seems to be a law of nature
that the maturity of nations, like that of individuals, is followed at no distant time by a more or less rapid decline;
and such has been particularly the case in those most eminent for learning. A corrupt and decaying condition of society naturally brings with it the third and last period in the
history of learning. Weakness, disguised at times under
extravagant and convulsive efforts at effect, takes the place
of a healthy and natural strength; affectation that of taste;
until in the gradual course of social dissolution, the power
of literary production entirely ceases.

In the history of English learning, the commencement and
the close of the first of these periods are distinctly perceptible. It begins with the triumph of the English language over
the Norman French, and terminates in the tumults of the
civil wars, which for a time absorbed the whole intellect of
the country, and left no room for literary effort. The great
poets that adorned this period are too familiarly known to
require to be mentioned. But this brilliant age was not distinguished by preëminence in poetry only. A multitude of
powerful writers in prose, among whom stands conspicuous
the gigantic figure of the illustrious Bacon, will render it
forever memorable in the annals of philosophy. It is remarkable, indeed, that the productions of the great writers
of this period, whether in poetry or prose, display the union
of the two highest qualities of the human mind, imagination
and thought, in extraordinary and almost equal degrees of
perfection. Bacon and Taylor, when it suits their purpose,
are as great poets as Shakspeare. Shakspeare and Milton,
when they choose to sound the depths of thought, can bring
up treasures hardly inferior in richness to those which fill
the store-house of the illustrious Chancellor. This combination of the highest excellences, so rarely found in connexion
with each other, gives to the period a peculiar character;
and though its brilliancy is tarnished by glaring and often

very gross deficiencies in taste, renders its products more valuable on the whole than those of any other in the history of learning.

While the last and one of the greatest ornaments of this school was still living, and before the publication of the greatest of his works, the close of the civil wars and the restoration of the Stuarts to the throne, opened a new era in the literature of the country, which corresponds with the second of those which I have just now described. The king and the principal courtiers had formed their taste in the French school of the age of Louis XIV., and were offended by the rudeness of the English writers of the preceding period. The men of genius and talent who sought their patronage and favor, looked, accordingly, to the French school for models in style. Dryden commenced the change, and though unfortunate on several accounts in the application of his talent, has left, as respects mere style, some of the finest specimens of writing in the language. The new manner which he introduced was copied and carried to perfection in the next generation by Pope, Swift, Addison, Bolingbroke and their contemporaries, whose brilliant productions throw so much lustre on the time of Queen Anne, that her reign has since been commonly described as the Augustan age of English literature. It would be more correct, however, to represent it as the opening of such an age, for it does not appear that there has been, since her day, either in substantial vigor of thought, or in correctness and elegance of form, any perceptible decline in the state of letters. The wits of Anne were succeeded by another generation, comprehending in poetry such names as Young, Thomson, Goldsmith, Collins, Cowper and Gray, and in prose, such as Hume, Johnson, Robertson, Gibbon, Junius and Burke. If the poets just mentioned, fell somewhat below their immediate predecessors in productiveness and power; the prose writers, on the other hand, rose decidedly above them. In the next generation, which is that of our own time, poetry recovered her honors, and the general standard of learning has been sustained at as high a point as ever, while the mass of products has been far greater than at any preceding period. As the political importance of the English race, taken together, is still in a state of rapid progress, we may reasonably expect that the present brilliant period in the state of literature will continue for a long time to come. If the results of the agitations in the mother country, which cannot yet be exactly anticipated, should be unfavorable to the political, and with it to the literary prosperity of England, we may hope that here, at least, where everything leads us to anticipate a long career of political progress and development, the course of learning will also still be onward; and that the rising brightness of the Western Hemisphere will replace, as they fade, the departing glories of the East.

The general characteristics of the present state of learning in England and America are, therefore, those which belong to the most mature and brilliant periods; —a healthy vigor, moderated and guided by a pure and correct taste. The present time may be regarded, in short, as a continuation, with a tendency to progress, rather than decline, of the Augustan age of English literature. But though agreeing in its general characteristics with that of the preceding century, the literature of our day is marked by some important distinctive qualities, to which I now propose, very briefly, to invite your attention.

Of these distinctive qualities, the leading one is a tendency to a revival of the spirit of the earliest period of our literature: —a renewed preference for substantial vigor of thought and feeling, over mere correctness of style; —a disposition to recur for models to the age of Elizabeth rather than to that of Anne. The immediate effect of the appearance of the first pure and finished works of art, in any department, is to fix the public attention, for the time, almost exclusively on the superficial qualities of form and style, and to produce in the artist a fastidious care upon this point, unfavorable to a free and expansive flow of thought and feeling. Something of this constraint may, in fact, be remarked in some of the poets of the middle of the last century, such as Goldsmith, Johnson, Gray and Collins, and also in the later productions of Rogers and Campbell, which belong to

the same school. Where society, and with it literature, are
tending to decay, a change like this marks the commencement of the gradual decline of letters, as in fact happened
in Greece and Rome. But where society is still in a state of
progress and expansion, some change of circumstances will
naturally, at no distant period, give a new impulse to literature. This impulse seems to have been given in England by
the general intellectual movement which preceded and produced the French Revolution. The great popularity of the
poems of Cowper was one of the first symptoms of an improvement in the public taste; but it was not till about the
time of the opening of the Revolution that it became apparent,
and its connexion with the political events of the day is sufficiently proved by the internal evidence afforded by the productions of the principal writers.

Then arose upon the literary world the brilliant constellation of poets, sometimes denominated the Lake school, of
which the chief ornaments were Wordsworth, Coleridge and
Southey. Though often ridiculed, and doubtless obnoxious in
some respects to severe criticism, they exhibited great
power, and have sustained themselves at the bar of public
opinion against their detractors. They were all, at the outset, warm and even violent friends of liberty, though they
have since seen fit to give in their adhesion to other principles. About the same time appeared Mackintosh, the most
powerful and elegant of the prose writers of the day; and not
long after him Moore, the most finished and sweetest of the
poets, undoubtedly the first of the lyric bards of his country. Both were ardent adherents of liberty. Contemporane-
ously with their appearance, a new spring came over the
enchanted gardens of romance which, since the days of
Fielding, Richardson and Smollett, had been overrun with a
luxuriant growth of rank but worthless weeds. This was the
great field for the literary glory of woman, who asserted
her claims to intellectual equality in the charming pages of
Burney, Radcliffe, and Edgeworth, much more effectually
than in those of Wolstonecraft and Godwin. Thus far the free
spirit of the age had operated spontaneously without much
regard to theory; but at length the Edinburgh Review, itself

one of the most brilliant literary phenomena of the time,
rescued criticism from the hands of the booksellers, and
employed it in explaining, directing, and encouraging the
spirit that prevailed in the world of letters. Finally, Scott
and Byron, the master-spirits of the time, made their appearance, and for a quarter of a century concentrated the
attention and divided between them, in nearly equal portions,
the admiration of the literary world.

Of this splendid literary constellation, the prevailing
characteristics were, as I remarked before, a fresh and
natural tone of feeling, independence and vigor of thought,
and a comparative carelessness of style. Most of the principal writers were attached, as I have said, to the political
doctrines of the age, and even the few who dissented from
them were so far influenced by its spirit, as to adopt, like
the rest, the new forms of literature. Scott, through life an
uncompromising Tory, displays in all his writings a greater
degree of originality and freshness, than almost any of his
contemporaries. Burke, naturally a champion of Liberty,
but driven by the excesses of the French Revolution to assume, for a time, the character of a partisan of Law, carried into his new vocation a power and freedom much greater than any that he had shown before, and in the splendor
and exuberance of his last productions entirely eclipsed all
the earlier labors of his life. Even Gifford, the champion of
the old school in politics and letters, though he never deviated in his original writings from the stricter forms of the
preceding age, was so far carried away by the taste which
prevailed around him, that he passed a great portion of the
last years of his life in writing commentaries on the dramatic poets of the age of Elizabeth.

Such, Gentlemen, is the first distinctive quality in the
literary aspect of the present time;—the revival of the
freshness and vigor of the earliest and best days of English
learning. I proceed to notice what I consider as its other
leading characteristic, I mean the great and hitherto unexampled popularity of learning.

The chief cause of the present popularity of learning is,
as you are aware, Gentlemen, the invention of printing.

This discovery forms the most important epoch in the history of modern Europe, and the one to which we must look for the origin of all the great changes, which distinguish the civilization of the last three centuries from that of those which preceded them. Before the invention of printing, literature had been the monopoly of a very limited number of persons, composed almost wholly of the clergy. The mass of the people, and a great proportion of the wealthier classes, could neither read nor write. A collection of a few hundred, or at most a few thousand books, which was then called a large library, was a treasure fit only for princes. The supply of books was kept up chiefly by the labors of the monks in the monasteries, most of which had their <u>Scriptorium</u> or writing-room, where the business was regularly carried on, but with what expense of time and labor I need not state. I recollect seeing at the Cathedral of Rouen in France one of two copies of the mass book, the preparation of which occupied the whole life of a scribe who had formerly been attached to that church.[2]

All this is now changed. The facility with which copies of the most extensive works are now multiplied, their comparative cheapness, and the extent to which they are circulated throughout the country, are matters of general notoriety. The influence of this change upon literature itself, and through literature upon the whole social condition of Christendom, has been of the highest importance.

The first effect of the invention of printing, and of the consequent cheapness of books, upon literature, was a great increase in the number of writers. For some time, however, they generally adhered to the old forms of composition. Methodical treatises on the several branches of science; regular histories; sermons and controversial tracts: in polite literature, plays and other poems constructed on the antique model, were the works which chiefly occupied the labor of literary men. After a while, however, the constantly increasing demand for books, and the necessity of accommodating the supply to the taste of a very numerous portion of the public, directed the activity of writers chiefly to two forms of composition which, if not

entirely new, acquired at this time an importance that they
did not possess before. This has gradually increased until
they have become, perhaps, the most prominent objects in
the present aspect of literature. I allude, Gentlemen, as
will doubtless readily occur to you, to the novel and the
newspaper.

Novels, though apparently one of the most natural as well
as attractive forms of literary composition, were entirely
unknown to the classical periods of Greek and Roman learning. Only two or three attempts of the kind have come down
to us from those periods, and these belong to the later ages
of both, and have little or no value. One reason of this may
have been the structure of society, in reference to the
forms of association among persons of different sexes; but
a still stronger one was probably the great scarcity and
value of the materials for writing. The first attempts in
modern times were the Romances of Chivalry, which formed
the delight of the higher circles in the middle ages, though
they were probably very little known to the people. They are
now remembered chiefly by the admirable work in which
Cervantes ridiculed them, and which furnishes itself one of
the finest specimens of the class of fictitious compositions.
To these succeeded the bulky pastoral romances of the age
of Louis XIV., until at length the happier genius of the English writers of the middle of the last century struck out the
path of a direct and true representation of nature. Crowds
of imitators followed in all parts of Europe; and this department of learning, although of recent invention, is
already perhaps the most voluminous of all, and is annually
enriched by the addition of thousands of volumes in all the
different languages of Christendom.

It is in this department of literature, as I have already
remarked, that female genius has achieved its principal
triumphs, and vindicated the claim of the sex to a full intellectual equality with man. The earlier and still immature
period of the French school was chiefly illustrated by the
labors of Mesdemoiselles de Scudery and de la Faye, and
in our own times we have been indebted to female pens for
a very large portion of the best works of this class. Without

adverting to a crowd of others of inferior celebrity, I need
only repeat, in justification of this remark, the illustrious
names of Burney, Radcliffe, and especially Edgeworth.
There is, in fact, in the nature of the novel, dealing directly
as it does in its usual and perhaps most attractive shape,
with the incidents and feelings of domestic life, something
that marks it out as a field peculiarly fitted for the exercise
of female talent. The elegant writers whom I have mentioned,
and the multitude of others who have essayed their powers
in the same line of composition, have introduced us successively to almost all the various forms of social life. Miss
Edgeworth, Miss Burney, and the greater proportion of
their fair fellow-laborers, prefer to expatiate in the draw-
ing-rooms and boudoirs of the fashionable world. Mrs.
Radcliffe, the Mighty Magician, as she has been called, of
the Mysteries of Udolpho, carries us back to the gloomy
and bloodstained abodes of the chivalry and churchmen of
the middle ages; while Scott, the great master, who has
given new dignity and increased popularity to this kind of
composition, like the chartered libertine whom he most re-
sembles, is equally at home in the palace and the peasant's
hut; and adorns his many-colored tissues at once with the
liveliest delineations of contemporary nature and the truest
portraits from history. Another class, perceiving the great
attraction of the novel, and bent on turning it to account for
useful purposes, have labored to make it the vehicle of
important instruction in moral and political science. In the
learned pages of Miss Martineau, for example, the hero, in
his stolen interviews with his devoted fair one, instead of
dwelling on the fooleries of love's young dream, selects for
discussion the more substantial subjects of rent, wages,
and the profits of stock. Her Ellas and Emmelines enliven
their moonlight bowers and morning boudoirs with disserta-
tions on the darkest points in political economy, which would
have done honor to the lecture-room of Adam Smith. But
experience shows that even political economy can be made
palatable in the form of a novel; and so general is the appetite for these attractive compositions that, in whatever
shape they appear, they are devoured by the public with

almost equal avidity, as the real politician feasts upon the
latest newspapers with nearly the same relish, whatever be
the nature of the contents or the partisan feelings of the publisher.

And this, Gentlemen, brings me to the other new form of
composition, which has acquired in our time such extraordinary importance; —I mean the newspaper. Although we can
hardly imagine, with our present habits of transacting business, how a government, and especially a popular government, could be carried on without newspapers, it is certain
that no such thing was known in any of the Republics of
Greece or Italy, nor indeed could have been before the invention of printing. The first newspapers are said to have
been published at Venice, and to have derived their name of
Gazettes from a small Venetian coin called Gazeta, which
was the price of a number. They began to assume some
degree of political importance, during the civil wars of the
seventeenth century, in England; but it is not until within the
last fifty years that they have become, —as they are now
justly styled, —a Fourth Estate, exercising a more powerful
influence on the public affairs of the countries in which they
are permitted to circulate freely, than the other three put
together. The political influence of the periodical press is
an inquiry of the highest moment, but which does not fall
within the limits of our present subject. I shall only remark,
that whatever dangers may be supposed to attend it in other
countries, differently constituted from ours, and however
it may be, as it doubtless is, abused among us, to promote
the purposes of faction or private malignity, it is yet, with
all its dangers and abuses, so necessary a part of the machinery of our political institutions, that they could not
possibly be made practicable in its absence. Scattered as
we are, over the vast extent of a whole quarter of the globe,
and yet required by the nature of the government to be
accurately and regularly informed of what is going on in
every part of the country, it is evident that the existence
and constant activity of the periodical press, are indispensable conditions of the practicability of our republican constitution. Without the aid of this efficient machinery for the

diffusion of information throughout the mass of the people,
and of the simultaneous improvements in the means of com-
munication among the different parts of the country, by
which the personal relations between their inhabitants are
so much facilitated and increased, it can hardly be doubted
that the Union would already have fallen to pieces from the
mere want of any sufficient principle of cohesion.

The political influence of the periodical press is, therefore, in this country, at least, with all its abuses decidedly
beneficial. Its effect on the state of learning has been by
some considered more questionable. It has been frequently
doubted, whether the great popularity which learning has
acquired in our time, will not exercise an unfavorable influence upon its progress and permanent value. It is urged
that the general diffusion of knowledge has a tendency to
render it superficial;—that the temptation held out by the
numerous periodical works that are constantly issuing from
the press, to hasty publication, discourages the persevering
study and mature reflection, which are necessary to the
accomplishment of works of finished excellence.

But these objections, Gentlemen, though not destitute of
plausibility, are not confirmed by experience, nor do they
stand the test of close examination. Where knowledge is
generally diffused through the community, there will doubtless be many more persons than there otherwise would be,
whose acquisitions are superficial and scanty; but for the
same reason a much larger proportion of those, who are
fitted by the superiority of their talents to distinguish themselves in any line of labor, will have the opportunity of taking the direction of science and learning. We should therefore naturally expect, that with the increased popularity of
learning, the number of profound thinkers, persevering
students, and really powerful writers would increase, instead of diminishing. The experience of the last century
very fully confirms this expectation. While the flood of
periodical literature has been constantly swelling through
the whole Christian world;—while the lighter sorts of publications have abounded to an extent, that was never known
nor dreamed of before;—the most abstruse and profound

scientific researches have been pursued with proportional perseverance, vigor and success; and the greater lights of poetry and eloquence have shone forth with more than ordinary brightness. The close of the last century, and the commencement of the present, were distinguished in Germany, by an extraordinary developement of metaphysical and antiquarian science; in France, by a great activity in natural philosophy; and throughout the Christian world, but more especially in England, by a splendid exhibition of superior power in eloquence and poetry.

In confirmation of the remark which I have just made, upon the influence of the diffusion of learning, and in further illustration of the general subject of the Address, permit me to advert very hastily to the character and merits of some of the principal ornaments of the English literature of our times. The suggestions that I may offer will, of course, be familiar to you, but on an occasion like the present, it is not so much the object to strike out new truths, or to illustrate dark passages, as to excite a sympathetic feeling, in regard to the pursuits which are common to us all, and to the illustrious men in whom we must all feel a deep and common interest.

Of the large and brilliant group of literary characters to whom I have adverted, Lord Byron is decidedly the most remarkable individual, and the one who may be considered as personifying and representing, more perfectly than any other, the spirit which prevails in the literature of the day. It might be said, perhaps, with safety, that no poet since the time of Pope, has exhibited any thing nearly so much power; —certainly none has attracted in nearly so high a degree the public attention. The circumstances of his private character and history, —his elevated rank in society, —his personal advantages, and even his personal defects, —his romantic adventures at home and abroad, —the generally wayward and eccentric course of his life contributed, with his real merit, and the almost miraculous facility with which he poured forth his poems, to render him for a time, the observed of all observers. His original taste seems to have been for the stricter forms of the school of Pope,

whose reputation he afterwards so powerfully sustained
against the attack of Bowles. His first feeble attempts in
verse consisted chiefly of imitations of the manner of the
preceding age; and in his next more vigorous effort, in
which he undertook to repel the incautious onset of the critical champions of the North, he approached more nearly to
the point and venom of the Wasp of Twickenham, than any
other subsequent poet. At this period, he felt, like most of
his countrymen, who are similarly situated, the disposition
to visit foreign countries; and it was, perhaps, fortunate
for his reputation, that the political circumstances of the
time induced him to turn his steps to regions better fitted
to enrich and stimulate a poetical temperament, than those
which compose what is commonly called the Grand Tour.
The sunny climes of Portugal, and the south of Spain,—the
gloomy desolation of the city of Minerva,—the strange but
splendid panorama of Constantinople and its neighborhood,
were the scenes of his first wanderings;—while the beautiful
banks of the Rhine, and the classic soil of Italy completed
the theatre of Childe Harold's Pilgrimage. From the business and fashion of the times,—from all the usual haunts of
the every-day world he seems to have studiously kept himself aloof, and his genius was probably none the worse for
it. In the charming language of one of his own poems,

> —— 'In the wilds
> Of fiery climes he made himself a home,
> And his soul drank their brightness. He was not
> Himself, like what he had been. On the sea
> And on the shore, he was a wanderer.
> He rested from the noon-tide sultriness,
> Couched amid fallen columns, in the shade
> Of ruined walls, that had survived the names
> Of those who built them. By his sleeping side
> Stood camels grazing, and some goodly steeds
> Were fastened to a fountain, and a man,
> Clad in a flowing robe, did watch the while;
> And they were canopied by the blue sky,
> So cloudless, clear, and purely beautiful,
> That God alone was to be seen in heaven.'

This was the true school for a young poet, and by studying
it, for three or four years, at the period of life when his
character was still ductile, he doubtless drew in a higher
inspiration than he would ever have reached, in the cold and
misty mountains of his native Scotland. He committed to
paper the first effusions of this new spring of genius and
poetry, in the midst of the scenes to which he was indebted
for it; and abandoning, at once, the formal manner of the
preceding age, adopted the verse of Spenser, which he man-
aged with more than the freedom and vigor of the age of
Elizabeth. Strange, however, as it may seem, his taste did
not keep pace with his talent. He still retained a lingering
fondness for the style of his first model; and on his return
from Europe, with the magnificent creation of Childe Harold
in his portfolio, his whole anxiety was to put to press with
all possible speed, a lame and pointless imitation of Horace,
in the manner of Pope, of which a few fragments only have
since been thought worth preservation. Luckily the judgment
of his friends was better than his own, and the moody hero
of his more successful labors, was chosen as the next representative of his genius. The rank, eccentricity, and
already acknowledged talent of the noble bard, attracted the
public attention at once, and the character of the work fixed
it forever. The immense applause which attested its success, produced its natural effect in exciting still further the
genius of the author, and he poured forth his subsequent
works, with a prodigality, not less admirable than their
surpassing power and beauty. He was now the literary idol
of the day, and basked for a time, in the full sunshine of
popular and fashionable favor. Then domestic calamities
assailed him; —the favor of the world deserted him; —and he
went forth a marked and melancholy man upon that second
Pilgrimage, from which he was destined never to return.
But though a change had come over his fortunes, and his
private reputation, there was none in the spirit of his
dream. Success had encouraged him; disgrace only goaded
him on to still more vigorous action. As he brooded in
gloom and exile, over his wrongs and sorrows, he felt the
secret springs of thought and feeling, opening with still

more depth and fullness in his bosom. The third and fourth
Cantos of Childe Harold, which he composed abroad, contain
with all the glow and freshness of the former ones, a new
train of refined sentiment and almost mysterious reflection.
In the sublime drama of Manfred, which was suggested by
his visit to the mountain scenery of Switzerland, his creative power seems to have reached its greatest height; and
here too, in some of the most brilliant passages, he points
directly to the particulars of his domestic trials. But whether his walk was in the sunny or the shadowy paths of life,
the forms of sublimity and beauty were constantly crowding
on his fancy; nor was there any visible decline in his power
of turning them to shape. His poetical course was all prodigality and pastime. His dramatic poems, the conclusion of
Childe Harold, even the lighter, and in a moral point of
view, less commendable productions of his later days, were
all instinct with life and vigor. The beautiful lyric effusion
on the fortunes of Greece, would have done no dishonor to
the harp of Pindar or Corinna; and the plaintive stanzas in
which the poet gives expression to the high and solemn mus-
ings, that occupied his mind on the last return of his birth-
day, have often been cited as among the happiest of his
productions.

The whole of them, however, various in form and subject
as they are, exhibit in high perfection the freshness of manner and manly freedom of thought, which I have pointed out
as the peculiar features of the new school of learning, that
has grown up within our own time, under the impulse of the
great intellectual movement, which led to the political agitations of the last half century. The tenor of Lord Byron's
writings also shows very clearly the close connexion between the moving principles of these agitations, and of the
new development of literary activity. He was not only a
professed partisan of liberal political principles, but he had
evidently studied much too deeply the writers of the last
century, who professed those principles in incorrect and
exaggerated forms, to the great injury of his moral sentiments and literary taste. Perhaps, however, the circumstances of his personal position in the world, may have

contributed even more than any of his studies, to produce
the unfortunate effects to which I allude. At all events it is
much to be regretted that the moral tone of a considerable
part of his works, is far from corresponding with their
poetical merit. He too often treats with open disrespect, not
merely the established institutions and received opinions of
his own country and time, but the sacred truths, which have
met the approbation of the wise and good of all ages, and
are recognised universally as the only possible basis of
society. He thinks deeply, but the chief result of his thoughts
is a sullen scepticism, at times degenerating into an open
and desperate revolt against the order of nature. There
seems to have been in the very foundation of his moral and
intellectual character, a principle of error that vitiated the
action of his mind in all its various moods. There is no
gravity in his seriousness;—there is no gaiety in his merri-
ment; one is the sullen gloom of suppressed fury,—the other
an insulting mockery of the best feelings, and the most important truths. Even his plaintive strains are a sort of
heart-rending lament, over the misery of his own condition.

> There's not a joy the world can give, like that it takes
>   away,
> When the glow of youthful thought is lost, in feeling's
>   dull decay.
> 'Tis not on youth's smooth cheek the blush alone that
>   fades so fast,
> But the tender bloom of heart is gone ere youth itself is
>   past.
>
> Then the mortal coldness of the soul, like death itself
>   comes down;
> It cannot weep for others' woes, it dares not dream
>   its own,
> That fatal chill has frozen o'er the fountain of our tears,
> And though the eye may sparkle still, 'tis where the ice
>   appears.
>
> Though wit may flash from fluent lips, and mirth distract
>   the breast

In midnight hours that yield no more their wonted hope
   of rest,
'Tis but as ivy leaves that round the ruined turret
   wreathe,
All green and wildly fresh without,—all dark and grey
   beneath.

Oh! could I feel as I have felt, or be what I have been,
Or weep as I could once have wept o'er many a vanished
   scene,
As streams, in deserts found, seem sweet, all brackish
   though they be,
So mid the wintry waste of life those tears should flow
   for me.

His friend and biographer labors to prove, that all this
wretchedness was merely ideal; but it corresponds too exactly with the course of the poet's life. How much happier
might have been his lot, if circumstances had given a different direction to his character from the beginning; or
even if in later life, recovering from the wild aberrations,
that are comparatively venial in the fervor of youth, he had
returned to his country, and employed his splendid powers
in the cause of truth and virtue! How glorious might not
have been his position at this moment, and perhaps for many
years to come, at the head of the literature of England; and
surrounded at the same time with all the adventitious advantages of elevated rank, and ample fortune! But it may be
doubted whether a different course of life, howmuchsoever
it might have improved the moral character of his writings,
would have tended to increase their poetical power and
beauty. The frantic energy,—the soul-subduing pathos,—the
wild flashes of levity, which are the highest elements of
poetry, and which enter so largely into Byron's productions,
result, perhaps, more naturally from the irregular work-
ings of a morally disordered nature, than from the healthy
action of the feelings, operating within the limits marked
out by a sound judgment and a correct and cultivated taste.
   In the Great Unknown, as he was for some years commonly

called, the competitor and rival, though at the same time, warm, personal friend of Lord Byron, we find almost all that Byron possessed, combined with almost all that he wanted to have rendered his existence as prosperous and pleasant to himself, as it was brilliant in the eyes of the world. With a poetical power hardly inferior to that of Byron, though exhibiting itself in a different way, and with less concentration and intensity, Sir Walter Scott united a steadiness of purpose and a felicitous moral temperament, which made his career as long and fortunate as that of his rival was short, fitful and disastrous. The inspiration of Scott seems to have been drawn, originally, from the rich sources of German poetry and romance. His first publications were translations of a romantic drama, by Goethe, entitled Goetz of Berlichingen with the iron hand, and of the celebrated ballad of Leonora by Büerger. In his original ballads, which followed next, and exhibited far more power, he pursued the same track. Nor did he, in his later works, ever appear to have lost entirely the impressions that first awakened his young genius. In the series of poems, commencing with the Lay of the Last Minstrel, he employs the same materials in substantially the same, though a more enlarged shape; and in the Waverley Novels he again presents them to us in a still more expanded form, and with all the detail and circumstance appropriate to this kind of composition. His first productions excited very little attention, although some of them exhibit, perhaps, a greater concentration of power, than any passages of equal length, in his larger works. The extent of his capacity was first made known to the world at large, by the Lay of the Last Minstrel. The freshness and spirit of the narrative,—the novelty and beauty of the imagery,—the wildness of the supernatural machinery, and above all, the entire originality which pervaded every part of it, struck the public mind with a sort of spell, which, though diminished at times, was not entirely removed, through the whole course of the author's long career. Marmion sustained and increased the impression, and the Lady of the Lake revived it in all its freshness. The rest of the series, whether published in the name of the

author or anonymously, had comparatively but little power;
and the bard had evidently exhausted his capacity for giving
attraction to this particular form of poetry, when Byron
blazed forth, like a splendid meteor, upon the literary fir-
mament. Scott felt himself eclipsed in the field of his former
triumphs, and with a prodigality of talent which could only
have been displayed by a mind of the highest order, struck
at once into a new track. Then commenced that astonishing
series of prose fictions, which, in popular effect, at least,
eclipsed alike his own poems, and those of his competitor,
and which form on the whole, the most remarkable literary
creation of the day. Then came forth, at the call of this
mighty enchanter, from the regions of fairy land, from the
walks of life in all its various forms, and from the monu-
mental vaults of history, that splendid array of characters,
which, for a period of fifteen years, passed in uninterrupted
succession, and with constantly increasing attraction before
the public. Coeur-de-Lion, with his noble frankness; Louis
the Eleventh of France, with his deep-laid policy; James
the First of England, with his awkward good nature, and
ridiculous pedantry,—the most learned fool in Christendom;
the gentle piety of Rebecca, and the dashing brilliancy of
Diana Vernon; the high-souled Roundhead, and the light-
hearted Cavalier; priests and pirates; fools and philosophers; with the hosts of their companions and attendants,
were all delineated with equal spirit and equal acceptance.
The appearance of each of these works was a sort of event
for the world at large. They were read alike by the grave
and the gay. The professed novel-reader devoured them as
a matter of course, while the careful mother, who, as a
general rule, withdraws this class of works from the eye of
her young family, made an exception in favor of the author
of Waverley. The grave magistrate was as eager to obtain
them, as the youngest of his students; and we are told that
when a celebrated Chancellor, of our own country, whose
occupations had prevented him from indulging, at all, in
miscellaneous reading, retired from the bench at sixty, the
first employment of his leisure was to go through the whole
series. Foreign nations united with the English and Ameri-

cans in giving a hearty welcome to these charming productions. They were translated into all the languages of Europe;
printed simultaneously at Edinburgh, Paris, and Philadelphia; and circulated with rail-road and steamboat rapidity,
from the banks of the Mississippi to the utmost limits of
Siberia. What treasures of delight and improvement has not
their illustrious author bestowed upon the whole generation
of his contemporaries! That his labors amused the vacant,—
that they lightened the heavy hours of languor, despondency
and illness,—that they occupied most agreeably, the occasional leisure of the busy, was much,—was enough of itself,
to entitle him to the public esteem and gratitude; but these
were far from being the highest of his merits. By his fine
taste, and the healthy tone of his morality, he rescued
poetry and polite literature from the service of vice, and
enlisted them on the side of good principles and good feelings. It is one of the attendant evils, of the diffusion of
learning, that its most attractive and beautiful forms are too
often employed as the agents of corruption. Almost the whole
drama of modern times, and a very large proportion of the
poetry and romance, pander directly to the vicious propen-
sities of our nature. In works which were intended to inculcate better principles, they are often connected with a
morbid softness, or a repulsive severity of sentiment, which
destroys their attraction. Scott avoided all these defects.
His moral tone is pure, but not ascetic; cheerful, manly,
encouraging, without the least tendency to license. His
heroes are not like those of Byron, Bulwer, and I am sorry
to add, of our countryman Cooper, highwaymen and heads-
men; nor are they on the other hand, like the Grandisons
and Orvilles of the last generation, faultless models of un-
attainable perfection. Like Shakspeare, to whom, in the
character and compass of his talent, he approaches more
nearly than any other writer, he presents to us a true picture of the world as it is, not enveloped in perpetual gloom,
as in Rasselas, nor yet illuminated by a constant glow of
pastoral sunshine, but a mixed scene, where men and women
act their parts as in real life, according to their several
positions and characters, and succeed or fail as the good or

bad qualities happen to predominate; where vice may achieve at times an apparent or temporary triumph, but where the only permanent and lasting goods are reserved for consistent, active and persevering virtue. When we recollect how much more extensively these excellent principles and feelings have been circulated by these writings, than they possibly could have been in any other form, can we hesitate to pronounce their author a great public benefactor? Can we hesitate to award to him, the oaken garland of civic desert, as well as the greenest laurel of literary glory?

The mind of Scott was wholly poetical, and the talent for abstraction was either naturally deficient, or but little cultivated. Hence his attempts in History, which requires,—to be treated in a superior way,—a great familiarity with general political truths, were comparatively unsuccessful. They are, however, brilliant, though sometimes hasty and incorrect delineations of the surface of public events, and would have been sufficient of themselves, to make a reputation for a less conspicuous writer.

The conduct of Scott in real life, corresponded with the moral tone of his writings, and he formed in both respects, the happiest contrast with his great rival in poetry. With a much less liberal allowance in the outset of the gifts of fortune, he became, in fact, to a very great extent, what I have said Lord Byron might have been, the ruling spirit of the literary world of his day. Of comparatively humble origin, he rose to wealth and rank, while Byron, by imprudence and extravagance of every kind, had lost in a manner the elevated social position to which he was born. While the heir of Newstead, abandoning the splendid abode of his ancestors, was passing a cheerless and solitary life in the inns and on the highways of Europe, his competitor for glory was adorning at Abbotsford, the home of his own creation with patrician profusion, and more than patrician taste and elegance. There he held his court,—the virtual monarch of arts and letters,—and received the homage of crowds of admirers that flocked to his residence from all parts of Europe. If the later period of his life was clouded with pecuniary embarrassments, they were not the result of his own

imprudence, and they gave him an opportunity of displaying
in fuller relief than before, the sterling uprightness of his
moral character. In presenting him in favorable contrast
with his great contemporary, I mean not, Gentlemen, to
pass a too severe judgment on the errors of Byron. I view
them in sorrow, rather than in anger, and am willing to
forget them in the admiration I feel for his genius. But how
much happier it is, when the great man is also good! When
the glorious lamp of genius pours its golden light upon a
long career of unsullied honor and every public and private
virtue! Few and far between, like the visits of angels to our
sublunary sphere, are the examples of this delightful combination; and never, perhaps, in the tide of time, has one,
on all accounts more remarkable and brilliant, been displayed before the world, than that of Scott. His mouldering
relics repose in his family monument in Dryburgh Abbey,
a spot congenial to his taste and temper,

> 'Where the cold light's uncertain shower
> Streams through the ruined central tower'

upon his tomb-stone, and the ivy spreads above it a royal
mantle of perennial verdure. The worshippers of poetry and
romance will delight to visit the spot at the hour when the
poet himself was wont to repair to his favorite haunt in
Melrose Abbey. But the whole world, says Thucydides, is
the sepulchre of illustrious men. Wherever the incompara-
ble works of Scott have penetrated, the admirers of genius
and virtue, though separated by thousands of miles from the
place of his residence and burial, will need no other monument to keep his memory green in their souls.

Of the writers of the present day, who have devoted their
labors to the graver topics of philosophy and history, there
is none sufficiently prominent above the rest to be considered as the type and representative of the whole. Sir James
Mackintosh, had circumstances been a little more favorable
to the full development of his power, would probably have
taken the lead of all his contemporaries, and stood forth the
master of eloquence, by as general an acknowledgment, as
Lord Byron did in poetry. His defence of the French Revolu-

tion furnished, perhaps, the fairest promise of future excellence, which was ever given by the first production of a still,
in some degree, immature writer; and this promise would
have doubtless been fully realized, had he been able to complete the great works which he had projected on the History
of England, and the History of Philosophy. His engagements
in the active business of the world; his love of society, and
of conversation, in which he greatly excelled; perhaps in
part a constitutional indolence of temperament, and finally
his early death, prevented him from carrying fully into
effect these extensive plans, and left us only some imperfect
specimens of what the finished fabrics would have been. In
these, however, and in his fugitive essays, we discover all
the elements of the highest excellence; a rich and copious
vein of thought, and a glow of deep and warm feeling, both
controlled in their expression by the constant supervision of
a pure and correct taste. The moral coloring of his works
is excellent; his philosophy is cheerful and encouraging; his
views of human nature, and of the prospects of society,
without being visionary, are of a lofty, bold and animating
cast. He drew his principles from the source, whence only,
as a French writer has justly remarked, good principles
can be drawn, the inspiration of a pure and generous heart;
and his eloquent expositions of them, enriched as they are
with all the stores of ancient and modern learning, are
admirably fitted to awaken in all, and especially in young
minds, uncorrupted and generous like his own, the contempt
for sordid and selfish pursuits, and the noble enthusiasm for
truth and virtue, which are the origin of everything really
valuable in practical conduct. In reading his works the only
regret we feel is, that one so good and great should have
been prevented by any obstacle, from doing full justice to
his admirable talents, in the amount and value of his finished
productions.

But though we find among the prose writers who are immediately contemporary with us, no individual sufficiently
prominent to stand forth as the acknowledged representative
of the literary spirit of the time, by looking back a few
years only we meet with one, who commenced his career in

the middle of the last century, but whose best and highest
efforts belong to the period of which I am speaking; and with
which he is fully identified by the genius and spirit of his
writings. You will perceive, Gentlemen, that I allude to no
other than Burke, in written eloquence the greatest name of
ancient or modern times, and the noblest representative and
exemplar in that department of the taste and talent of the
present age. Mackintosh, as you know, though his first
effort was an attempt to refute the most powerful one of
Burke, obtained very soon after a more correct view of his
principles, and delighted through life to acknowledge him as
his master. One of the best critics and greatest men of the
last century, advises the young student, who is endeavoring
to form a good English style, to devote his days and nights
to the volumes of Addison. With all just deference to the
authority of Dr. Johnson, and without disparagement to the
real merit of the Spectator, I would rather hold up to the
ingenuous youth of our country, as at once the richest treas-
ury of just and deep thought, and the finest example of a
free, flowing, copious, and at the same time powerful,
pointed and manly style, the writings of Edmund Burke.
These, Gentlemen, I would venture to propose as the man-
uals of daily and nightly study in preference, though not to
the exclusion of Addison: not for the purpose of servilely
copying them in the mere forms of language which ought, in
every case, to be the spontaneous effusion of the full mind
and heart, but of imbibing, as far as may be, the noble
spirit that breathes through every part of them, and forms
the real source of their whole literary and philosophical
value. The style of Burke, considered as a form of the English language, is undoubtedly one of the most finished and
splendid that has ever been exhibited. It displays throughout
the happy and difficult union of all the richness and magnif-
icence that good taste admits, with a flowing ease of construction. In Burke, we see the manly movement of a well-
bred gentleman: in Johnson, an equally profound and vigorous
thinker, the measured march of a grenadier. We forgive the
great moralist his stiff and cumbrous phrases in consideration of the rich stores of thought and poetry, that are con-

cealed in them; but we admire in Burke, as in a fine antique
statue, the grace with which the large and flowing robe adapts
itself to the majestic dignity of his person. But with all his
literary excellence the peculiar merits of this great man are
perhaps the faculty of profound philosophical thought, and
the moral courage which led him to disregard personal inconvenience in the expression of his sentiments. Deep
thought is the informing soul, that everywhere sustains and
inspires the imposing grandeur of his eloquence. Even in
the Essay on the Sublime and Beautiful, the only work of
pure literature that he attempted, there is still the same
richness of thought, the same basis of divine philosophy,
to support the harmonious superstructure of the language.
And the moral courage which formed so remarkable a feature in his character is another point, which also recom-
mends it to attention as a model and a study. It was a remark
of the ancients that the first requisite for excellence in oratory, is to be a good man: a rule of criticism, which I fear
would settle pretty easily the claims of some pretenders to
distinction, even in our comparatively uncorrupted country.
But it seems to be a law of nature that the highest degree of
eloquence demands the union of the noblest qualities of
character, as well as intellect. To think is the highest exercise of intellect: to say what you think, the boldest effort of
moral courage: and both these things are required for a
really powerful orator or writer. Since eloquence without
thought is a mere parade of words, and no man can express
with spirit and vigor any thoughts but his own. The principal
of one of the Jesuits' Colleges, one day inquired of Rousseau by what art he had been able to write so well. 'I said
what I thought,' replied the somewhat unceremonious
Genevan,—conveying in these few words the severest censure of the system of the Jesuits, and the best explanation
of his own.

   Edmund Burke, therefore, Gentlemen, is the person who
may fairly, as far as written eloquence is concerned, be
regarded as the noblest representative of the literary spirit
of the age; the person whose writings may be safely recommended as the finest models of style as well as the richest

storehouse of the truest, deepest, soundest political wisdom.
To us, Gentlemen, as republicans, they are invaluable, because they present the theory of free government in a safe,
guarded and practicable form. The friends of freedom, who
had previously written upon the subject in ancient and in
modern times, disgusted with the abuses of arbitrary power
which came under their own observation, and having little
or no experience of the actual operation of better institutions, had generally failed in attempting to embody, in a
practicable shape, the spirit of liberty which gave so much
ardor and beauty to their eloquence. The Republic of Plato, —
the Utopias of More and Harrington, and various other essays of a similar character, though delightful to read, offer
little or nothing that can be turned to account, by the practical statesman. Montesquieu and Locke are in some, though
in a much less degree, obnoxious to the same objection.
Machiavelli, perhaps the most powerful genius that has
applied itself systematically to the exposition of political
science, in avoiding this error runs into the opposite one,
and offers as a theory of government, the unscrupulous employment of violence and fraud in their most revolting forms.
Rousseau, the most eminent political writer that preceded
Burke, and one of the most brilliant and popular of the class,
advanced his demoralizing principles, in a nervous, pointed
and fascinating style, which took deep hold of the public
mind of Europe, and had formed, in a manner, the prevailing opinion, when Burke commenced his political and literary
career. Warmly attached by character, education, and the
circumstances of his life to the cause of liberty, but in-
structed by a long course of practical experience, and in his
later days by the excesses of the French Revolution, Burke
avoids with equal care the errors of Machiavelli and of
Rousseau, combines with a firm and enthusiastic faith in
Liberty and Virtue, the strictest regard for Law and Order,
and the soundest good sense in the application of means, and
thus brings out an idea of government which is clear of all
solid objections. Nor is his wisdom the less valuable because
it is presented to us, not in the form of a systematic treatise, but in the course of a free and rather desultory discus-

sion of the great public events of the time, and especially
those of the French Revolution. It is to this very circumstance, on the contrary, that we owe in part the warmth and
vigor of the style which the author would not have displayed
to the same extent in a formal treatise. I think I may say
with safety, Gentlemen, that there is nothing in secular
learning superior to the magnificent productions of Burke:
nothing that approaches more nearly to the sublime effusions
of the Hebrew prophets which, like them, were called forth
by the grand political events of the times. The writings of
Burke remain for the instruction and warning as well as
admiration and delight, of all future ages, a perpetual commentary on the astonishing and fearful tragedy of the French
Revolution,—a splendid beacon on the breakers upon which
the political pilots of the continent in his day ran their whole
fleet aground. We may well say of him as the noble Coriola-
nus in Shakspeare prophesied of his infant son;

> —— 'Thou shalt be
> To shame invulnerable, and stick in the wars
> Like a great sea-mark, standing every flaw,
> And saving those that eye thee.'

He was answered, as you know, repeatedly answered,—
Mackintosh answered him,—Wakefield answered him,—Price
and Priestley answered him,—Paine answered him;—and,
Gentlemen, how did he reply? As the beacon to which I have
likened him, replies by fresh torrents of light to the waves
that beat and howl round its base, so the great champion of
well-ordered liberty replied to his obscure adversaries; he
replied to them by overwhelming them with new floods of
eloquence and wisdom; he replied to them by saving them,
whether they would or not, from the dangers into which their
delusions were hurrying themselves and their country. And,
Gentlemen, he did save them: to the influence of his writings
alone, it is to be attributed, that England was rescued from
the revolutionary maelstrom that swallowed up most of her
contemporaries. Their answers were forgotten,—his works
remain, and will be coeval with the literature of Christendom.

But, Gentlemen, the hour reminds me, that I have already trespassed too long on your attention. I have endeavored to present to you, a rapid sketch of the leading characteristics of the present period in English literature, and have held up to you some of its brightest ornaments, as examples, fitted to inspire a generous emulation, and to give it the safest and most honorable direction. What remains then, Gentlemen, but to invite you with friendly, but earnest entreaty, to persevere in the good work for which we are associated? Our country calls loudly upon us, who have had the fortune to enjoy the advantages afforded by her best institutions of education, not to prove untrue to the high trust that has been committed to us. When, in ancient times, a citizen of Lacedemon repaired to Delphi, to inquire in what country he should best consult his happiness by fixing his residence, what was the answer of the oracle? *ΣΠΑΡΤΑΝ ΕΛΑΧΕΣ ΤΑΥΤΑΝ ΚΟΣΜΕΙ.* Do your best for your own Sparta. If this was a just and noble sentiment in its application to Sparta, with what transport should it not be echoed by the citizens of this our favored country? Sparta, celebrated as she is in the annals of the world, occupied a little barren, rocky territory, on the shore of the Mediterranean, not larger than one of your counties. For us the field of honorable labor, of usefulness, of glory, stretches far and wide, over half the globe,—from ocean to ocean,—from the orange bowers of the tropics, to the icebergs of the arctic circle. The generations that preceded us,—our gallant and generous ancestors,—redeemed this vast domain from barbarian occupation and foreign thraldom. It was the boast of Sparta, till the time of Epaminondas, that her women never saw the smoke of an enemy's camp. It is our boast, Gentlemen, that our women have seen the smoke of an enemy's camp at every stage in our national existence, and have seen as often the fires that produced it extinguished in defeat. It was the fortune of our young Republic to be born and cradled in the midst of alarm and danger. Our fair country-women beheld, too often, the smoke of an enemy's camp, when for a hundred and fifty years in succession, the savage lurked with his firebrand and tomahawk, behind their cottages. They beheld it in the war of

independence, when a ruthless invader wrapt Falmouth in
flames, and left your mothers but two hours time to rescue
their persons from infamy, and you, their children, from
destruction. They beheld it, during the last war when the
blaze of your burning libraries enlightened the midnight
skies of Washington and Baltimore. Then, Gentlemen, they
saw it for the last time. Never more shall the sacred soil of
our country be polluted by the step of a foreign foe. Thanks
for this to the rivers of blood that have flowed in your defence, on every sea and every shore! Thanks for this to the
hecatombs of gallant and patriot victims who sacrificed
themselves for their country on a thousand battle-fields,
from Philip's war and Lovell's fight, to the closing scene at
New Orleans! By sea and by land; on the lakes and on the
ocean; with ships and with squadrons; in forts and in the
field; by day and by night, we have every where met the
enemy, and they were ours.

From the danger of foreign invasion, therefore, Gentlemen, your fathers, by their valor and virtue, have secured
you. They have done far more. On the vast and glorious
heritage, which their bravery redeemed from savage occupation and foreign thraldom, their wisdom erected the
temple of regulated Liberty. No brilliant castle in the air,
to be swept into nothing by the first political commotion; but
an edifice of solid structure and deeply laid foundations,
destined, we trust, to withstand for many centuries the
shocks of passion, and the mining inroads of time. Already
has it passed the dangerous ordeal of the first generation.
The billows of foreign invasion have spent themselves in
harmless fury at its base. Once and again, the earthquake
throes of faction have shaken it from beneath, but it fell not
for it was founded on a rock. Already have the nations begun
to look to it from abroad, as the grand model of political
architecture. 'Beautiful from situation,—the joy of the
whole earth,—is Mount Zion on the sides of the north.' Yes,
Gentlemen, to the wisdom of our fathers, we are indebted
for social institutions, which justly command the admiration
of the friends of freemen; which have been the exemplar of
all the Governments since instituted abroad and at home;

which our parent country, proud and justly so, as she always
has been, of her constitution and laws, is hastening to imi-
tate. Under their auspices the country has advanced in its
career of prosperity, with a rapidity before unexampled.
Cities, empires,—Lowell, Ohio, our whole western Paradise, justify the statement,—rise from the bosom of the
earth like exhalations. The wilderness blossoms like a rose.
The very rocks and sand-banks,—witness Nantucket,—witness all New England,—pour forth products, more rich and
abundant, than ever came from the gold and diamond mines
of Peru or Golconda. New forms of government, that had
hitherto been regarded as the visions of philosophic dream-
ers, too beautiful to be ever realized on this terrestrial
sphere, are going on in quiet operation, in full view of an
astonished and admiring world. As a political power, the
country has taken, at the outset of its course, its position
among the leading states of Christendom.

  Independence and liberty, the great political objects of all
communities, have thus been secured to us by our glorious
ancestors. In these respects, Gentlemen, we are only required to preserve and transmit unimpaired to our posterity,
the inheritance which our fathers bequeathed to us. To the
present, and to the following generations, is left the easier
task of enriching, with arts and letters, the proud fabric of
our national glory. Our Sparta, Gentlemen, is indeed a
noble one. Let us then do our best for it.

  Let me not, however, be understood to intimate, that the
pursuits of literature or the finer arts of life, have been,
at any period of our history, foreign to the people of this
country. The founders of the Colonies, the Winthrops, the
Smiths, the Raleighs, the Penns, the Oglethorpes, were
among the most accomplished scholars and elegant writers,
as well as the loftiest and purest spirits of their time. Their
successors have constantly sustained, in this respect, the
high standard established by the founders. Education and
Religion,—the two great cares of intellectual and civilized
men,—were always with them the foremost objects of attention. The principal statesmen of the Revolution, were persons of high literary cultivation; their public documents

were declared, by Lord Chatham, to be equal to the finest
specimens of Greek and Roman wisdom. In every generation,
our country has contributed its full proportion of eminent
writers. Need I mention names in proof of this? Recollect
your Edwards, erecting in this remote region, the standard
of Orthodoxy, for enlightened Protestant Europe. Recollect
your Franklin, instructing the philosophers of the elder
world in the deepest mysteries of science; her statesmen in
political economy, her writers in the forms of language. In
the present generation, your Irvings, your Coopers, your
Bryants, with their distinguished contemporaries, form,
perhaps, the brightest constellation that remains in the literary hemisphere, since the greater lights to which I have
pointed your attention already were eclipsed; while the
loftier heights of mathematical, moral and political science
are occupied with not inferior distinction, by your Bow-
ditches, your Adamses, your Channings, your Waylands
and your Websters.

In this respect then, Gentlemen, our fathers did their
part; our friends of the present generation are doing theirs,
and doing it well. But thus far the relative position of England and the United States has been such, that our proportional contribution to the common literature was naturally
a small one. England by her great superiority in wealth and
population, was of course the head-quarters of science and
learning. All this is rapidly changing. You are already
touching the point when your wealth and population will equal
those of England. The superior rapidity of your progress
will at no distant period give you the ascendancy. It will
then belong to your position to take the lead in arts and letters, as in policy, and to give the tone to the literature of
the language. Let it be your care and study not to show your-
selves unequal to this high calling, —to vindicate the honor
of the new world in this generous and friendly competition
with the old. You will perhaps be told that literary pursuits
will disqualify you for the active business of life. Heed not,
Gentlemen, the idle assertion. Reject it as a mere imagination, inconsistent with principle, unsupported by experience.
Point out to those who make it, the illustrious characters

who have reaped in every age the highest honors of studious
and active exertion. Show them Demosthenes forging by the
light of the midnight lamp, those thunderbolts of eloquence,
which

> 'Shook the arsenal and fulmined over Greece—
> To Macedon and Artaxerxes's throne.'

Ask them if Cicero would have been hailed with rapture as
the father of his country, if he had not been its pride and
pattern in philosophy and letters. Inquire whether Caesar,
or Frederic, or Bonaparte, or Wellington, or Washington,
fought the worse because they knew how to write their own
commentaries. Remind them of Franklin, tearing at the
same time the lightning from heaven, and the sceptre from
the hands of the oppressor. Do they say to you that study
will lead you to scepticism? Recall to their memory, the
venerable names of Bacon, Milton, Newton, and Locke.
Would they persuade you that devotion to learning will withdraw your steps from the paths of pleasure? Tell them they
are mistaken. Tell them that the only true pleasures are
those which result from the diligent exercise of all the faculties of body and mind, and heart, in pursuit of noble ends
by noble means. Repeat to them the ancient apologue of the
youthful Hercules in the pride of strength and beauty, giving
up his generous soul to the worship of virtue. Tell them
your choice is also made.—Tell them with the illustrious
Roman orator, you would rather be in the wrong with Plato,
than in the right with Epicurus. Tell them that a mother in
Sparta, would have rather seen her son brought home from
battle a corpse upon his shield, than dishonored by its loss.
Tell them that your mother is America, your battle the warfare of life, your shield the breastplate of Religion.

Notes

The text is based on the separate print of 1834, republished
here by permission of the Bowdoin College Library: "An Address to the Phi Beta Kappa Society of Bowdoin College, on the
Present State of Polite Learning in England and America, Delivered at Brunswick, Me., September 3, 1834, By Alexander
H. Everett. Boston: —Charles Bowen. MD CCC XXXIV."

    1. "We will go to Athens."
    2. [Original footnote:] The state of things in this respect
was then precisely the same as it had been among the Greeks
and Romans. The scarcity of books, and the accidents to
which they are, under these circumstances, liable, are cu-
riously illustrated by the fortune of the works of Aristotle,
which is related by Strabo, Plutarch and some of the other
Greek writers. This great man, whose opinions have exercised a stronger influence on the mind of Europe than those
of any other individual, was for a long time in danger of
being known to posterity only by tradition. It was his habit,
as it was that of the other Greek philosophers, to give instruction orally in his school, and he appears not to have
published his works during his life; having intended them
probably as memoranda to be used in his lectures. By his
will he bequeathed them to his pupil Theophrastus, the author
of the work on Characters, who succeeded him in the Lyce-
um, as some say, with express instructions not to make
them public, although this is denied by others. At all events,
it seems, that Theophrastus did not publish them, but after
keeping them during his life-time, bequeathed them by his
will, with his other books, to Neleus. Whether this person
was by character, wholly insensible to the advantages of the
diffusion of knowledge, whether he thought that philosophy,
like some other sorts of nectared sweets, would grow richer
by being stored in a cellar, or whether, as some say, he

only sought to keep his treasure out of the reach of a great
book-collector of the day, the king of Pergamus, who was
rather unscrupulous in his modes of acquisition, does not
distinctly appear; we only know that the disposition which he
made of his library, including the works of Aristotle, was to
place it in a subterranean vault, or cave, which he constructed
expressly for the purpose, and where it remained a hundred
and sixty years. At the end of that time one of his posterity,
who happened to explore the lower regions of his residence
for some other purpose, found the books, as may well be
supposed, in no very flourishing condition, half eaten up by
the worms, and nearly destroyed by the humidity of the
place. With a knowledge of these facts we can hardly wonder, that the text of Aristotle should be occasionally a little
obscure. The scanty remnant of these literary treasures,
which the worms and the moisture had spared, was now
brought forward and sold to a wealthy Athenian, named Apel-
licon, who kept them until the invasion of Greece by the
Romans, when they were carried by Sylla to Rome, and
placed in his own library. There they became known to
Tyrannion, a Greek scholar of eminence, who had been invited to Rome by Lucullus, and was on terms of intimacy with
Sylla's librarian. Tyrannion had a large library of his own;
and he succeeded, by what process is not known, in obtaining possession of the copy of Aristotle belonging to Sylla.
By him it was probably communicated to Cicero, with whom
Tyrannion was contemporary, and who bestows in his philosophical works repeated and splendid encomiums on the
Stagyrite; characterising his style as a river of flowing gold.
    Thus, was the only existing copy of the works of this great
master,—at all events, the one to which Europe was indebted
for the knowledge of his philosophy,—buried for nearly two
centuries in a damp cellar, and only rescued by an accident
before the moisture and the worms had completely destroyed
it. Even this was a better fortune than that which befel the
works of many other writers of the highest merit. Of Epicurus, Menander, and a whole list of philosophers, poets and
historians, we have nothing left but the names. In the general wreck of civilization that took place on the invasion of

the Roman Empire by the barbarians, most of the few books
then in existence perished. The still fewer that survived this
catastrophe were exposed to new danger from the mistaken
piety of the monks, who purposely destroyed them as profane
and dangerous; or valuing the material on which they were
written, more than the work itself, washed out the poet or
the philosopher for the purpose of obtaining a blank sheet of
parchment. The ingenuity of the scholars of the present day
has hit upon a process by which the writing thus erased may
be restored, and their laborious and persevering researches
have already been rewarded by the discovery of several
valuable fragments of ancient literature, including a considerable portion of the lost treatise of Cicero on Government.

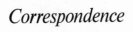

Correspondence

Correspondence

To Lucy Everett

Mrs. Lucy Everett.   Boston. USA.

St. Petersburgh.   Dec. 31. 1809

I can hardly express to you, my dearest mother, how much I was delighted with receiving your affectionate letter dated September 13th, which arrived about ten days ago. It was very short, which I should have been tempted to be very sorry for, if not half angry, were it not that the little previous notice you had of the opportunity, was a reason perfectly sufficient to account for this circumstance. If you could but form an idea of half the delight it gave me to receive those letters, I know you would improve a great many opportunities that I fear you neglect. After receiving the packet I sat eight or ten minutes looking at it, and anticipating the delight I should have in reading the letters and for as much as half an hour afterwards I could not help shedding tears for mere satisfaction. I dare say you feel happy at receiving my letters, now I am so far from home, but it seems to me that it cannot be a matter of half so much interest to you provided you know from time to time that I am well, as it is for me, who am away from all my family and acquaintance. I am delighted with this opportunity of sending home and intend to write a great many letters: it is by a courier in the service of the Emperour, going off to Paris with dispatches for Count

Lahlen, the Russian Minister for America. Of course the letters will go perfectly safe. Though I do not grudge any trouble for the sake of conveying letters to you, and improve every opportunity however slight in the hopes that you will do the same, yet I must confess, there is more comfort in writing letters and long ones, where one is pretty sure they will go safe.

Your letters were not half particular enough: you must allow me to chide you for it my dear mother, though I feel no anger in my heart. You only tell me that every thing goes on pretty much as usual: and if I had been on a weeks excursion to Dorchester, to Exeter or to Ludbury and just returned home, that would be a satisfactory account, but, alas! here I am four thousand five hundred miles from home and you only tell me, that every thing goes on pretty much as usual. I want to be informed of every little circumstance that has taken place in the family and neighborhood, of every thing, however small in appearance relating to any of my acquaintance, of all the parties and balls, and sleigh rides that take place. I wanted very much to know whether Bigelow was still in Boston, as he talked of going on to Philadelphia to spend the winter, whether Isaac Hurd, or Frank Parkman or Foster Coffin had sailed for England as they all talked of it: whether J. Cogswell had returned from his last voyage: whether Ebenezer has opened his office yet, whether Charles is in Boston and a thousand &&'s. So you see how natural it is after enjoying a great pleasure to complain that it is not great enough. But one thing I cannot excuse: neither you, nor any of the family that wrote, said one word about dear little Enoch. Even Sally, in enumerating what schools she and Thomas and John go to forgot to mention him. To be sure I cannot help concluding that he is well but when one is away from home one wants something particular. Not one word about Uncle Huse and his family. Complaining again: how I [sic] ungrateful I am. You will think however what it is to be so far over the hills and waves and forgive me.

No doubt you want to hear something about me. I have been very fortunate as to my health. The climate has affected almost all the Americans here as it generally does all

strangers very severely, but I have not had a days sickness
with it. Every body tells me that I have gained a great deal
of flesh and that I look much better than I did in Boston and
on the passage—as the Apostle says "I partly believe it."
You recollect no doubt that I had lost some flesh before leaving America and was a little thinner than usual. The cold of
this climate is by no means terrible. Yesterday was the
coldest day we have yet had. It was about fifteen or twenty
degrees on the thermometer below the coldest weather that
we have in Boston. Yet on that day I was out all the morning,
sliding on the Ice-Hills with a party. This is a particular
diversion, practiced by the Russians of all ranks[,] classes,
ages and sexes and is in substance the same with the ceremony practiced by the American youth under the name of
"sliding downhill." On that day the cold was 12 degrees below 0 on Farenheits thermometer but in general it has not
been far from freezing point. It is the custom here to take a
great many precautions against the cold. I wear flannel next
to my body all over: When I go out I have a great coat for
walking, lined with fur, with a high cape that comes up
round the ears and almost covers the face: for riding it is
usual to have another coat or as they call it a <u>shoob</u> which is
a loose great coat, wadded all over and quilted, or lined
with fur. Most people prefer the first way, for one of these
shoobs lined and trimmed with fine fur costs from six to
eight hundred dollars. I have also large boots lined with
flannel to draw on over shoes and stockings or over other
boots: —Fur-caps are considerably worn: —The common people wear universally a sheep skin dressed with all the wool
on and turned inwards: they make a loose coat out of it, tied
with a belt round the waist and on their heads a thick cap
lined with wool. But they are so hardy that they often leave
their sheepskin coats and all their other garments open on
the neck and bare them to the cold.

Mrs. Adams and Miss Johnson, to wear when they ride
out, (for they never think of walking at this season) have
immense silk-cloaks lined with fur, weighing more than I
should dare to say with velvet boots lined with wool. They
have both of them suffered amazingly from ill health since

they have [word omitted]: always taking cold at the least ex-
posure and frequently confined to their chambers with it for
several days. Charles their little boy, who was two years
old on the passage, has been remarkably well. He used to be
very amusing on the passage except that his mother indulged
him a little too much. He is a fine boy however. His father
makes him speak French and English and he speaks one
nearly as well as the other. He is very fond of me.

At present, which is now seven or eight weeks since our
arrival, we are still at a hotel which is at least but an unsettled way of life. The difficulty of obtaining a house, convenient and suitable in every respect has made this unavoidable: But Mr. Adams has at least succeeded in engaging
one, which we are to enter upon soon and in my next letter
I shall probably be able to give you an account of my local
situation. So high are rents here, that he is obliged to pay
for this house ready furnished indeed, four thousand rubles,
which is at present equal to 1200 or 1500 dollars. Other
expenses are also very high here.

As to my manner of spending my time here. I live rather
a pleasant life, see a good deal of company, attend a good
many balls and affairs of that kind, and in these respects
have only to regret that I am absent from so many friends in
America. Petersburgh is a very gay place in the winter
season and it is expected of foreigners here to go into society very much. I have been so little time here that I have not
of course contracted any very intimate acquaintances but in
some future letters I may possibly amuse you with remarks
on a few characters here well worth observation and as I
become more familiar here and more acquainted with the
city I shall perhaps trouble you sometimes with a description
of the churches, palaces and other publick buildings. At
present, though I have not said half that I want to, I must
stop. In addition to this, you will see several other letters
to others of the family and I dare say will be quite tired with
them all, but I can assure that nothwithstanding all my prolixity and loquacity I am still your most affectionate and
devoted Son:

[Massachusetts Historical Society]

To Edward Everett

St. Petersburgh.   Jany. 1. 1810

I was charmed with your letter, my dear Edward, excepting that it was not half long enough. Instead of giving me at least half a dozen pages, filled with interesting particulars about College, Boston, Politicks or any thing you allowed me, only two which indeed contained for the quantity as much interest as one often finds in two pages. I was considerably surprised at the election of Mr. McKean as successor to Mr. Adams in the Professorship of Oratory. His talents perhaps are equal to the place but it will require with him an entirely new line of study to qualify him to fill it. His passion has always been the Mathematicks and if I may judge from some personal acquaintance with him and observation on his writings he is not much given to the genus rhetoricum. Indeed I have heard him say as much. His comfort is however that as far as reading will give it him, the science lies in the compass of a literature not very extensive. His natural or confirmed taste he will probably find it difficult to alter.

I was not much surprised at the Assignment of the parts in my Class at Commencement, though three years ago I should have stared a little had it been said that Thomas would perform the English Oration and Charles Burroughs the Latin and they would have wondered as much. —I hear no news in any of your letters of my friend Ticknor or Parkman, concerning whom I am quite anxious. Pray mention every body and every thing when you write again and do not be frightened at the length of the letter[;] the longer it is the better I shall find it.

You wish me to make large extracts from my journal particularly respecting the voyage. This request has no doubt been perfectly satisfied by letters received long before this will be. I can inform you, however, that if ever you take a

long sea-voyage expecting variety or amusement you will be
egregiously disappointed. The six weeks that intervened
from the time we left Boston till we reached Christiania and
again the fortnight from Elsinore to Copenhagen—had their
pleasures to be sure as they passed, but I seldom past any
time more irksome or disagreeable. Every thing like quiet
is a stranger to a ship. It is not that one is sick, that one
cannot sleep sound or feed well but the tossing and rolling of
the ship tears up all comfort by the roots. If it rains it is
dark and damp below and wet & stormy above. If it blows you
can not think of sitting or even sleeping in peace: if it does
not blow, God in his mercy defend us from a calm. Thirteen
days were we loitering at the distance of about three hundred
miles from Fair Isle and the breath of heaven never once
blowed upon us. Heaven bless me! what frowns of the captain! what gloom of the crew, what despondency in the cabin.

The sea is not without its <u>agremens</u>[1] and I have certainly
shown you its worst side but very little exaggerated. The
prospects from time to time are beautiful. The view of the
clear blue sky, sprinkled with stars on a fine moonlight
evening, with a long line of light streaming from the heavens
across the sea is enchanting. —Nothing is more inspiriting
and lively than a fine morning, the sun just risen clear and
the ship scudding handsomely before a brisk clear north-
wester. The motion of the ship as it plunges down and rises
over the waves that are then high gives the idea of activity.
The waves are a clear blue garnished with white foam as
each breaks and disappears and often on such a morning
another ship seen in the distance gives a pleasant variety.

The most enchanting prospect I ever saw was that when we
passed the Island of Hogland about sixty miles from Cron-
stadt. I think I have mentioned it before in one of my letters
but it will bear repetition. After a fine clear morning we
came in sight of Hogland and came up within about twelve
miles of it at sunset. The moon was at full. The sun went
down on one side and left the sky variegated with most beautiful colours, on the other the moon rose over the island
without a cloud and almost eclipsed the two lights that glim-
mered on two hills below. The passage north is dangerous:

we came up with it at midnight, the pilot takes his station
amidship and calls out every few minutes to the Helmsman
"Steady, so[.]" "Steady" steers the helmsman: in a few minutes the strait was passed and the lights began to retire. The
next week an American ship was wrecked at this very passage.

We saw no Dolphins on the passage: they are found in
more southern Latitudes. Large sculls [schools] of porpoises
played round the ship from time to time and now and then we
saw a great whale "Wallowing unwieldy enormous in his gait."

I have the more willingly dwelt thus long on our voyage because I really have not been long enough in Petersburgh to
give any very interesting description of its locale or inhabitants. At the same time in confining myself to the marine
part I have omitted the most interesting occurrences of the
passage, our adventures at Christiania in Norway and at
Copenhagen. The former, which had all the romantick features of the days of chivalry were described I think in a letter to Hale in part.

In a literary point of view Petersburgh is at present completely beneath notice: —It is even less distinguished for its
men of genius and science than it was in the days of Catherine. —In the acquisition of languages, the Russians of respectable birth are indeed superior to perhaps any other
nation in the world. I attribute it to the great number of foreigners residing here: but it is a literal fact that you
scarcely meet a Russian of high standing that does not speak
two or three and even four or five foreign languages. French
is spoken by them universally and with great purity: German
is almost as common: English and Italian are more rare but
by no means infrequent.

This is the fourth letter that I have written home for this
conveyance and I will stop for very shame. I know you will
never forget to write to me and be very particular and diffuse
or even prolix. You need not put my name on the outside, but
direct to me and then put on the cover directed to the address
of Mr. Adams. The outside should be written very plain: for
where the language is not known, there is great danger of
miscarriage. If you have opportunities, be so kind as to

send files of the latest newspapers and in some of the
spring-ships, if there is a safe conveyance, I should like to
have you send me ten, or twenty volumes of the latest English works, if there are so many worth seeing, for all intercourse is entirely stopt here. I shall improve the opportunity
of one ship's return to send out two or three little trinkets
if I can find any thing curious.

I was delighted with Sarah's letter[2] and shall take the
first opportunity to give her a long answer in French, which
I hope Lucy and she have not forgotten. I shall be very much
disappointed if I do not find them perfect at my return. When
you write, tell me whether Mama has left Boston and when
it is intended. I long to see Thomas, and John, and Enoch:
they will be grown almost double before I see them: —

Farewell[.]   Your affectionate brother: —

P.S. A happy new year to you: may it be pleasant, prosperous and profitable: marked with improvement and filled with
pleasure: —The same to Mama and brothers & sisters: —

Memorandum of books to be sent out in the Spring (Included in the above) N.B. You will be very careful to put these
and whatever else you send out in the spring, into the same
ship, by which Mr. Gray sends out to Francis and then they
will be safe.

Adams's Lectures.
· Elliott's Biographical Dictionary (The Dr. will give me
      one, if you ask him.)
   Several new English volumes if there should any come
      out worth sending.

Of my own books: —

Spanish Grammar & Dictionary.
Persian Grammar.
Port Royal Greek & Latin Grammar.
Marmion.

[Massachusetts Historical Society]

To Andrews Norton

Boston.   26. Feb. 1814

Mr. Norton.

Dear Sir—In thinking over the matters discussed at our
meeting on Thursday, it occurred to me that some alterations in the plan then proposed and accepted would be likely
to promote the success of the Repository:[3] and I take the
liberty of communicating them to you for your consideration.
Every body knows the <u>vis inertiae</u>[4] inherent in all large
bodies and I fear very much that a publishing committee to
be chosen in rotation would not bring to the execution of
their duty the ardor, & perseverance so requisite to the conduct of a work of this kind. —Now my plan is this: that you,
who are the father of the work and best qualified by ability,
direction of studies, leisure and probably the paternal interest you must feel in keeping it up, to take the direction of it,
should be permanent and perpetual Editor. —The society of
Gentlemen might have their quarterly meeting and be holden
to contribute as largely as they would be on the present arrangement. —Thus the work would derive every possible
advantage that could be received from the present plan &
would secure in addition that interest, attention and zeal
which I humbly conceive can only be effected by Editorial
Unity.

There is I think but one objection to this, which to be sure
is a very strong one—that one person cannot be expected to
give up his time to [word omitted] without any consideration.
It might however be worth considering that the labor would
not be very much increased and that under such a system
the work might probably produce a decent profit. —

Under such an arrangement it would be advisable to take
all proper measures to make the work popular and it would

be worth thinking of, whether any thing could be done by
adopting the idea suggested by Dr. Bigelow at the meeting
and altering the present arrangement of the matter so far as
to let the articles in the different departments succeed each
other indiscriminately and whether the objection which you
then made & which is certainly possible might not be allevi-
ated by attention to the arrangement of individual pieces.

You will excuse my freedom in suggesting these ideas. I
feel much interested in the work and extremely anxious that
it should proceed. Whatever plan may be adopted, my feeble
exertions shall be given to it, with as much cordiality, I
venture to say, as is felt by every member of the society:
but I candidly confess that I cannot entertain very sanguine
expectations of the success of the plan adopted last Thursday. It is an excellent system but it wants a sail. —I should
be much obliged to you, if you would take these ideas into
consideration & shall be really happy if any suggestion of
mine has an influence in introducing what I think so great an
improvement in the system.

Respectfully your friend & humble serv.

A. H. Everett

[Harvard University Library]

To George Ticknor

Brussels. Jany. 25. 1819

My dear George.

When I was making up the debtor and creditor account of
our correspondence at the time I wrote you last, I forgot one
letter which you must have written me, though I never received it. I have been informed by Edward that you sent me

from Göttingen an account of the German Tugendbund,[5] which
in consequence I suppose of my vagabond life never came to
hand. If you have a copy of that letter I should be greatly
obliged to you to send it me—If not perhaps you can refer me
from memory to the most accurate and copious sources of
information upon the subject. In this place I can get no German books whatever and shall be obliged to send particularly
for every thing I want. —Pray let me know if you have any
intelligence of Bancroft who went out to Gottingen last summer to study. They have had a battle I see since between the
students and the Military and I have some fears that he was
among the killed. I hope not, as I want a correspondent in
Germany.

Yours ever.

AHE.

[Dartmouth College Library]

To John Pickering[6]

The Hague   Dec. 17. 1821

Dear Sir.

I received a few days since with much pleasure your very
friendly letter of the 7th of Sept. accompanied by two copies
of your memoir on the Indian languages and a copy of your
translation of Wyttenbachs method of instruction. I beg you
to accept my thanks for your obliging present of two of these
papers; and am truly sensible of this proof of your remembrance. I have transmitted to Professor Boke the memoir
intended for him and also the translation of Wyttenbach. This
I have no doubt will interest him, as well from his acquaintance with the distinguished author, as from the civil mention

of himself which you have introduced in a note. I do not learn
that any biography of Wyttenbach has yet appeared. His own
life of Ruhnken, which you have probably seen is a charming
work, and one of the finest specimens of modern Latin to be
met with. I doubt whether his successor, though a good
scholar and an industrious man, will ever pay so handsome
a tribute as this to his masters memory. If any thing should
be published upon this subject, I shall take the liberty of
sending it to you.

Although I can take no positive interest in the study of the
aboriginal dialects of our country, as you justly suppose, as
well from the want of any acquaintance with the subject as of
means to investigate it here, I still think it a branch of
learning of very considerable importance; and rejoice to find
that you have been able to devote so much time and attention
to it and with such good effect. These languages ought certainly to be explored sufficiently at least to ascertain whether they throw any light upon the early periods of history and
whether any affinity can be traced between them and the
languages of the old world. This question once settled, the
pursuit would perhaps in other respects be unprofitable. But
this is itself a point of great consequence; and considering the
extraordinary results of a similar [word omitted] that have
been obtained by the study of the eastern languages, we have
no reason to despair of success in our own quarter. The intimate affinity between the Sanscrit and Teutonic tongues,
which has lately been discovered in Germany, and which I
think is noticed in your memoir, is perhaps the most curious
philological fact, that has ever been brought to light and
promises to illustrate very strongly the ancient history of
Europe and the world. I had read your paper in the Memoirs
of the academy, before I had the pleasure of receiving it
from you. The plan you recommend for writing these languages, appears to be extremely judicious, and well fitted
to effect the objects you have in view.

I admire the enthusiasm, which appears in the introduc-
tory remarks to your translation of Wyttenbach on the subject of education. There is room enough for improvement in
most of our institutions: and if an increased attention to

Latin and Greek in schools and colleges is really as desirable as you suppose it to be, I sincerely wish that your efforts and those of your friends in the vicinity of Boston to encourage this branch of study may meet with all possible success. I must frankly confess however that I doubt very much the expediency of insisting upon these studies as a part of general education in our country. Classical literature will always constitute one of the most elegant and important objects of philosophical research, as well for the beauty and perfection of its forms, as for the importance in every point of view of the facts with which it makes us acquainted: and it is much to be wished that our higher institutions should possess in libraries and professorships the necessary aids for pursuing these studies. I hope we shall never want a sufficient number of finished classical scholars, who have appropriated to themselves the whole stock of European learning connected with the subject and are able to sit in judgment upon the philosophical conclusions to which European scholars have been led by these researches, and if necessary to revise and correct them. This is a point of improvement which in our country we have not yet fairly reached: and until we have, though politically independent of Europe, we are intellectually in the situation of colonies. On this point there can be no difference of opinion. But the acknowledged importance of classical studies as a branch of general learning does not clearly prove their value as the basis of popular instruction: for the same argument might be used to shew that every schoolboy should be taught Arabic and Sanscrit, or the Indian dialects, to which you justly attach so much importance, but which you would never think of introducing into common schools. Whether there are still any good reasons of a different kind why the Greek and Latin languages should be made the principal object of attention with all our young men for several years of their lives, is a larger inquiry, into which you have probably entered much more fully and deeply than I have: and your conclusion seems to have been in the affirmative. I take the liberty of adding a few remarks which tend a different way, more from a wish of communicating with you upon an interesting subject, than from any hope of presenting you with new or valuable thoughts.

The great argument in favor of making the study of the classics the basis of general education is authority and experience. This method has been regularly pursued in every part of modern Europe during the period when Europe has been gradually acquiring an undoubted intellectual superiority over the rest of the world. The presumption therefore would seem to be in favor of the system of education, which has produced such results. But this argument though decisive in itself, appears to me when properly considered, to weigh at present against the classical system of education rather than in favor of it: for the same causes, which formerly made it convenient that all persons intended for liberal pursuits should study Latin (and Greek as subsidiary to it) now operate in a different direction: and make it convenient for all such persons to study the vernacular tongues of their respective countries. Formerly all professional and political business was transacted in the Latin language; which was also employed by the learned throughout Europe in writing and conversation. At that time it was not a matter of expediency but of absolute necessity that every well educated man should read, write and speak Latin with ease and elegance. This substantial reason, and not any fancied advantage in the way of mental discipline to be derived from the study, I take to have been the moving cause why the classical tongues were made the basis of education. The great intellectual progress of the European nations, as far as it is connected with methods of education, proves therefore the great advantage of studying thoroughly in youth the language which is afterwards to be employed in the business of life. When, therefore the state of society underwent a complete change in this particular, as it has done within the last two or three centuries, and when the Latin language was everywhere superseded by the vernacular tongues for all purposes of business, literature and conversation, the argument of experience and success immediately began to weigh in favor of giving these languages a preference over the Latin, as the basis of education. The study of Latin and Greek is however still kept up to a great extent in Europe by the force of habit: but there is hardly a doubt that it will ultimately fall into disuse with the state of society which led to it, and will only be preserved as a branch of curious learning. With us the state of society in question never existed, and the system of education, naturally resulting from it, of course never prevailed in any considerable degree. The attempt to establish it now must I think be unsuccessful and likely as far as it succeeds to do more harm than good as well from the inutility of the Latin and Greek languages in the business of life, as from the false direction given to the students mind by his attention to them, and the consequent neglect of other more important studies.

In fact of what utility is a knowledge of these languages to the mass of professional men: for whose advantage the general system of liberal education is intended? Our clergymen no longer write or preach in Latin: our lawyers neither argue nor plead in it: nor do our physicians speak it at their consultations. The books that are of use in all the professions are now written in the modern languages and the ancient writers have long been translated. The little knowledge of Latin and Greek necessary or convenient in the professions in consequence of the remains of former usages which still hang about them: might be acquired as a part of professional learning in a few weeks or months. These languages have therefore ceased to be of any direct utility. And although I have sometimes heard of certain indirect advantages in the way of mental discipline or improvement in taste, which are supposed to arise from the study of them, I confess that most of the remarks I have met with to this effect have appeared to me exceedingly vague and visionary. For with regard to taste—we know that this is acquired by familiarity with the best models of a language in its written and spoken forms. Of what use then for this purpose is the assiduous study of another and a different language? Persons who have already thoroughly studied the British classics in prose and verse and derived all the advantage from them in point of taste which they are capable of bestowing, may give themselves doubtless some farther improvement and perfection by exploring in a subsidiary way the sources of the language in the classical and kindred modern dialects. But to pursue the latter studies as principal and not as subsidiary ones for this purpose: and to do it, as is done both in England and America, to the neglect of the native models, is in my opinion an error little short of absurdity.

It is sometimes said that in point of fact we find no good English writers who have not made a study of the Greek and Latin languages: and this is thought to prove that we must necessarily learn Greek and Latin in order to write good English. It is true in general, though not universally, that our good vernacular writers have had some tincture of ancient learning: which indeed they could not well avoid considering the usual course of education. But it would be quite unsafe to trace their excellence to this source: and it is frequently found that of two or three writers who naturally come into comparison with each other, the merit is in the inverse ratio of their attainments in ancient learning—as in the case of Shakespeare and Ben Jonson. Supposing however, what is very probable, that an author by profession would derive great benefit from studying the best ancient writers— still we are to recollect that the object of general education is not to form professional authors but accomplished citizens—and in a literary point of view—to enable the student to use his own language with correctness and elegance—for which purpose it is obvious that the most direct and effectual method is to study his own language. If in after life he is led to enter upon the profession of authorship he will then pursue the additional studies that are proper to fit him for it.

With regard to the great advantage supposed to accrue from attending to the ancient languages in the way of intellectual discipline, I confess myself unable to make out very clearly the nature of them; and as far as I understand what is intended, to perceive their reality. "We know not," says a writer in the October number of the N. A. Review, "that there is any thing which in the discipline of the mind can supply the place of the study of the Latin and Greek. We know of no means to be compared with this for the purpose of communicating the power of quick and delicate discrim-

ination, and of imparting clear perceptions of the difference
of words and things." Now in this, as in most other expressions of the same opinion, there is a vagueness in the language which makes it difficult to understand precisely what
is meant. The talent of discriminating with quickness and
delicacy among the words and phrases of our own language,
so as to judge instantaneously and instinctively what are
correct and incorrect, elegant and inelegant—is equivalent
to good taste in language: and is acquired, as I observed
before, not by studying foreign languages but by the assiduous perusal of the good English writers in prose and verse.
What is meant by obtaining clear perceptions of the difference of words and things is rather doubtful. The writer may
perhaps intend that it is a very useful thing to investigate the
nice shades of meaning under which the same word presents
itself in different languages; we may find for example by
studying foreign languages that <u>virtue</u> with the Romans meant
<u>courage</u>, while with the French and English it means <u>good
morals</u>; and with the Italians a taste for the fine arts. But
these and other such points are matters of curious philological and philosophical research and have little to do with the
common uses of language in the ordinary business of life.
The best mental discipline is, in general, that which supposes the greatest intellectual activity: and this is not required
for the acquisition of foreign languages. Composition in
prose and verse, and the discussion, whether in writing or
extempore discourse, of controverted questions in the different departments of knowledge, are at once more active
intellectual exercises than the study of Latin and Greek and
a better discipline for the faculty of just and ready discrim-
ination in the employment of words and ideas.

   This consideration leads me to notice another objection to
the present system of classical studies, still stronger perhaps than their positive inutility—which is the false direction
they give to the whole course of education and the neglect
they occasion of pursuits that are really important and necessary. The two great objects in the literary part of education are to supply the fund of knowledge wanted for entering
upon the business of life and to form the intellectual habits

and tastes which are most suitable for turning it to account.
Of these two objects, both of which are indispensable in a
finished education, the formation of tastes and habits is still
more essential than the acquisition of positive knowledge;
because a deficiency in the latter respect may be supplied to
a certain extent with comparative ease at any point in life,
while in the former it is altogether irremediable. Of these
habits the most important are those of writing and speaking
the English language with facility, correctness and elegance.
These are the principal literary qualifications, which are
wanted for the transactions of all sorts of professional and
public business, for social intercourse, and even for conducting scientific and literary investigations with reputation
and success. Now these objects are so little attended to in
our schools and colleges that they may be considered as
wholly over looked. No attempt is made to initiate the student into the beauties of English literature—which ought to
be the first step in the progress of forming his taste and
preparing him for the exercises of composition and declamation. No attempt is made to form the habit of extempore
speaking in public—so necessary in some of the professions,
so agreeable and convenient in all the walks of life, and so
useful as a mere intellectual exercise. And even English
composition though nominally an object of attention, is so
little pressed, that it is quite impossible for the student to
acquire the proper tastes and habits, which demand continual practice for a length of time. I remember that during the
four years I passed at Cambridge I was called upon, in
themes and forensics, for about a dozen pieces of composition. I noticed at that time the want of attention on the part
of the institution to composition and declamation was so obvious, that the students, though not generally over fond of
imposing upon themselves any labour which they could avoid
had formed voluntary associations for improvement in these
arts.

The effect of this inattention to our own language is, as
might be expected, a pretty general ignorance of its first
principles even among persons of liberal education. Good
books, as is well known, we have none, not so much for this

as for some other reasons: but take up a printed paper of any
description and from any quarter—a President's message—
a Governor's speech—a diplomatic despatch—a sermon—a
report in Congress or a state legislature—or any of the thousand proclamations and publications that are continually
coming out, and it shall go hard but you find if not absolute
bad grammar, which however is far from being out of the
question, barbarous and inelegant constructions and unauthorized words in abundance. Your townsman, Dr. Bently,
being now no more, may be mentioned without offence as an
example of a man of fine genius and most extensive knowledge, who from defective education could not write an intel-
ligible sentence in his own language. There are some excellent remarks upon this point in the N. A. Review No. 1 New
Se. which I cannot refuse myself the pleasure of quoting.
"Good plain English grammar—the true old fashioned discipline of noun and verb—is after all the great crux of our
draughters of reports, our makers of speeches, and our
writers of despatches. Eloquence, stile, effect, these are
easy matters: and you cannot take up a report on the Semi-
nole war, or a statement of the affairs of the Bank, but you
find it as flowery as a May morning. But what the orators
have gained among us, the grammarians have lost: and a
rank flourishing solecism has shot up under many of the
most promising plants in our oratorical gardens. So far has
this run, that some charitable persons have cast about for a
remedy. And as it is a practice in some foreign universities
for the ingenuous youth, before taking their degree, to employ a veteran under the name of a <u>grinder</u>, to teach them a
few phrases of customary Latin, so these benevolent persons
have recommended that our eloquent men of the description
alluded to should, before appearing in public, employ some
competent person to grind a little English into them." As the
same defective system prevails in England, so the same result is observable there to nearly as great an extent: and it
is rare to find a composition of a public or professional
man; which is not deformed by some barbarous and ungram-
matical passages. To cite a single instance: the public despatches of Lord Londonderry—are among the most inelegant

compositions to be met with any where. Nay—the literary
champion of the Radicals has had the triumph of criticising
with success the speeches from the throne.

The want of a proper training in the art of public speaking
is, if possible, still more perceptible in the wretched appearance generally made by the students of our colleges at
their exhibitions, in the almost universal defect of grace and
power in the manner of our professional and political orators, and I may add, in the absence of fluency and eloquence
in common conversation, which forms so unpleasant a distinction between the educated men of England and the United
States and those of the Continent of Europe. More than this,
the prospects of young men educated for the pulpit and the
bar, are often wholly blasted, by the effects of this unfortunate system. After passing ten or twelve years in laborious
and expensive preparatory studies, they finally come to their
professions without having even attempted to form the habit
of public speaking, or having been reminded by any of their
instructors of its necessity. At their first trials under such
circumstances they almost necessarily acquit themselves
very indifferently. The indulgent public attributes their ill
success to a want of talent or attention. Their reputation is
blighted in the bud: they become dispirited and indolent; and
instead of rising to the heights of their professions and turning their large advances of time and money to good account,
they are too happy to find refuge from absolute want in some
obscure nook of the social fabric—some village school—or
clerkship—and toil hardly through life for a painful and
scanty subsistence.

How then is this state of things to be improved? Not merely by sending the whole rising generation upon voyages of
discovery in the literature of distant nations and past ages—
not by training them in Greek, Latin and Hebrew, or even in
French, Spanish, Italian and German—studies which are all
good in their way and for those who have time and inclination
to attend to them but which are not the proper basis for a
system of general education. The mass of students, whose
principal object is to write and speak English, must leave
all these fine foreign luxuries of literature and condescend

to learn the thing they want to know, that is, English. And in
order that this may be done thoroughly it is necessary that
English should be made the basis of their instruction and the
principal object of attention. Instead therefore of being particularly anxious that our boys may one day vie in their
knowledge of Latin with the sons of Westminster and Eton,
I shall be for myself quite satisfied, if the time ever comes
when our young men, upon leaving college, shall be familiar
with our own literature and be able to speak and write English with ease[,] correctness and elegance. The remark of
the old Roman lawyer applies here I think with still more
force than in the connexion in which he used it—Turpe est
patrici et nobili et causas oranti linguam in qua versarentur
ignorare.[7]

Without entering into the details of a system of education,
for which our own language and literature should serve as a
basis, it is easy to see what would be its general course.
After learning to read and write, the student should begin to
peruse the good English authors in prose and verse commencing with the easiest and such as are best suited to his
comprehension and going on in order through the whole list.
His reading should be directed by his instructors and his
judgment aided by their critical observations and explana-
tions. By this course of reading his literary taste would be
formed. As soon as his faculties admitted of it he should
begin to compose in prose and verse, and to declaim extempore: & should do this, not three or four times a year, as
we did at Cambridge, but three or four times a week or
every day. These exercises, with the perusal and reperusal
of all the books that form the circle of elegant English literature should make up the whole course of discipline in the
literary part of education. It is sometimes said that if boys
are not taught Latin and Greek, there will be nothing to occupy their time. Those who hold this opinion forget that the
object of education is to form habits and tastes as well as to
supply facts. Facts are soon learned: languages are easily
acquired: but the formation of habits and tastes demands in
the happiest subjects a long course of discipline and exercise: and the part of life that can be given up to education is

not too much for this purpose. I am bold to say that a student who should commence this course of exercises at eight
or ten years old and continue it under judicious direction till
the age of one and twenty would afterwards find that every
moment of time thus occupied had been employed to the best
advantage. These exercises would however engage only a
part of his attention at any one period, because they relate
only to the literary part of education. The acquisition of the
necessary stock of positive knowledge, professional and
general, must be carefully attended to in connexion with
them. Health, morals and manners must also be provided
for in this as in every other system: and in these respects
as in most others our existing establishments would admit of
great improvement. One incidental advantage of the change
here contemplated in the system of liberal education would
be that the two sexes might be brought up much more nearly
on the same principles than they are now. Independently of
merely professional studies and of public speaking the
course of discipline for both might be the same: and their
minds being thus nourished from the same copious fountain
of our native literature, they would have a rich store of
common thoughts and feelings upon general and important
subjects. At present the two divisions of society, who are to
live together and to make each others happiness are brought
up as it were in two separate worlds, and have not three
ideas in common, of such at least as result from education.

   I owe you a thousand apologies, my dear Sir, for this long
dissertation into which I have been betrayed by the interest
of the subject, and which I fear will not only prove tedious;
but appear too much at variance with some of your own
views. I have made these imperfect suggestions, however,
with the less hesitation, because I know that from your better judgment and longer experience you will be able to correct them at once where they are fallacious or unfounded.
With renewed thanks for your kind remembrance, which you
will think I have but ill repaid with this tiresome homily,
I remain, dear Sir, your very sincere friend and obedient
Servant.

[Massachusetts Historical Society]

To Edward Everett

Edward.

We are still waiting impatiently, my dearest brother, for
news of your marriage and are anxious to felicitate you and
our new sister upon so happy an occasion.[8] —I received this
morning a letter from John dated at Geneva the 7th current.
He had come on foot from Paris and appeared to be pretty
well satisfied with his expedition. After exploring the neighborhood of the place where he now is he proposes to return
immediately to The Hague. He expresses a strong desire to
be with you at home, and talks of embarking for the United
States immediately after his arrival here. I have little doubt
that he will conclude to return this autumn or early in the
Spring. —Since I wrote you last we have had a flying visit
from Washington Irving. He staid a day here &dined &passed
the evening with us. —His conversation was very gay and
amusing, though somewhat too highly seasoned with scandal
and forming in this respect a complete contrast with the
sugar & water of the Sketch book. He appears from his own
account to be quite recherche in the best London society; and
talks with much familiarity of the Machinuk of Donegal—Mr.
Greenwood, Miss Lydia White and other persons probably of
great merit though but little known out of their own circles.
He was quite exhausted with a round of gaieties and being
troubled besides with a sore leg was going to recruit himself
at the warm baths at Aix-la-Chapelle. He told us a variety
of anecdotes of most of the principal literary characters and
especially of Mr. Campbell,[9] whom he represented under
a very unfortunate and ludicrous point of view, from what
precise motive I did not learn. The biography [10] he formerly
wrote of Campbell shows that he was then an enthusiastic
admirer of his work & character. He spoke with some dis-
satisfaction of the Review of Bracebridge Hall in Campbell's
Magazine and perhaps this is the source of the evil: although

I rather attribute it to mere levity and the propensity to
scandal inherent in the atmosphere of polished society. It
was enough to make a man laugh or cry—according as his
mood might be—to hear Irving tell the story of Campbells
remonstrating against a passage in the biography above mentioned in which he is said to have mutilated Gertrude of
Wyoming [11] in deference to the judgment of his friends. He
warrants the sweet bard of the Pleasures of Hope in a big if
a mean and constricted spirit talking noisily through a row
of pinched lips in a whiney pitiful voice and interlarding every
[word omitted] these words with a d—n. G-d d—n it—Mr. Irving. You must alter that passage—Why d—it, the people
will think I am one of those d—d fellows that are afraid by
G-d, to say what they think. Delicacy! why G-d d—n it, I
write as other people do, &. —This may possibly be a fair
specimen of his conversation: but I confess I prefer believing
that Irving has heightened a trifle. I was very well pleased
to learn from him that Murray has undertaken to circulate the
Review. Irving speaks very highly of it and represents it as
being much liked by all that see it. John mentions in his
letter that he saw the April No. at the Athenaeum in Geneva.

The papers today bring the news of a crisis in Spain which
will decide the fate of the parties at issue for some time to
come & probably against the King. The royal guard has re-
volted and at the last dates had just made an attack upon the
constitutional troops in the heart of Madrid and been repulsed
with loss. Who is at the head of the movement is not yet
clear—but there is very little doubt who is at the bottom of
it. The priests will never be easy as long as this member-head
remains upon his shoulders; and this I fear will not be a great
while should the present crisis finaly [sic] turn in favour
of the Cortes. After this there can be no confidence or mutual understanding between the parties. —The probability of a
war in the East seems to be at an end although the Turks are
continuing their massacres and have just slaughtered 87
hostages of the principal inhabitants of [word omitted] in
cold blood. So much for the age of humanity & civilization.
My wife joins in love to you & the family.

July 17 [1822]   [Massachusetts Historical Society]

To George Ticknor

New York. June 6. 1825.

I ought to have acknowledged sooner, my dear Ticknor, your
kind note received the evening before we left Boston with its
enclosures for Paris. I am truly sensible to your attention
and hope that I may be able to render you in return some
little service at Madrid or wherever else the fates may send
me.

We had a very prosperous journey to this place but in ar-
riving found that it would not be practicable to get away so
soon as I had wished—for under all the circumstances I did
not wish to prolong my residence much in this renowned city.
But the Don Quixote which sailed the 1st. proved to be a
Jonah vessel (200 tons) and inconvenient for her sire. The
name it is true was not ill-suited to my purpose but on other
respects the appearances were so unpromising that I concluded to sacrifice the name. The Montano which sailed the
5th was already taken up and the first that offered was consequently the Edward Quennel. She luckily happened to be a
very fine vessel and on her we have accordingly taken passage for the 15th. All this detail of packets & their names
must be vastly amusing to you & Mrs. T. but you know by
experience that when a man is preparing for a voyage his
head, & par consequent his pen, think upon nothing else.

I saw Mr. King the day before he sailed. He looked more
feeble than he did at Washington and was rather trite. I had
upon my tongue the solve venercenteur[12] but happily suppressed it. —Besides him we have seen here the literary
Lions: They were all assembled at the Sedgwick menagerie
and made a very handsome show. I was much pleased with
Miss S.—a little disappointed in Bryant. Anderson seems to
be an intelligent man malgré a very foolish Review that he
wrote of my book on Population in the Atlantic Magazine.
—The first No. of the New York Review is out.[13] If it does

not gain strength as it goes on, our friend Sparks is in no
danger. The Baron is here or rather was and is now gone up
to West Point. He seemed to be a cup too low but was cheer-
ing himself up with Kant's Religion innerhalb die grenzen
der reiner Vernunft[14] and is no doubt better by this time.

As you take no part in politics I need say nothing to you of
the objects of my mission: Mrs. T. who is fast ripening into
a stateswoman will be pleased to know that she may expect
about six months hence some important advices from Madrid. Give my best love to her with that of my wife (who will
however write before we sail) and tell her that we wish her
well through that state which ladies—however much they may
love their lords—are generally as anxious to be out of, as
they are to be in it.[15] —Let us hear from you as often as possible and believe me yours with high esteem & affection.

                                        A. H. Everett

[Dartmouth College Library]

To George Ticknor

                          Madrid.   April 20. 1826.

My dear Ticknor.

I send you herewith the manuscript copies which you requested in your instructions to me before I left Boston, as
far as they could be obtained. Copies of the other works that
you mention are probably not to be had. We shall however
not forget them and if any accident throws them in our way
shall certainly profit by it. When I say we and our I mean to
speak of Mr. Rich[16] and myself—he being the person by
whose aid I have been able to execute your commission as
far as I have done it. The copies of Timoneda were made

from a printed copy in his possession which contains two of
the three dramas entire and a fragment of the other. This,
as Mr. R. tells me—is the only copy known to exist: and the
work had become so rare as to be wholly forgotten (the fate
to which its literary value probably entitles it). Some of the
savans [17] in their Sepcutrnant [18] denied to Mr. Rich that
Timoneda ever wrote any plays.

I also send herewith a copy of the work on the Voyages of
Columbus which is on your list and has just appeared. This
is one of the small paper copies. A few were printed on
large paper and if you would also like to have one of these it
can be procured. This work is the first of a series of publications on the same subject. The next in order will be Voyages of Amerigo Vespucci. Let me know whether you wish to
have these works transmitted to you regularly as they appear, and if so whether you prefer the large or the small
paper copies.

The cost of the manuscripts—at $3 each is $27
and that of the Columbus—   4
making   31
which you can pay over at your convenience to my brother
Edward.

Your friends here are well and frequently inquire for you.
The Nuncio in particular requested me not long since to recall his name to your remembrance. When I told him that
you had delivered a course of lectures on Spanish literature
he said that if you published it he should be greatly disappointed if you did not send him a copy. He has lately been
named Bishop of Sarole and is soon to quit this station, upon
which occasion he will receive—according to custom—the
Cardinal's hat. —He is mentioned as a probable future Candidate for the Papacy.

My wife sends her best love to Mrs. T. to which I beg you
to add mine & am very truly yours.

A. H. Everett

To William H. Prescott

Madrid.   Sept. 5. 1827

W. H. Prescott Esq. —

My dear Sir.

I enclose herewith Mr. Rich's note of the last articles purchased for you with his receipt for the cost, and will beg the
favour of you to pay over the amount to my brother Edward.
If you have any further occasion for my services in the way
of procuring books I hope that you will command them without reserve. It is highly agreeable to me to contribute to
the success of any well conceived literary undertaking and
particularly so one in which you are interested.

Since I had the pleasure of writing to you I have seen in
the newspapers an advertisement of a new work by Hallam
on the Constitutional History of England[19] which may perhaps supply you with some useful materials. I was not much
struck with his Middle Ages, as I mentioned in a former
letter: but as I read it or rather looked it over very hastily
at a time when my attention was a good deal distracted with
other matters, I do not feel entire confidence in my judgment respecting it. The European Critics, Continental &
British, generally agree in placing Hallam very high: but I
rarely think it prudent to pin my faith upon the sleeves of
these gentry. Those of us who are initiated in the mystery of
reviewing know pretty well what value to set upon the dicta
of the critical journals.

Apropos of this: I have just received the 2d. No. of
Walsh's Review containing an article upon my America.[20]
I could not help thinking upon reading it as Alceste in the
Misanthrope says of the effect of some of her tirades upon
the company present—Par la samblue, Messieurs, je ne

croyais pas etre si plaisant que je suis.[21] —The Reviewer
makes himself as merry with the political system of Christendom & the eventual influence of Religion and Govt. as if
he were considering a jest book; & finally winds up by gently
reprimanding me for treating grave subjects with too much
flippancy. The critic who I understand is a promising young
Philadelphian of the name of Wharton writes in the spirit of
a petulant boy and will learn better as he grows older: but I
cannot readily excuse Walsh, whose personal relations with
me (in defect of any other reason) ought to have prevented
him from inserting an article which is evidently intended to
injure the work & its author. The ends of my fingers have
been itching to take him in hand, ever since I read the piece.
My privy council are, however, of [the] opinion that it does
not require an answer and I shall probably be governed by
their advice.

Irving has lately sent off the greater part of his life of
Columbus which will appear simultaneously in England and
the United States. I have not read the whole of it, but I am
satisfied that as a literary work it will be much superior to
Scott's Napoleon.[22] The latter seems on the whole to have
disappointed the public, and as far as I have had opportunity
to examine it I must needs say (in my poor opinion) with
reason. The effect will be I fear injurious to his general
reputation—We may say of him as Tacitus does of the Roman
Emperor Galba—Omnium convenia capax imperii nisi impe-
rasset.[23] His brilliant success in poetry & novels had thrown
such prestige about him that we all thought him capable of
any thing: but his failure (if it be one) in regard to Bonaparte, will probably induce the public to look a little more
narrowly into the real merits of his other works.

Pray let me hear from you occasionally—when los Reyes
Catolicos[24] will afford you leisure.

                        Yours very truly

[Massachusetts Historical Society]

To Jared Sparks

Madrid.   Oct. 22. 1827

Dear Sir.

I send you herewith an article upon Paraguay and her Supreme and Perpetual Dictator[25] which I hope you will find to
the purpose. —The book reviewed does not seem to have been
much noticed in our journals (as few are but such as come
through English channels) and the matter, which has some
intrinsic importance may therefore be to a certain extent
new. I have been able to add some particulars from personal
knowledge and private memoirs in my possession. —This
article will of course be in good season for the April No.
and I shall endeavor to send you another for the same probably on the Sculptor Canova,[26] having lately received a complete collection of engravings from all his works accompanied with a biography and with Commentaries by the Countess
Albrizzi. —The article upon Baron de Stael[27] transmitted
with my letter of the 5th ult. has doubtless come to hand.
If not let me know it and I will send you another copy.
     Since I wrote you last, I have received your friendly and
interesting Epistle from Mount Vernon[28] and also the July
No. of the Review, both which were long in reaching me,
having been accidentally detained at Gibraltar. I was glad to
find that you had struck out the allusion to Dr. Channing[29]
at the close of the article on M'Culloch[30] for two reasons,
one (being the first of the two mentioned by you) that I had
lugged him in rather ungracefully and as it were by the head
& shoulders & the other (not mentioned by you) that he would
have certainly been more angered by the somewhat dispar-
aging mention of his previous labours than flattered by the
encouraging prospect held out in regard to his future ones:
and as I really intended to be civil to him, I should have

counterworked my object. —As respects what you say of his
intellectual habits & theories, I am hardly competent to
judge as I have but a slight personal acquaintance with him
& have not heard him preach above some half a dozen times.
After reading your letter I looked over again his Review of
Milton and Greenwood's article on the Growth of the Mind,[31]
which, you say, was written with a view to Dr. C.'s notions.
With all due deference to the Stone Chapel (backed too by
your authority) I must own that I think Sumner Street has the
best of the argument. —Admitting (as is done by both) the
possibility of social improvement I see no reason why we
should assume the present state of civilization in Europe and
America as the nee plus ultra[32] any more than that of China
or New Holland. —How does it appear for example that the
best & wisest men of a thousand years hence may not be a
good deal wiser and better than John Locke whom Mr. Greenwood seems to hold up as the type of possible perfectability?
Locke was a shining light in his day but as good old Robinson
said of Calvin—he saw not all things—even of those we may
add that are now visible. How much of his works on Religion,
Government and Philosophy is already obsolete! Thousands
of the present generation much inferior to Locke in talent
are nevertheless wiser upon all these points—In other words
the standard of civilization in regard to these makes it higher than he left it. There is little or no doubt in my opinion
that it will be still higher two or three centuries hence than
it is now. To say precisely in what the future improvements
will consist would be to make them; but for any individual
to affirm that none can be made because he can form no idea
of such as have not been made is an evident non sequitur.
—On this point therefore—much as I respect Mr. Greenwoods
judgment of which I have a high opinion—I cannot but think
Dr. Channing in the right. —I was altogether very much
struck with the article on Milton by the latter. There are no
doubt weak points about it, but there is a fine fresh vigorous
enthusiastic spirit in it that pleased me greatly and gave me
a stronger impression of power in the author than I posit [?]
any American, or indeed European publication that I have
lately read. —Depend upon it that you would render a service

to the cause if you could among you, work up the Doctor into a fuller development of some of the hints on Mental & Moral Philosophy which he has thrown out in this piece.

I owe my thanks to you and John Gray for the article on my book.[33] His remarks on the style are sufficiently flattering to satisfy the amour propre of any author; and as the style is in fact the whole book (Vid. my former letter) there is the less reason to be alarmed at the few exceptions taken by Gray to the matter. My observations on Religion in the chapter on South America have been caviar to him as well to most other readers, including even our strongminded and free thinking friend Prescott. —I am not displeased to find myself alone in my opinion upon this subject, for, as I am certain of being in the right, my theory—if it differ from that of all the world, will turn out to be a grand discovery, and I have only to establish it to the satisfaction of all the world, in order to become a famous politico-religious Reformer— a sort of new fashioned Martin Luther. I do not see that I need to despair of ultimately giving my name to a new Icon and obtaining a niche in the temple of fame with the Muggletons & the Hopkinses: I shall however as you will naturally suppose—set about the preliminary arrangements very much at my leisure.

While writing this letter I have received yours of the 3d. of Sept. and am truly happy to learn from it that you are confirmed in the plan of coming to Europe. It will not only answer a good purpose as respects your immediate objects, but will be on all accounts an agreeable and useful excursion. —No man among us, who is naturally good for any thing, can visit the old countries without material benefit: and if there were any case in which the Coelum non animum[34] of Horace were completely verified the fact would only shew that the individual in question had much more of the Animal about him than of the Animus. —I mentioned in a former letter that I thought of taking a trip into France & England next spring, if the state of the public affairs here should afford the necessary leisure. I still retain this intention, and think it altogether probable that I shall be able to execute it. At all events I anticipate with confidence the pleasure of meet-

ing you either here or in some other part of Europe. —As
respects your access to the public archives of the different
kingdoms, I imagine that there will be no great difficulty.
Sir Walter Scott was allowed to use them with freedom, I
believe both in France & England, for his Napoleon; and so
was Ion[35] for his historical work. The application should be
made in each country through the channel of our Ministers,
& it would be proper to obtain from the Secretary of State
precise instructions to them to facilitate your object. —You
may depend upon all the aid that I can give you here, and
although this Govt. is rather more mysterious than most of
the others I think that they would accede to any request of
the kind that I should make. —Should you come to this country you will be able at any time to get a passage home from
Gibraltar. —Let me beg you by the bye to order my Review
when sent direct from Boston to that place to be addressed
to Hill and Blodget instead of the Consul.

I have lately intimated to my brother Edward that I thought
it advisable for him & you to attempt to effect a pacification
with Ticknor in order to keep him to your standard.[36] —This
might easily be done by a few advances on your side and
would answer a useful purpose. I will drop a word upon the
subject in a letter which I have occasion to write soon to
Ticknor & this—if you choose to follow it up—will serve as
an opening to the negotiation. —Ticknor, tho' a little hasty—
has excellent points about him & it is really a pity that he
should go over to the enemy. I hope that you will not forget
to make some arrangements with the twin brothers.[37] They
are so superabundantly modest that you will get nothing from
them without urging; but when they are once engaged they
will persevere, and even furnish you, as I said before, with
exactly the kind of matter you most want—that is—taste,
sentiment & poetry. —When fairly set to work they will be
worth the whole of Walsh's Septuagint. —If you have no article engaged upon Miss Sedgwick's new novel,[38] you might
apply to William (of Springfield) for one. He would do it con
amore as he is personaly [sic] attached to the author & thinks
highly of the book. —Miss Sedgwick by the bye should be
properly noticed & encouraged. It gives me pain to see a

second rate poetess like Mrs. Hemans[39] (acknowledged as
such in her own country where they are better judges than
we are)—taken up & trumpeted for a genius—while Miss S.
a much superior person—is comparatively overlooked.
—Oliver Peabody will also review with pleasure any thing
you may send him in the way of polite literature and with a
little practice will be worth ten of Wallenstein, who is—entre
nous—rather too prosaic—but nevertheless has his value.
—Irving has finished his life of Columbus and sold the MS. to
Murray for 3000 guineas. He is in a fine active vein, and is
already breaking ground for a Moorish Romance. But let
that be a secret. —I remain, dear Sir, your very faithful
friend & serv.

A. H. Everett

[Harvard University Library]

To George Ticknor

Madrid.   Jan. 7. 1828

My dear Ticknor.

Your letter of the 15th of May was a long time on the passage and I have been much longer in answering it than I intended, having been waiting untill I could accompany my
letter with such of the books on your last order as I was able
to procure. I put the list into Rich's hands without delay;
and now return it enclosed with his annotations, from which
you will learn that all the articles have either been sent already or cannot be procured excepting the Chronicle of
Alonso el Sabio which is herewith transmitted. I should have
despatched this two or three months ago; but Washington
Irving saw fit to borrow it, and would have kept it till the

day of judgment had I not lately recovered it from him as it
were by main force. The price of the book, as noted by Mr.
Rich on the enclosed paper, is eight dollars which you will
please to pay over to my brother Ed.

I learn with pleasure from your letter that Walshs Review[40] is likely to succeed. Not, as you may well suppose,
from any great personal interest that I have in it since he
has thought proper to perform upon my last work[41] the operation technically called cutting up and will probably do the
same by any other that I may publish hereafter. But I fear
him not: and as respects the general effect the Review will
be of service to the cause of letters. Nor do I apprehend with
you that it will injure the North American. I should rather
suppose, on the contrary, that competition would operate
favorably by rousing up the spirits of Sparks and his con-
tributors which had begun in some degree to flag. I can
vouch for one that I felt myself singularly excited by the
joint effect of the last mentioned motive and of Walsh's lam-
poon upon me and forthwith set to work much more actively
than I should have done under other circumstances. Hale,
whose aid is of more importance, may not improbably be
wrought upon in a similar way. —I regret to learn—which by
the bye you do not mention—that you have seceded from our
standard and enlisted under Walsh. This is owing I suppose
to your brouillerie[42] with Sparks and with Edward: but I see
not why you should allow them to influence your public proceedings. We are all fellow labourers in literature as well
as in politics for the honour of Old New England (excuse the
bull) and however we may make mouths at each other at
home we ought to unite cordially against the common enemy.
I see not indeed for that matter—if I may take the liberty of
saying so—why the aforesaid brouilleries, which, as far as
I know any thing of their origin, are not founded in any very
serious injuries on either side should be allowed to divide
old friends for life. What says the Scripture? Be angry and
sin not. And again: Let not the sun go down upon your wrath.
In other words: There is no harm in pouting a little occasionally provided you make up before you do each other or
the public any mischief. I am not deep enough in the history

of your controversies to know from whom the first advances
ought to come, but in this age of Coalitions & Combinations
there could hardly be much difficulty in bringing about a rec-
oncilement: and the one who does the most towards effecting
it will have the satisfaction of knowing that he is the best na-
tured fellow of the three. I have intimated as much in late
letters both to Sparks & Edward, and should be truly happy
if the hiatus I have thus given should produce a rapproche-
ment among you not only on account of the reward promised
in Scripture to the Peacemaker, but because we should in
that case have the advantage of your aid on the Review.
—I cannot in fact reconcile it to my notion that you should
contribute to a work which has declared war against me
without cause. Mrs. Ticknor will, I trust, approve these
suggestions & employ her mediation in effecting the desired
object.

    You inquire how we like our residence at Madrid. Of this
you can judge pretty well for yourself: since every thing remains exactly as when you were here. The Constitution
passed over the country like a high wave over a ship at sea
in a storm, and has left no traces of its passage. As to public amusements, Lions, et id genus omne,[43] we are as you
know miserably deficient, but as I have long ago supped full
of these horrors I suffer little or nothing from the want of
them. —The corps diplomatique is well composed and forms
of itself an intelligent and polished circle of society. We see
but little of the natives, who associate together in their own
Tertulias[44] & are not very anxious to communicate with foreigners. Your old friend the Nuncio has quitted the field and
his successor the Archbishop of Athens (post vario casus)[45]
has arrived. He is perhaps somewhat less polite and learned
than his predecessor of Tyre but by way of compensation is
much more gay or rather goguenard[46] —a far more essential qualification for a high ecclesiastical dignitary in their
holy apostolic countries. At a regular diplomatic dinner
given a few days ago by Count Brunetes I happened to be
placed at table between the said Archbishop & another rev-
erend churchman, whom you may perhaps have known—Gar-
cia [?] now Councillary of the Crusade and Archdeacon of

Madrid. I expected, as you may naturally suppose, to be a
good [deal] edified by the neighborhood of the two Arches and
was hugging myself in the expectation of hearing a learned
colloquy upon the three persons of the Trinity—the fine points
of Calvinism or the thirty nine articles of the Church of
England. Instead of this the worthy Archdeacon (a lad of
some fifty five or three score years) entertained us with a
disputation upon the thirty things that go to make up a completely piety [sic] woman which he debated at length with
much complacency, although Bayle[47] (not in general very
mealy mouthed upon these matters) declines going beyond
the three or four first. See his Dictionary article Helen.

Wilkie[48] the painter, whom you know by reputation if not
personally, has been here for some time, & makes an agreeable accession to our society. He is in bad health and is not
able to work much but is getting on slowly with a charming
picture of the interior of a Spanish Parada. He is a fine,
cool, intelligent Scotchman, not unlike Robert Owen in his
manners & person but without his extravagant theories or his
length of note. He keeps much with Irving & we also see him
frequently. He told me soon after his arrival that there is
now for sale at London a valuable collection of paintings belonging to the succession of Mr. West[49] & that the heirs
would dispose of them on reasonable terms. He seemed to
think that they would form an excellent foundation for an
American gallery. As you are meditating something of this
kind at Boston, it might not be amiss to institute an inquiry
upon the subject. West's merit, though perhaps overrated
a little just before his death, is admitted by all to be of a
sterling character, and his paintings have a peculiar value
as [?] they [?] are the work of a countryman. The collection
could probably be bought en bloc much cheaper than the
same number of equally good pictures could be procured in
any other way.

I hear nothing farther respecting the controversy between
the two Cardinals about the baptism of Brunetes daughter.
We have nothing new in the literary line nor are we likely to
have unless the next livraison of Navarete[50] which I shall
certainly send you. Pray let me know when you write what

you think of my theory or rather that of Llorente[51] upon the authorship of Gil Blas.

My wife is in flourishing condition and joins with me in sending a thousand good wishes upon the new year to yourself and Mrs. T.

—Yours cord. AHE.

[Dartmouth College Library]

To George Ticknor

Madrid.   July 12. 1828

It is a long time my dear Ticknor since I have had any news from you. I take for granted that my letter of Jan 7. and the Chronicle which followed it have been duly received. I have been favoured in the interim with a copy of your Edition of Haven's Remains[52] for which I presume that I am indebted to you and beg you to accept my thanks. The life is very judicious and elegant, saying neither too much nor too little, and saying what it says in the best manner—I was I confess, rather disappointed in the Remains, though perhaps unreasonably, as they include little or nothing that was prepared for publication, and what is not prepared for publication can seldom be completely fitted for it. All the articles however are evidently fruits of a naturally superior and highly cultivated intellect and evince at the same time the best moral qualities. —Had Haven lived I am satisfied that he would have given us some really valuable works. His taste seems to have turned more & more towards letters as he advanced in life, and his fortune gave him opportunity to follow the best of it. The most agreeable of these fragments are the observations on foreign countries, and I can not but regret

that Haven had not done more in this way. It is unfortunate
in general that our intelligent travellers so seldom publish
any thing upon their return from Europe. Few books are so
instructive and certainly none so entertaining to a mature
mind as good travels; and I do not quite agree with you in a
remark, which I recollect, you once made when I was talking with you upon this subject and urging you to publish your
own travels that works of this kind belong to a low order of
writing. A book of travels admits of the display of every
kind of merit whether of style or substance that can belong
to any composition, excepting those that are proper to the
highest strains of impassioned eloquence & poetry; and these
are also excluded from philosophy, history, and other sorts
of writing that are generally esteemed as of the first class.
No man whatever may be his pretentions, need be ashamed
to place his name by the side of Humboldt, Clarke, Dr.
Johnson, Mad. de Stael and Châteaubriand.—Even Herodotus
the great father of all prose writing is as much a traveller
as a historian. The few examples we have had of American
travels have not, it is true, been of a nature to raise the
standard of the genus among us, or to stimulate others: but
in this as in other cases Fools rush in &. If Walsh had published two or three volumes of such letters from Europe as
those he inserted in his American Review, he would have
given us a better book than any he has yet written, or probably will write. Haven too, had he drawn up—as he might
have done with little trouble soon after his return—a copious
narrative of his travels, would have left us a far more valuable legacy than his present Remains, interesting as they
are. And you, who had much better opportunities for observation than either of them & possess a much more ample
stock of materials than they can have had, might digest
them, with great credit to yourself & advantage to the public
into two or three separate works—as for example, one on
Germany—another on Spain—a third on France, Italy, or
England &. Pray think seriously of this, and as life is
short, put your shoulder to the wheel at once. Believe me
you cannot turn your time, talents, and materials to better
account; and will thus give your name a great immediate

popularity at home and abroad, which will form an excellent
basis for the success of any other and more solid labours
which may suit the greater maturity of a later period of life.
—I say this without disparagement to your Spanish, French
& German lectures, all of which, you will, I hope successively publish; but which as they are already written you
might revise, correct and enlarge in connexion with other
undertakings of the kind I have mentioned.

This however is by way of digression although it has turned
out rather a long one. To go back to Haven: —I was much
struck with the depth and warmth of religious feeling exhibited in some of his writings, and cannot but hope that it may
be properly considered a sign of the times and an indication
of the prevalent state of feeling among the higher circles of
our society. Taking the people though we have perhaps quite
enough—not to say a great deal too much—of what passes
under the name of Religion and is in fact a more or less un-
happy expression of the religious principles & feelings that
are inherent in our nature, and cannot be suppressed, though
they may be misunderstood and misrepresented. What we
want is a more enlightened view of Religion and a more
pointed application of it to the conduct of life including political affairs. Our most enlightened divines even of the liberal
school seem to waive voluntarily the advantage of the religious sanction even for the duties of ordinary morality. Thus
Mr. Palfrey fills up his discourse against Intemperance with
statistical calculations on the waste of life occasioned by it.
This is well to come in aid of higher; but what is any mere
detail of cyphers for effect compared with the desolating
picture of a heavenly spirit, hawked at and killed, as it
were, in its pride of flight by the devil of vicious indulgence,
forfeiting its lofty destination and its hopes of a more intimate union with the universal principle of Life—Intelligence
& Love—and degrading itself perhaps irretrievably, to a lower sphere of being. This is the religious view of the matter,
and it must certainly make a very different impression upon
every feeling mind (and every mind when properly addressed
is a feeling one) from the others. As to the influence of
Religion in political affairs: the very theory of the subject

is forgotten: and so completely has the public opinion become vitiated in relation to it that it is now thought the perfection of wisdom to exclude religious motives entirely from the business of Govt. or, as it is commonly expressed, to establish a complete separation of Church & State. This is nothing less than a complete separation of Morality & Religion. The few remarks of a different tendency, which I hazarded & in which I set forth the erroneous heresies that religion was the basis of morals and the only solid foundation of any political fabric were so much at variance with the received notions & common language of the day that the people really did not know what to make of them. —The theory is equally forgotten in England, although very ably exposed in a work of no older date than Hooker's Ecclesiastical Polity [53] —which contains as I have since had reason to suppose although I did not know it at the time of writing my book having never read Hooker—a development of the same notions on this subject as are briefly intimated in my America. But who now thinks of reading Hooker? Who knows any thing of him except the single sublime sentence, so often quoted, which is however enough of itself to render his name immortal as it has done, and which in fact contains in two lines the substance of his great work, and of the theory to which I allude. —If our present political institutions shall hereafter require—as is not improbable—to be strengthened by the introduction of any new principles, it will not answer for us to recur to the worn out and exploded European machinery of hereditary rank & magistracy—which have heretofore been always kept in view by the friends of a stronger system among us—but we must go higher to the ever active and living spring of Religion. Underneath—in the noble oriental ellipsis of Scripture—Underneath the Everlasting Arms.

You will gather from these observations that what I said in my book on the subject of Church & State was not—as you appeared in a passage in one of your letters to suppose, thrown out merely for effect as a startling paradox, but was a suggestion—which [was] considered as of the highest importance—The subject is however—if not too serious at least much too large for a letter and I must leave it. I enclose one of Rich's Circulars, of which you will doubtless receive others from himself. He left us yesterday with his family for Bilbao where he will embark for London. —I also enclose a prospectus of a Spanish translation of Bouterwek with notes which will be I think to you an interesting work. I am well acquainted with the translators particularly Contino who is the son of a wealthy Mexican Count now an emigrant in this Kingdom. He is from his love of letters quite a rara avis among the Spanish nobility, and possesses a fund of zeal and activity besides a good deal of talent. He gave me a copy of the first sheet as it came from the press which I enclose as a specimen of the style & execution. The paper is to be like that of the prospectus. The first volume appears in September and the rest afterwards in succession. I shall take care to send them to you, as they come out. Navarrete's next volume will also be out in September. Irving is at Seville, working away at his Moorish Chronicles. I hear but little from him & suppose that he is too busy to write many letters.

I hope you took in good faith and acted upon the pacific overtures in my last letter. Edward, to whom I wrote at the time to the same effect answered me that he desired nothing better. From Sparks I have not heard on this or any other subject for months past, but he is naturally an Israelite without guile & derives too much advantage from your friendship to wish to be on bad terms on this subject. I hope that when you write you will make me a favourable report on this subject. It will give me as much satisfaction to bring about a better understanding among you as it would to conclude the treaty of Mutual Indemnities with this Govt. which I have been hammering at for two years and shall I fear, leave it in the same state in which I found it. This I trust will not be the case with the one in question.

Mille choses, as usual, from my wife to Mrs. Ticknor in which I beg leave cordially to join. Let me hear from you as often as you have leisure and inclination to write, and believe me ever yours most truly.

[Massachusetts Historical Society]

To Manuel Gonzales Salmon

His Excy. D[on]. Manuel Gonzales Salmon
Principal Secretary of State

Sir.

I have the honour to acknowledge the receipt of Y[our]. E[x-cellency].'s letter informing me of the King's gracious assent to my request that my countryman Mr. Washington Irving might be permitted to examine the documents relating to the Life and Voyages of Christopher Columbus, which are preserved in the public archives at Seville.

I pray Y. E. to convey to H[is]. M[ajesty]. my respectful thanks for this flattering & acceptable mark of his Royal favour, and avail myself with pleasure of the occasion to offer Y. E. the renewed assurance of my sincere respect & esteem.

Madrid   Aug. 19—1828—

[Massachusetts Historical Society]

To Henry Wadsworth Longfellow

Boston.   March 25. 1832

My dear Sir.

I received your letter of the 19th but was prevented by a pressure of business from answering it by return of mail. I am glad to hear that you are preparing the article upon the Italian dialects.[54] —I will immediately make inquiry of Prof.

Ticknor respecting those of which you wish to obtain specimens. —He will be more likely to have them himself or to
know where they are to be found than any other person in this
neighbourhood.

   You will perceive that in preparing your article for the
press I have made a few alterations and omissions. —The
public feeling upon every thing connected with the subject of
religious belief is so extremely sensitive that it becomes
necessary to observe a caution in treating it which under
other circumstances might appear excessive. —The great
length of Mr. Davies's article on the North-Eastern Boundary[55] —which I was obliged to print and which considerably
exceeded the number of pages I had calculated as for it—
compelled me to omit your notice of Mrs. Child.[56]

   As to your suggestion on the subject of the appointment of
Secretary of Legation, it would give me great pleasure to
forward your views by any means in my power. —The nomination of the Secretary has been generally left to the Minister
and the only method of obtaining the place is by making interest with some person who has received the superior
appointment. —If Mr. Peeble by his late ambitions in recon-
ciling Maine to the acceptance of the award should have so
far recovered his favour with the Hero as to receive another
mission—which is altogether probable—your family connexion
with him and your literary reputation would recommend you
very strongly to his notice. —Should any nomination of minister be made which would put it in my power to employ my
personal influence in determining the appointment of the
Secretary, I should, if you desired it, propose you very
readily. I am not sure that the place—if you obtained it—
would realise your expectations. It is not a very agreeable
one especially for a married man without fortune. I have
tried it, married & single, and can speak from experience.
—Expertus metuit:[57] —Nevertheless every man must be
happy in his own way and one man's experience furnishes no
precise rule for another.

   My wife is much indebted to you and Mrs. L. for your

friendly remembrance and cordially joins with me in the
best wishes to you both.

I am, dear Sir, yours very truly & faithfully

A. H. Everett

[Harvard University Library]

To Henry Wadsworth Longfellow

Boston.   April 27. 1832

My dear Sir.

I will, with much pleasure, preserve and return to you the
MMS. of the articles which you may hereafter send me.
—I thought very favourably of your last. The alterations
which I made were, in almost every instance, concessions
to the extreme delicacy of the subject, rather than emenda-
tions either of the style or substance. —I am very happy to
find that the next is in preparation and shall depend upon it
for July. —We have already begun to print and I should be
glad to have it as soon as you can conveniently furnish it.
—Mr. Ticknor tells me that he has put into your hands every
thing that he has on the subject of the Italian dialects and
there is no other source to apply to in this vicinity so that it
will not be in my power to furnish you with any additional
materials. —As to Mrs. Child I will, if you please, consider
her a little longer.

I have seen some mention of a Western Quarterly Review
& should not be surprised if such a thing were attempted, but
it would not survive the first year. —The three editors—if
there are so many—are probably Chase, Walker and Flint.

I have received a copy of your Italian Grammar but have
not yet had time to read it. I incline to agree with you in the
opinion that the place of Secretary of Legation—although not
on all accounts a very eligible one especially for a married
man—is better than the one you hold. Not that the office of
a Professor is in itself objectionable but that the College is
in a tottering & uncertain state. —It will give me very great
pleasure—to use the little influence which I might have with
my political friends—should they again come into office—in
introducing you into the diplomatic line. —The prospect of
such an event is not at present so flattering as we could
wish, although I do not, on the other hand, consider it so
desperate as the good Jackson men would fain have us believe it to be.

Our friend Irving is coming out with a new Sketch Book for
which I expect great things. Cannot you give us something in
the form of travels or sketches in prose or verse about
Spain? The subject is excellent and almost new. Your recollections are now more fresh than they will ever be hereafter. —You will say that you have no time but what says the
old adage? —The more a man does the more he may. —Let
us hear from you then without delay. It is no slight motive
for publishing in that you are sure of a favourable Review
which may not always be the case.

My wife joins me in sending our best with cordial regards
to yourself and lady.

Yours very truly.　A . H . Everett

[Harvard University Library]

To Henry Wadsworth Longfellow

Boston. July 20. 1833

Dear Sir.

I received this morning your letter of the 16th and agreeably to your desire, reply to it with pleasure by return of mail.

The place in the Legation at Madrid, which you suppose to be vacant is not so. Mr. Walsh was superseded some months ago by Mr. Arthur Middleton of S. Carolina. It is not improbable that the chagrin resulting from this circumstance may have precipitated his death. —Had there been a vacancy I would with much pleasure have used my influence, such as it is, in your favour: but appointments under the present administration are so entirely and exclusively a business of political jobbing—most especially where New England is concerned—that I do not believe you could have obtained this. —Better or at least other times will come round after a while: and if you retain the inclination to taste the sweets of the diplomatic career—dulcis inexpertis[58] —it is altogether probable that sooner or later you may be gratified.

Outre-Mer was duly received and I pray you to accept my best acknowledgments for it. I shall endeavor to get a notice of it into the next Review although if you intend to publish one or two numbers immediately it might be expedient to delay the notice till January and take them up together. You can inform me, if you please, what your preference would be in this respect. —The first number is very sprightly & entertaining and must, I think, be popular. The subjects are, as you say, somewhat light but the work is intended for light reading and would not accomplish its objects or obtain success if it dwelt on topics of a grave character.

The subject which you propose to treat for the Review will

furnish a very attractive article and I shall depend upon having it for the next number.

If I hear of any thing that would be likely to suit Cortes
I will certainly inform you.

My wife joins in affectionate remembrances to Mrs. Longfellow.

Yours very truly & faithfully

A. H. Everett

[Harvard University Library]

To Jared Sparks

Washington. D.C.

April 13. 1838

Dear Sir.

I send you enclosed the conclusion of the Life of Warren.[59]
It is made up, as you will see, in part, from my address at
Charlestown on the anniversary of the battle of Bunker's
Hill. I have endeavored to mark out such parts of the color-
ing, as appeared to be too high for simple biography and
have generally, I hope, brought it down to a proper tone.
If you find any thing that appears to be too rhetorical you are
at full liberty to expunge and alter at discretion.

If you find the chapters too short you will, of course,
modify the division as you think proper.

I have at home a genealogical deduction of the several
branches of the Warren family for two or three generations
before and after the General. It was sent to me by Judge
Newcomber of Greenfield. If you think it expedient to append
it to the Life I will furnish you with it on my return.

I mentioned in the life the fact that the bullet was taken from Warren's body by Mr. Savage of the Custom House. In my address at Charlestown I exhibited it to the audience not long after which I received an anonymous letter through the post office assigning certain reasons why the bullet could not be genuine. I had thoughts of preparing a note upon this point, which should include the letter with comments upon it, shewing why the objections are not satisfactory. Not having the letter with me I could not do it now & having promised you the life for the first of March, I did not like to delay it any longer. If you think such a note would add to the interest and value of the article I will give it to you after my return. The discussion, though not important, is precisely of that kind that might perhaps amuse the curious antiquarian.

Please to acknowledge the receipt of the three parcels of the Life under cover to Mr. Gelpin.

I have given Mr. Hale an order upon you for the sum due to me as compensation for writing the article which you can pay to him at his and your convenience.

I am, dear Sir, with great regard

very truly and faithfully yours.

A. H. Everett

[Harvard University Library]

To Lydia H. Sigourney

Roxbury.   Oct. 25. 1839.

Dear Madam.

I have received your letter of the 19th inst. and am greatly obliged by your friendly expressions on the subject of the address. A collection of several detached efforts of this

description into a volume would be an affair of very little
labor and would not interfere at all with any original works
which I might have in contemplation. —I owe you many thanks
for your suggestion in regard to a work on the history of
English Poetry. —I have in my head a number of projects,—
mostly of a historical character,—but the rambling and unsettled life which I have led, has hitherto prevented me from
seriously undertaking any extended work. Should circumstances ever be favorable, I should probably attempt something on the history of modern Europe,—which I have had
occasion to study more than any other subject. —I should be
able to introduce into a work of that kind a review of the
polite literature of the different countries with perhaps better effect than if it were treated in separate essays. The true
office of Poetry seems to be to relieve and adorn the serious
business of life; and Criticism never appears to more advantage than in connexion with a record of public events.
Mr. Prescott's book is a fine example of the effect of that
method.

I agree with you in thinking that Pocahontas is the finest
subject for poetry which our history or perhaps that of the
world can furnish. —The best models for narrative poetry
are the works of Scott and Byron, but it would be rather dangerous to follow closely in the track of either. I am not myself partial to long narrative poems; and if I intended to
treat the subject of Pocahontas, I should be rather inclined
to do it in prose. The prose novel or Romance seems to be
the true Epic of modern times. Verse, which, to be good for
any thing, should possess the greatest possible concentration
of thought and perfection of language, is hardly the proper
form for a protracted work. Its triumph is in short lyrical
pieces, like your own,—to which it gives a diamond-like
polish and brilliancy. In a prose novel you would have no
trouble with the name of Smith, which, as you suggest, would
be inadmissible in verse. The History of Virginia by Smith
himself, including his own adventures previously to his expedition to America, would, of course, be the most important parts of your materials. The marriage of the heroine
with Rolfe would form a regular catastrophe and take her off

your hands at the close in the most approved way.

In a work of this kind a mixture of the comic has a good effect and there are some incidents in the early history of Virginia which would afford very good materials for this purpose. I allude particularly to the importation of a cargo of young women from England to meet the demand for wives, which, it seems, at that time greatly exceeded the supply. On the arrival of the ship which bore this precious freight there was of course an active competition among the bachelors for the fair prizes; and in order to reconcile conflicting claims as well as possible, it was determined to put up the newly arrived ladies at auction, the minimum price for a wife being fixed at a hogshead of tobacco. The 'fragrant weed,' as you are aware, was at that time the circulating medium of the colony. This little incident might, I think, be wrought up into two or three very comic scenes or chapters, that would serve as episodes to the body of the work.

Excuse these too hasty lines and believe me with the highest regard, dear Madam, very truly & faithfully yours.

A. H. Everett

P.S. Goethe expresses the same opinion which I have ventured to give in regard to long narrative poems. See his conversation with Eckerman lately translated and published in this country.

[Connecticut Historical Society]

To Lucretia O. Everett

Havana.   Dec. 19. 1840

My dearest wife.

I have been intending ever since I came here in the spring,
to take some convenient time for visiting the slave market.
Just before my return to the United States in the spring,
I set out to go, in company with Mr. Fernander,—an employé
in Mr. Knight's house, but we were prevented from reaching the place by the miserable state of the roads. Last week
Mr. Wert proposed to me to take a seat with him in his
Volante, and drive out before breakfast to the Barracoon,
where the market is held.

We started about 7 (the breakfast hour being 9) after first
taking a cup of coffee to fortify the stomach. The morning
was one of the finest I have ever known:—the sky clear:—the
air fresh, and the thermometer about 70°. The distance is
from three to four miles, and the road for a part of the way
very pleasant as it passes through the two Paséos, which lie
just without the walls of the city. For the last two miles the
road is bad and the country not particularly agreeable although as green and fresh at this season, as the neighborhood of Boston is in June. The Slave market was formerly
just at the termination of the new Paséo, and we passed on
our way the Barracoon, that was then used, and which is now
occupied as a villa by Jorcade, one of the principal slave-
dealers of the place.

These Barracoons, or, as we say, barracks,—for the
word barracoon is the argumentative form of the other,—are
ranges of one-story buildings, enclosing a square court. The
new one, where the market is held, is quite extensive, and
contained, when I was there, from five to six hundred slaves.
The buildings, and every thing about them, are kept in very

good order. The superintendent's quarters are on the left,
as you enter the court: —the kitchen at the extreme corner
opposite, and the rest of the sides are filled up with the
buildings, occupied by the negroes. A number of them were
loitering about the court in the sun; but the greater part
were in the buildings. We went into two of the largest rooms,
in each of which there were from 150 to 200. In one they
were sitting in a row round the sides of the room, doing nothing: in the other they were seated in the same way, but were
engaged in a kind of musical exercise. One of them was pa-
rading the whole length of the room, back & forward, holding
in his hands a kind of wooden instrument, with which he appeared to mark the time for the music. The rest continually
repeated a short, monotonous chant, with which they kept
time by clapping their hands. The effect was rather doleful,
but we were told that it was one of the sports of the old
country.

The slaves, while in the Barracoon, are fed abundantly on
salt fish, dried beef, and plantains, in order to restore, as
soon as possible, their vigor and good looks after the ex-
haustion of the voyage. It is observed here, as in the slave
markets of the east, —that they are anxious to be sold. I was
rather curious to see the operation of buying and selling, but
there was no purchase the day I was there. The whole trade
is now against law, but is connived at by the Government,
who receive a regular payment of $8 a head for every slave,
that is landed on the island. The annual importation is calculated at about 20,000; and the spoils are divided among two
or three persons, —the Captain General receiving the Lion's
share. —The whole business is—as Mr. Webster said of the
tariff law, —a mass of abominations, and the island is no
better than another Algiers on a large scale; but the moral
sense of the people is so completely blinded by habit, that
instead of being shocked at the existence of such a state of
things, they are shocked, on the contrary, at the mere suggestion of any plan tending to disturb it.

Since I wrote, our house has been filling up with new com-
ers, chiefly by way of New Orleans, and is now crowded. Mr.
Wert has a letter today from Mr. Wickoff, charge d'affaires,

and principal Knight Errant to the "divine Fanny,"[60] —ordering lodgings for her, and her party, so that we may expect their arrival from day to day. This will be as important an event here, as the election of General Harrison to the Presidency in the United States.

We are also in expectation of a visit from Mrs. Van Rensselaer—ci-devant Miss Talmadge, with her husband, for the improvement of her health, which, I am sorry to hear, is not in a good state.

I had a letter yesterday from Mr. Woodbury, requesting me to accept the place of Commissioner for building the new Custom House, rendered vacant by the resignation of Mr. Bancroft. He "regrets to state that it is not in the power of the department to offer me any pecuniary compensation for my services, which will however, be chiefly of an advisory nature, and will not engross much of my time." The Commission consists of three persons, the two others being Robert G. Shaw, and S. S. Lewis. Both these, if I am not mistaken, receive in some way,—I believe in commissions or disbursements,—a pretty handsome compensation. The third Commissioner has always been, untill the resignation of Mr. Bancroft, the Collector: and he, being well paid in other ways for all his time, was expected to work for nothing upon this Commission. —It seems hardly fair to expect the same from me: and if my absence from home did not prevent me from accepting the appointment, I should say as much to the Secretary. He wrote to me at Boston, in apparent ignorance of my being here, although I had the honor of seeing Mrs. Woodbury at New York on my way, and although I have written some letters to Mr. Forsyth, since I have been here, which ought to have been talked about in the cabinet. Probably just at the time when he wrote, there was but little thought, of any thing except the elections.

There is nothing new, since I wrote, in the way of business. The Knights go today to their estate to pass the Christmas holiday. I shall, perhaps, go next week upon the same errand with Osgood to his namesake's place, but I am not quite sure. —I was kept awake the greater part of last night by my next door neighbor, a Spanish lady, who was seized with a violent fit of colic, and was singing out <u>Dios mio</u>! and <u>muy mala</u>! at the top of her voice for three hours in succession. Luckily she is better today, and I trust she will be well enough before night to give her neighbors a chance of sleeping.

P.S. Dec. 20. I was interrupted, in the middle of this sheet yesterday, and will now fill up the two remaining pages with a Postscript, although there is not much more of consequence to be said. To begin where I left off, I am happy to find that my fair Spanish neighbor is mending rapidly, and, though still indulging occasionally in a few <u>Ohs</u>! and <u>Ahs</u>! had, on the whole, a quiet night, which gave me a chance of enjoying one too. She is a young married lady of fortune from Principe, on the other side of the island, who had come up to the Havana to participate in the gaieties of the season. Being thus "bent on pleasure," without having, like John Gelpin's wife, "prudent mind" to keep her desires in check, she began her career by eating too much ice-cream, and brought herself nearly to death's door.

The Knights did not go to the country on Saturday, as they intended, and I had the honor yesterday of dining with them. Mr. Audubon and his ladies, Mr. Delessart of Paris, and one or two other gentlemen made the party. —Nothing transpired of importance. The principal topics of conversation in the <u>beau monde</u> are the opera, and the expected arrival of the "divine Fanny." The latter, being the last in the order of time, excites, just at present, the strongest sensation. She has no engagement here, and the Manager of the theatres was supposed to be half inclined not to make her an offer, from an opinion that her performing would injure the opera, and that he should, on the whole, lose by her. —He accordingly gave out that he was going to New Orleans on the next steam-boat, and if he had done it, would of course, have been, at the time of Miss Fanny's visit, absent from the Havana. —This report getting wind threw the whole city into consternation, and might have produced very serious results had it not been for the energetic conduct of the Governor, who, hearing of the manager's intention, and feeling the exigency of the case, determined at once on a <u>coup d'etat</u>.

Accordingly, on Saturday evening, he sent for the Manager
into his room at the theatre, and, after giving him a suitable
reprimand for his perverse and treasonable designs, ordered
him premtorily [sic] to engage Fanny on the best terms he
could make, or else to give up the theatre to some body who had
a better notion of the responsibilities of the place. The manager of course acquiesced, and we shall, in consequence,
have the unspeakable satisfaction of seeing as much of the
charming Fanny's silk stockings, as we please, or rather,
as she pleases; and, in general, she is pretty liberal in her
allowance. I was in the Governor's room at the opera last
evening, and heard the whole story from himself. I took the
liberty of indulging in a little pleasantry upon the importance
that is given to this dancing girl, but His Excellency intimated in reply that it was, after all, no joking matter, and,
least of all, on the part of our countrymen, whose heads had
been turned as completely as theirs possibly can have in-
stancing the conduct of the Baltimore people in talking of her
horses.[61] —I could not but admit that his objection was just.
—I am still without letters from home, but, as there are a
number of vessels coming in today, I calculate with confidence on receiving some. With best love to all I remain,
your affectionate husband. A. H. E. vid P.S. page 1.[62]

P.S. 2d. Dec. 21. I had no means of despatching this letter
yesterday, and am thus enabled to add on a second P.S.,
that after writing the first I received a letter from Judge
Bullard of New Orleans, offering me, in the name of the
Trustees of the Jefferson College, the Presidentship of that
Institution.[63] This is the place about which you will recollect
there was some correspondence last year, when the plan
fell through in consequence of the former, or rather present,
incumbent not resigning, as was expected. The Judge says,
that it is now certain, that he will resign: —expresses the
great regret and disappointment, that were felt by the Trustees at not being able to engage me last year, and wishes me
to give him an answer by the return steam-boat. I shall give
the same answer that I did last year: —a conditional acceptance with liberty to withdraw after examining the situation

of the College on the spot, —if I desire it. The Judge does not say when the place will be vacant. As I am now, as it were, in the neighborhood (the steam-boat runs in three days) I think I shall take a trip to New Orleans pretty soon, and reconnoiter. —The salary is $4000 a year and a house. —More of this anon: in the mean time I will thank you not to mention the subject to any one out of your immediate family.

[Massachusetts Historical Society]

To Lydia H. Sigourney

Jefferson College. La.   Jan. 13. 1842

Permit me, my dear Mrs. Sigourney, to offer you, as I do most cordially and sincerely, the good wishes of the season. I hope that you may meet through the year with all the success, poetical and personal, that you deserve, and that, I am sure, is as much as you need to desire. I trust that before the end of the year we shall be favored with an account of your visit to Europe. —The inclination of the day is decidedly for travels; and yours will be received with strong interest. You will find no difficulty in producing a book of higher cast, and a more attractive character, than that of Miss Sedgwick, which I have read since I wrote to you last. She is, in parts, a little too green, and dwells throughout too much in mere gossip. Your mind is more poetical than hers, as well as more religious and, for both reasons, will attach itself, in preference, by a natural instinct, to scenes and objects of a loftier nature. The majority of lady writers do not rise above the atmosphere of the tea-table, which is the element of the common novel, and have a constant downward tendency towards the kitchen. Most of them write books on housewifery, including Miss Sedgwick: —a few only—such

as Hannah More, Mad. de Stael, &, when they quit the region
of ordinary life, soar instead of sinking; and, in all these
cases, as in all cases of a real intellectual superiority in
men, the elevating power will be found, I think, to reside in
a strong sense of Religion,—which I understand in its largest
extent, as you will see by my including Hannah More and
Mad. de Stael in the same category.

I am getting quite impatient to make the acquaintance of
our fair Princess, and am proud, as you may well suppose,
of the share you kindly allow me, in her paternity. If she
inherits any of the amiable graces of her mother she must
be a very attractive personage. I saw her in the bookshops
at New Orleans on a late visit to that city, but did not care
to introduce myself to her in the midst of a crowd,—believing that I should enjoy her company more in a quiet tête-à-
tête at my own hermitage, where I shall expect to see her
arrive with a letter of introduction from you in due season.[64]
—It is true that our public have not yet shewn much taste for
the red race: but, in justice to the world, it must be owned,
on the other hand, that they have hitherto been presented in
a rather questionable shape. Cooper made them very popular, and I flatter myself that our Pocahontas will be a decided favorite. After making her acquaintance I shall take the
liberty, my personal relations to her to the contrary notwithstanding,—to give my opinion of her in print.

I am glad that you saw Carlyle. —His peculiarity of manner is occasionally carried to an unpleasant excess, but,
whatever may be his faults (& every one has them of greater
or less importance) he is decidedly at the head of the present race of English writers:—far above Macaulay, for example, who is puffed so extravagantly by some of our ridiculous
bookseller-critics.

We are, it is true, as you say, rather on "the outside of
the world," in this quarter; but you must not suppose that
we are entirely beyond the domains of elegance & letters.
On the contrary, we are just at this moment setting ourselves
up to be the arbiters of taste for the whole country. The first
number of the "Southern Quarterly Review" makes its appearance this month under the auspices of the Rev. D. K.

Whitaker, lately of Charleston, S. C. The first article, which
I saw in print last week at New Orleans, poured a broadside
into the whole periodical press from the Lady's Book to the
N. A. Review. It is written by the Editor. I have been requested to contribute, and shall occasionally give some thing.
Whatever northern critics may say of her, our Princess shall
have justice done to her in the "generous South."

I regret to learn that you have been suffering with Influenza.
Complaints of that kind are unknown in our delightful climate
—we have had no weather yet that would be called at the North
cold. I set out my peach-trees, pomegranates, and rose
bushes in the middle of December, and some of them are already budding. —I could say more on this attractive theme,
but will not condemn you to the toil of deciphering any more
of my scrawling palimpsest. Believe me, dear Madam, most
truly & faithfully your friend & obed. sert.

A. H. Everett

[Connecticut Historical Society]

Notes

The text of each piece of correspondence is based on the
autograph, used by kind permission of the institution cited
in brackets at the conclusion of the letter.

1. Agréments seems intended: "pleasures."
2. Everett's sister Sarah married Nathan Hale in 1816.
Lucy Everett was a younger sister.
3. Frank Luther Mott lists the full title of this publication
as The General Repository and Review—first issue, January,
1812; last issue, October, 1813. Founded at Harvard, the
Repository published articles in four departments: Theology,
Literature, Review, and Intelligence; and even though it

remained basically a Harvard periodical John G. Palfrey later claimed it as a forerunner to the North American Review. Mott notes that "in the middle of its second year, the Repository was turned over to 'A Society of Gentlemen,' who issued the July number and, after a long interval, an October number; and with that publication ceased." (A History of American Magazines, I [1930], 277-278.) Everett's letter to Norton indicates the unfulfilled hope of continuing the publication of the Repository.

4. "The strength of inertia."

5. "League of Virtue," a secret society of German students, 1808-1816, formed to free North Germany from the yoke of Napoleon.

6. John Pickering (1777-1846) was described by Franklin Edgerton in "Notes on Early American Work in Linguistics," Proceedings of the American Philosophical Society (July, 1943), 27, as "one of the two greatest general linguists of the first half of the Nineteenth Century in America."

7. "It is base for a patriot and a nobleman pleading causes to be ignorant of the language in which they will be delivered."

8. Edward Everett married Charlotte Gray Brooks on May 8, 1822.

9. Thomas Campbell (1777-1844), Scottish poet.

10. The publisher Charles Nicholas asked Irving to write an introduction for a volume of Campbell's selected verse; the result was a eulogy of Campbell that revealed Irving's limited style as a biographer. (See Stanley T. Williams, The Life of Washington Irving, I [New York, 1935], 120-122.

11. Campbell's poem "Gertrude of Wyoming" was published in 1809.

12. Solve venerantur seems intended: "Relax, they are being worshipped."

13. First issue, May, 1824; last issue, April, 1825.

14. Everett is slightly inaccurate in quoting Kant's title: Die Religion innerhalb der Grenzen der blossen Vernunft (1793): "Religion Within the Bounds of Mere Reason."

15. George and Anna Ticknor's daughter, Susan Perkins, died in 1825 when she was but a few weeks old.

16. Obadiah Rich (1783-1850) is frequently mentioned as the agent who secured Spanish books requested by George Ticknor and William Hickling Prescott.

17. Savants seems intended: "scholars."

18. "Septuagint" seems intended.

19. Henry Hallam (1777-1859). Constitutional History of England from the Accession of Henry VII to the Death of George II (1827).

20. "America," The American Quarterly Review, 1 (March and June, 1827), 494-520.

21. Sacrebleu misquoted as par la samblue: "By Jove, Gentlemen, I didn't think that I am as amusing as I am."

22. Life of Napoleon (1827).

23. "Capable of all things except ruling an empire."

24. Ferdinand and Isabella. Prescott's memoranda for 1827 (George Ticknor, Life of Prescott [1864], 84-85) indicates that he was engaged in serious reading and research for Ferdinand and Isabella, published in 1838.

25. "Revolution in Paraguay," North American Review, 26 (April, 1828), 444-478.

26. "Life and Works of Canova," North American Review, 29 (October, 1829), 441-478.

27. "De Staël's Letters on England," North American Review, 26 (January, 1828), 163-196.

28. Jared Sparks was at Mount Vernon engaged in editing the papers of George Washington and the diplomatic correspondence of the United States ministers abroad, and foreign ministers in this country during the Revolutionary War.

29. William Ellery Channing (1780-1842). "Remarks on the Character and Writings of John Milton" (1826).

30. "M'Culloch's Political Economy," North American Review, 25 (July, 1827), 112-153.

31. F. W. P. Greenwood, "Growth of the Mind," North American Review, 24 (January, 1827), 56-68.

32. Ne plus ultra seems intended: "ultimate."

33. "America," North American Review, 25 (July, 1827), 169-183.

34. Caelum non animum mutant qui trans mare currunt: "They who race across the sea change not their minds but

their place."

35. Literally transcribed; "Irving" seems intended, however, perhaps in abbreviated form.

36. David B. Tyack in George Ticknor and the Boston Brahmins (Cambridge, Mass., 1967), 122, discusses this controversy.

37. Everett's two brothers-in-law, Oliver William Bourn Peabody and William Bourn Oliver Peabody.

38. Catharine Maria Sedgwick (1789-1867) published Hope Leslie, or Early Times in the Massachusetts in 1827.

39. Felicia Dorothea Hemans (1793-1835).

40. Robert Walsh (1784-1859) began publication of the American Quarterly Review in 1827; the journal continued for a decade.

41. The "cutting up" was Wharton's review of Everett's America (1827) in the American Quarterly Review, 1 (March and June, 1827), 494-520.

42. "Disagreement."

43. "And all that breed."

44. "Circles."

45. "After various misfortunes."

46. "Bantering."

47. Pierre Bayle (1647-1706). Dictionnaire historique et critique (1697).

48. Sir David Wilkie (1785-1841).

49. Benjamin West (1738-1820).

50. Martín Fernández de Navarrete (1765-1844). At Everett's request Irving had come to Spain in 1826 to translate Navarrete's history of Columbus.

51. Juan Antonio Llorente (1756-1823). Observations Critiques sur le Roman de Gil Blas de Santillane (Paris, 1822). Everett reviewed this book in "Who Wrote Gil Blas?," North American Review, 25 (October, 1827), 278-307, reprinted in Critical and Miscellaneous Essays, First Series (Boston, 1845), 28-66.

52. Nathaniel Haven of Portsmouth was on the Liverpool packet in 1815 when Ticknor and Edward Everett sailed for Göttingen. He died at an early age and Ticknor edited his papers: The Remains of Nathaniel Appleton Haven. With a

Memoir of His Life (Cambridge, Mass., 1827).

53. Richard Hooker (1554?-1600). Of the Laws of Ecclesiastical Polity (1594). The "single sublime sentence" on which Everett dwells here is probably the following: "Of Law there can be no less acknowledged than that her seat is the bosom of God, her voice the harmony of the world."

54. "History of Italian Language and Dialects," North American Review, 35 (October, 1832), 283-342.

55. C. S. Davies, "North-Eastern Boundary," North American Review, 34 (April, 1832), 514-564.

56. Lydia Maria Child (1802-1880).

57. "He who has been tried, fears."

58. "Sweet to those who have experienced."

59. Life of Joseph Warren, in Jared Sparks, ed., Library of American Biography (25 vols., Boston, 1834-1848), First Series, Vol. X, 93-183. Warren (1741-1775) was a Boston physician and Revolutionary officer, killed at the battle of Bunker Hill.

60. Fanny Elssler (1810-1884), Austrian ballet dancer.

61. In The Chronicles of Baltimore; Being a Complete History of "Baltimore Town" and Baltimore City from the Earliest Period to the Present Time (Baltimore, 1874), J. Thomas Scharf includes this entry among the 1840 events: "In July Miss Fanny Elssler appeared at the Holliday Street Theatre and created great excitement; some of the single seats brought as high as $3.50 each, being a premium of $2.50. On one occasion the horses were taken from her carriage, and she was drawn to her lodgings by enthusiastic young men." (Page 502.)

62. The second postscript was written vertically across page one; two lines were written vertically on page two.

63. Judging from other surviving correspondence, Everett must have left this position some time between May 1842 and July 1843.

64. Pocahontas and Other Poems (1841).

Bibliography

The state of Alexander Hill Everett scholarship is embryonic, as I have suggested—confined largely to passing references, to quoted correspondence in studies of Everett's more famous contemporaries, and to studies of the Spanish influence on American literature. Stanley T. Williams, for example, cites fifty-four single references to Everett in The Spanish Background of American Literature (2 vols., 1955; rpt. Hamden, Conn., 1968), but each reference is very brief. No critical study or biography has appeared in print. I have published two groups of letters: "The Everett-Longfellow Correspondence," American Transcendental Quarterly, Part One (Winter, 1972), 2-15; and "Mrs. Sigourney's Friend and Mentor," The Connecticut Historical Society Bulletin, 36 (July, 1971), 77-91.

Although Everett's books are now appearing from time to time in reprint and microprint, largely because of their incidental interest to economic historians, they are not consistently available even in libraries with substantial collections. Access to the journal articles continues to depend upon the availability of the North American Review and other nineteenth-century periodicals.

The Massachusetts Historical Society has the primary collections of unpublished material—the Alexander Hill Everett Papers and the Everett-Peabody Collection. The former deposit includes the official correspondence that Everett conducted when he held government posts abroad, a vast number of letters and reports primarily of interest to the historian. Although the citation of specific items is beyond

247

the scope of this bibliography, these holdings obviously represent a major source for any study of Everett. Smaller collections of letters are in the various libraries cited below,
and doubtless still others exist.

   The present list of Everett's writings is limited to those
items whose authorship has been conclusively identified. The
stream of Everett's occasional publications apparently began
in 1808 with his contributions to the short-lived Monthly
Anthology and Boston Review, and articles, reviews, poems,
and addresses continued to flow from his pen until shortly
before his death. Material of this sort usually appeared un-
signed in the nineteenth-century periodicals; although Everett's authorship has been established for perhaps the great
bulk of what he wrote, numerous stray pieces have no doubt
gone unnoted in the available indexes.

   The point of departure for this bibliography is an excellent
earlier work by Fred Somkin, "The Writings of Alexander
Hill Everett (1790-1847), A Partial Checklist," Bulletin of
Bibliography, 23 (January-April, 1963), 238-239. In addition to the citations given there, I have furnished individual
entries for Everett's articles in the Monthly Anthology and
Boston Review and the North American Review, listed the
known collections of his correspondence, and keyed each of
the journal articles later republished in Critical and Miscellaneous Essays to its location in the collected volumes (the
entry "C&ME 1st, 2," for example, indicates that the article
in question reappeared as the second article in the first
series of Essays).

I. BOOKS

America: or a General Survey of the Political Situation of
   the Several Powers of the Western Continent, with Conjectures on their Future Prospects. By a Citizen of the
   United States, Author of "Europe," &c. Philadelphia,
   1827; English ed., London, 1828; German ed., Hamburg,
   1828; Spanish ed., trans A. X. San Martin, Northampton,
   Mass., 1828.
Critical and Miscellaneous Essays, To Which are Added a

Few Poems. Boston, 1845-?1846. Republishes selected
periodical writings, identified among the listings below.
Critical and Miscellaneous Essays, Second Series. Boston,
1846.
Europe: or a General Survey of the Present Situation of the
Principal Powers; with Conjectures on their Future Pros-
pects: By a Citizen of the United States. Boston, 1822;
English ed., London, 1822; 2d ed., London, 1823; Ger-
man ed., trans L. H. von Jacobi, 1823.
Life of Joseph Warren, in Jared Sparks, ed., Library of
American Biography (25 vols., Boston, 1834-1848),
First Series, Vol. X, 93-183.
Life of Patrick Henry, in Jared Sparks, ed., Library of
American Biography (25 vols., Boston, 1834-1848), Sec-
ond Series, Vol. I, 209-398.
Müller, Johannes von. The History of the World . . . (Tr.
from the German) . . . Compared throughout with the
original, rev., cor., and illustrated by a notice of the life
and writings of the author, by Alexander H. Everett.
Vols. 1-2 (of 4), Boston, 1840.
New Ideas on Population: with Remarks on the Theories of
Malthus and Godwin. Boston, 1823; English ed., London,
1823; 2d ed., Boston, 1826; French ed., trans C. J.
Ferry, Paris, 1826.
Poems. Boston, 1845. Duplicates the verse in C&ME 1st,
above.

II. PERIODICALS

American Annual Register

"History of the United States" (the section entitled "Bank of
the United States"), 8 (1832-1833), 1-21.
"History of the United States" (the section entitled "Admin-
istration of Andrew Jackson"), 7 (1831-1832), 1-15.
"Opinions in South Carolina," 5 (1829-1830), 62-142.
"Spain," 5 (1829-1830), 414-418.

Boston Daily Advertiser (newspaper)

Report of Fanueil Hall speech, November 11, 1835.

Boston Miscellany of Literature and Fashion

"Aranjuez," 2 (July, 1842), 1-8.
"The Hermitage of Candoo," 2 (July-December, 1842), 174-
   178.
"Madame de Sévigné," 1 (January-July, 1842), 80-89.
   (C&ME 1st, 1)

Boston Quarterly Review

"The Currency," 2 (July, 1839), 298-326
"The Currency," 3 (January, 1840), 80-116.

General Repository

"Musaeus' Popular Tales," 4 (July, 1813), 91-105.
   (C&ME 2d, 3)
"Resources of Russia," 4 (July, 1813), 136-.
"The Martyrs of Chateaubriand," 3 (January, 1813), 169-181.

Godey's Lady's Book

"The Sabbath," in Critical and Miscellaneous Essays, First
   Series (1845), 458-463. (C&ME 1st, 13)

Independent Chronicle and Patriot (newspaper)

"Letters from England," June 11, 14, 21, 28; July 16, 19;
   August 6, 16, 23; September 17. Boston, 1817.

Monthly Anthology and Boston Review

"Abuse of Words," 5 (September, 1808), 493-495.
"Apologue," 6 (May, 1809), 302.
"Article 1" (one-line tribute to Nathaniel Fanning; no other

title), 6 (February, 1809), 126.

"Biography," 5 (November, 1808), 590-591.

"Blair's Grave," 5 (August, 1808), 425-427.

"Blair's Grave," 6 (February, 1809), 86-87.

"Castiglioni's Travels in North America," 5 (July, 1808), 389-391.

"Corinna," 6 (March, 1809), 159-160.

"Corinna, or Italy by Madame de Stael Holstein," 5 (June, 1808), 336-339.

"Eloquence," 6 (June, 1809), 382-383.

"Epitaph," 6 (May, 1809), 301.

"Epitaphs," 5 (August, 1808), 427-428.

"Facilis Descensus Averni," 5 (December, 1808), 655-656.

"Florian," 5 (June, 1808), 308-309.

"Grecian Song" (translation), 7 (July, 1809), 29.

"Grinke's Oration," 6 (June, 1809), 421.

"Hopkin's Oration," 7 (July, 1809), 61-62.

"Horace," 5 (June, 1808), 309.

"Horne Tooke," 6 (May, 1809), 299.

"Imitation," 6 (February, 1809), 84-85.

"James I," 5 (June, 1808), 308.

"Laudes Cantabrigiae," 5 (December, 1808), 658.

"Law," 6 (February, 1809), 84.

"Lines in Memory of John T. Gilman," 5 (April, 1808), 212.

"Love" (translation from Lorenzo), 5 (October, 1808), 549.

"Magi Gotamenses," 5 (August, 1808), 430-433.

"Manto," 6 (January, 1809), 23.

"Marmion," 5 (October, 1808), 561-564.

"Modern Chivalry," 5 (September, 1808), 498-508.

"Modern Chivalry," 5 (October, 1808), 554-558.

"Peiresc," 5 (October, 1808), 549-550.

"Petropoli, V.A. Kal. Sextil," 9 (December, 1810), 401-402.

"Philip IV," 6 (May, 1809), 302.

"Pierce's Oration," 6 (February, 1809), 122-123.

"Poems by George Crabbe," 6 (January, 1809), 57-59.

"Remarker, No. 43," 6 (April, 1809), 228-231.

"Retrospective Review," 6 (June, 1809), 422-427.

"Saul," 5 (October, 1808), 548-549.

"The Admirable Crichton," 5 (May, 1808), 251-252.
"The Odyssey," 6 (April, 1809), 241-242.
"Theocritus and Virgil," 6 (June, 1809), 376-379.
"To Correspondents," 6 (June, 1809), 427.
"Trifle," 6 (April, 1809), 239.
"Versio Latina," 6 (February, 1809), 103.
"York and Lancaster," 5 (October, 1808), 550.

New England Magazine

"The French Revolution," 1 (July, 1831), 190-202.

North American Review

"American Library of Useful Knowledge," 33 (October,
    1831), 515-530.
"American Poets," 33 (October, 1831), 297-324.
"Anecdotes of Morellet and His Contemporaries," 15 (Octo-
    ber, 1822), 319-340.
"Bigelow's Travels in Malta and Sicily," 35 (July, 1832),
    228-255.
"British Opinions on the Protecting System," 30 (January,
    1830), 160-216.
"Canova and His Works," 10 (April, 1820), 372-386.
"Chinese Manners," 27 (October, 1828), 524-562. (C&ME
    1st, 12)
"Cicero on Government," 17 (July, 1823), 33-75. (C&ME
    1st, 10)
"Cushing's Reminiscences of Spain," 37 (July, 1833), 84-
    117.
"De Staël's Letters on England," 26 (January, 1828), 163-
    196.
"Dr. Channing," 41 (October, 1835), 366-406.
"Early Literature of France," 38 (April, 1834), 358-381.
"Early Literature of Modern Europe," 38 (January, 1834),
    158-177.
"European Politics," 21 (July, 1825), 141-153.
"Exhibition of Pictures at the Athenaeum Gallery," 31
    (October, 1830), 309-337.

"Fidler's Observations on the United States," 37 (October, 1833), 273-314.
"Geoffroy on Dramatic Literature," 10 (April, 1820), 291-316. (C&ME 1st, 5)
"Hale's Geography," 31 (October, 1830), 460-462.
"History of Intellectual Philosophy," 29 (July, 1829), 67-123. (C&ME 2d, 10)
"History of Philosophy," 18 (April, 1824), 234-266. (C&ME 2d, 5)
"Hodgson's Memoirs of the Berber Languages," 35 (July, 1832), 54-74.
"Immigration," 40 (April, 1835), 457-476.
"Imprisonment for Debt," 32 (April, 1831), 490-508.
"Irving's Alhambra," 35 (October, 1832), 265-282.
"Irving's Life of Columbus," 28 (January, 1829), 103-134. (C&ME 2d, 4)
"Life and Character of Jefferson," 40 (January, 1835), 170-232.
"Life and Works of Canova," 26 (October, 1829), 441-478. (C&ME 1st, 8)
"Life and Writings of Schiller," 16 (April, 1823), 397-425. (C&ME 1st, 4)
"Life of Bernardin de St. Pierre," 13 (July, 1821), 200-227. (C&ME 1st, 3)
"Life of Henry Clay," 33 (October, 1831), 351-396.
"Life of Rousseau," 15 (July, 1822), 1-21. (C&ME 2d, 8)
"Literary History of the Eighteenth Century," 12 (April, 1821), 246-268.
"Lord Byron," 20 (January, 1825), 1-47.
"Louis Bonaparte," 11 (October, 1820), 239-271.
"Malthus on Political Economy," 28 (April, 1829), 368-388.
"Memoirs of Casanova," 41 (July, 1835), 46-70.
"Memoirs of the Queen of France," 18 (January, 1824), 1-33.
"Men and Manners in America," 38 (January, 1834), 210-270.
"Mirabeau's Speeches," 15 (July, 1822), 73-93.
"Mrs. Butler's Journal," 41 (July, 1835), 109-146.

"Nullification," 36 (January, 1833), 205-275.
"Origins of the Old Parties," 39 (July, 1834), 208-268.
"Peace Societies," 6 (November, 1817), 25-45.
"Politics of Europe," 27 (July, 1828), 215-268.
"Politics of Europe," 30 (April, 1830), 399-454.
"Popular Education," 40 (April, 1835), 511-536.
"Posthumous Works of Madame de Staël," 14 (January, 1822), 101-128. (C&ME 2d, 2)
"Private Life of Voltaire," 12 (January, 1821), 38-60. (C&ME 1st, 6)
"Progress and Limits of Social Improvement," 38 (April, 1834), 502-538.
"Rae's Political Economy," 40 (January, 1835), 122-141.
"Rémusat's Chinese Grammar," 17 (January, 1823), 1-13.
"Revolution in Paraguay," 26 (April, 1828), 444-478.
"Sir James Mackintosh," 35 (October, 1832), 433-472. (C&ME 1st, 9)
"Sismondi's Julia Severa," 15 (July, 1822), 163-177.
"Speeches of Messrs. Story and Webster," 12 (April, 1821), 340-365. (C&ME 1st, 11)
"Stewart's Moral Philosophy," 31 (July, 1830), 213-267. (C&ME 2d, 7)
"Sunday Mails," 31 (July, 1830), 154-167.
"Swallow Barn," 36 (April, 1833), 519-544.
"Tales of the North-West," 31 (July, 1830), 200-213.
"The Annuals," 38 (January, 1834), 198-209.
"The Art of Being Happy," 27 (July, 1828), 115-139. (C&ME 1st, 7)
"The Art of Preserving Beauty," 32 (April, 1831), 444-453.
"The Cherokee Case," 33 (July, 1831), 136-153.
"The Laws of Population and Wages," 33 (July, 1831), 1-28.
"The Linwoods," 42 (January, 1836), 160-195.
"The Union and the States," 37 (July, 1833), 190-249.
"The Washington Papers," 39 (October, 1834), 467-494.
"Thomas Carlyle," 41 (October, 1835), 454-482.
"Tone of British Criticism," 31 (July, 1830), 26-66.
"Usury and the Laws of Usury," 39 (July, 1834), 68-111.
"Wheaton's International Law," 44 (January, 1837), 16-29.
"Who Wrote Gil Blas?" 25 (October, 1827), 278-307. (C&ME 1st, 2)

Southern Quarterly Review

"La Havane," 7 (January, 1845), 153-196. (C&ME 2d, 9)

The Token

"Lord Vapourcourt" (1831), in Critical and Miscellaneous
  Essays, Second Series (1846), 452-475. (C&ME 2d, 11)

United States Magazine and Democratic Review

"Contemporary Spanish Poetry," 14 (April, 1844), 395-
  408.
"Enigma" (poem), 1 (October, 1837), 81-82.
"Funeral of Goethe, from the German of Harro Harring"
  (poem), 11 (November, 1842), 471-475.
"Greenough's Statue of Washington," 14 (June, 1844), 618-
  621. (C&ME 2d, 6)
"Mrs. Sigourney," 11 (September, 1842), 246-249.
"Sketch of Harro Harring," 15 (October, 1844), 337-347.
  (C&ME 2d, 1)
"Specter Bridegroom. A Poem Imitated from the German of
  Bürger," 12 (June, 1843), 587-592.
"The Condition of China," 21 (November, 1847), 397-410.
"The Discovery of America by the Northmen," 2 (April,
  May, 1838), 85-96; 143-158.
"The Malthusian Theory. Discussed in a Correspondence be-
  tween Alexander Hill Everett and Professor George Tuck-
  er of the University of Virginia," 17 (October, November,
  December, 1845), 297-310; 379-391; 438-444.
"The Re-Annexation of Texas," 15 (July, 1844), 11-16.
"The Texas Question," 15 (September, 1844), 250-270.

III. PUBLISHED ADDRESSES AND PAMPHLETS

"A Defense of the Character and Principles of Mr. Jefferson; being an Address delivered at Weymouth, Mass., on
  the 4th of July, 1836." Boston, 1836.
"A Discourse on the Progress and Limits of Social Improvement; Including a General Survey of the History of Civili-

zation. Addressed to the literary societies of Amherst College . . . August 27, 1833." Boston, 1834.

"A Few Notes on Certain Passages respecting the Law of Nations, contained in an Article in the North American Review, upon the work entitled 'Europe,' . . . By the Author of that Work." Boston, 1823.

"A Letter on the Texas Question" (from the Democratic
Review for September, 1844). New York, ?1844.

"Address delivered at Jefferson College . . . June 30, 1841,
on Assuming the Functions of President of that Institution."
New Orleans, 1841.

"Address of the National Republican Convention to the People of the United States," Journal of the National Republican Convention (December 12, 1831), 17-28.

"An Address delivered at Charlestown, Mass., on the 17th
of June, 1836 . . . in Commemoration of the Battle of
Bunker Hill." Boston, 1836.

"An Address delivered at Salem on the Eighth of January,
1836 . . . in Commemoration of the Victory of New Orleans." Boston, 1836.

"An Address delivered before the Massachusetts Charitable
Fire Society . . . May 28, 1813. . . ." Boston, 1813.

"An Address delivered before the Massachusetts Horticul-
tural Society . . . September 18, 1833." Boston, 1833.

"An Address delivered before the Peithessophian and Philo-
clean Societies of Rutgers College, on the Literary Character of the Scriptures. . . ." New York, 1838.

"An Address to the Literary Societies of Dartmouth College,
on the Character and Influence of the German Literature.
Delivered at Hanover, N.H., July 24, 1839." Boston,
1839.

"An Address to the Phi Beta Kappa Society of Bowdoin College, on the Present State of Polite Learning in England
and America . . . September 3, 1834." Boston, 1834.

"An Address to the Philermian Society of Brown University,
on the Moral Character of the Literature of the Last and
Present Century . . . Providence, R.I., September 4,
1837." Providence, 1837.

"An Oration delivered at Holliston, Mass. on the Fourth of

July, 1839. . . ." Boston, 1839.

"An Oration delivered . . . before the citizens of Boston on the 5th of July, 1830." Boston, 1830.

"British Opinions on the Protecting System . . . Reprinted with a few alterations from . . . the North American Review, for January, 1830." Boston, 1830.

"Character of Gen. Jackson and Mr. Van Buren, in 1832; also Notions of Anti-Masonry, By the Same Author, in 1833." Boston, 1836.

"Eighteen Hundred and Twenty: A Poem. Part first." London, 1821.

"Memorial of the New York Convention, to the Congress of the United States . . . of the Friends of Domestic Industry Assembled at New York, October 26, 1831. . . ." Baltimore, 1832.

"Remarks on the Governor's Speech. By an American. . . ." Boston, 1814.

"Report of the Committee on Education, on so much of the Governor's Message as Relates to the School Fund." Boston, 1835.

"Strictures on Nullification . . . From the 'North American Review'." Boston, 1832.

"The Conduct of the Administration . . . Reprinted from the Boston Daily Advertiser and Patriot." Boston, 1832.

IV. MANUSCRIPT SOURCES

American Philosophical Society, Philadelphia, Pennsylvania: 10 miscellaneous manuscript letters.

Baker Memorial Library, Dartmouth College, Hanover, New Hampshire: 10 manuscript letters to George Ticknor.

Boston Public Library, Boston, Massachusetts: 7 miscellaneous manuscript letters.

Connecticut Historical Society, Hartford, Connecticut: 9 manuscript letters to Lydia Huntley Sigourney.

Davis Library, Phillips Exeter Academy, Exeter, New Hampshire: 4 miscellaneous manuscript letters.

Georgia Historical Society, Savannah, Georgia: 2 miscellaneous manuscript letters.

Haverford College Library, Haverford, Pennsylvania: 4
miscellaneous manuscript letters.

Houghton Library, Harvard University, Cambridge, Massachusetts: 28 manuscript letters to Henry Wadsworth Longfellow.

Houghton Library, Harvard University, Cambridge, Massachusetts: 31 manuscript letters to Jared Sparks.

Houghton Library, Harvard University, Cambridge, Massachusetts: 9 miscellaneous manuscript letters.

J. Pierpont Morgan Library, New York, New York: 2 miscellaneous manuscript letters.

John Hay Library, Brown University, Providence, Rhode
Island: 3 miscellaneous manuscript letters.

Massachusetts Historical Society, Boston, Massachusetts:
unpublished Everett Papers.

Massachusetts Historical Society, Boston, Massachusetts:
unpublished Everett-Peabody Collection.

Massachusetts Historical Society, Boston, Massachusetts:
unpublished letterbooks.

New Hampshire Historical Society, Concord, New Hampshire: 1 miscellaneous manuscript letter.

Pennsylvania Historical Society, Philadelphia, Pennsylvania:
5 miscellaneous manuscript letters.

South Caroliniana Library, University of South Carolina,
Columbia, South Carolina: 4 manuscript letters to Hugh
Swinton Legaré.

Yale University Library, New Haven, Connecticut: 9 miscellaneous manuscript letters.

Index of Names

Martineau, Harriet, 153
Mary, Saint, 114, 118-119, 130
Mason, William, 127
Mazarin, Jules, 130
Menander, 178
Milton, John, 18, 28, 30, 45, 47, 58, 63, 109, 127, 128, 142, 144, 146, 176, 213
Mirabeau, Honoré Gabriel Victor Riqueti, Comte de, 30
Montesquieu, Charles de Secondat, Baron de La Brède et de, 17, 31, 170
Moore, Thomas, 9, 14, 26, 83, 149
More, Hannah, 240
More, Thomas, 170
Moreau, Jean Victor, 31
Mudo, El (Juan Fernández Navarrete), 114
Murillo, Bartolomé Esteban, 114, 116-120, 121, 123, 125
Murray, John (1778-1843), 206, 216
Murray, William, 53

Napier, John, 11
Napoleon I (Napoleon Bonaparte), 19, 25-30, 31, 33-35 passim, 46, 114, 176, 211
Navarrete, Martín Fernández de, 219, 224, 244n
Nelson, Horatio, 18, 28
Newton, Gilbert Stuart, 132, 138, 140n

Newton, Isaac, 9, 63, 76, 176
Norton, Andrews, xiv, 191

Oglethorpe, James, 174
Olivares, Gaspar de Guzmán, Conde de, 122
Ovid, 53
Owen, Robert, 219

Paine, Robert Treat (1773-1811), 56
Paine, Thomas, 171
Palfrey, John Gorham, x, 222, 242n
Penn, William, 174
Percival, James Gates, x
Pericles, 145
Perkins, Thomas, 125
Philip II of Spain, 112, 116
Philip IV of Spain, 122
Pichegru, Charles, 31
Pickering, John, xiv, 193, 242n
Pindar, 159
Pindar, Peter (John Wolcot), 133
Pitt, William, Earl of Chatham, 175
Plato, 63, 142, 170, 176
Playfair, John, 11
Plutarch, 177
Pocahontas, 232, 240
Polycarp, Saint, 112
Pope, Alexander, 66, 147, 156-157, 158
Pradt, Dominique de, 28
Prescott, William Hickling, x, xiv, 210, 214, 232

ELIZABETH EVANS, Associate Professor of
English at the Georgia Institute of Technology,
received her Ph.D. degree at the University of
North Carolina, Chapel Hill. Her current
scholarly interests are reflected in published
articles on A.H. Everett, Thomas Wolfe, Doris
Betts, Edith Wharton, W.J. Snelling, Flannery
O'Connor, and other American and British
writers.